SCREENED IN

Anthony Silard has provided leadership development coaching and training to thousands of CEOs and senior executives of Fortune 100 companies, small businesses, and the world's largest nonprofits, including GE, Disney, Nokia, Bank of America, IBM, CARE, Save the Children, and the American Red Cross. He has also coached political leaders, including G-20 cabinet ministers. He has taught leadership at various universities around the world, including IESE Business School, Claremont McKenna College, California State University San Bernardino, the Monterrey Institute of Technology, INCAE Business School, and the International University of Catalonia and has lectured on leadership at Harvard, Stanford, Georgetown, the University of California at Berkeley, George Washington University, Cal Poly Pomona, and ESADE Business School. Anthony has received numerous awards for his work, including Harvard's Robert F. Kennedy Public Service Award, was named Visionary of the Year by the PBS series *The Visionaries*, and was featured at the Presidential Summit for America's Future and America's Promise. Anthony holds a PhD in leadership from IESE Business School, which he received with First-Class/Excellent Distinction, a Master's in Public Policy focused on leadership from Harvard University, and a BA from the University of California at Berkeley. He also served in the Peace Corps in Kenya for two years. Anthony is CEO of the Global Leadership Institute and President of the Center for Social Leadership. He lives with his wife and two children in California.

Praise for *Screened In*

"The game of life was thrown a major curve ball when the first iPhone was released in 2007. If loneliness, anxiety, and depression are the indicators—as Anthony Silard compellingly makes the case, with a raft of largely unknown research to back him up—then most of us are striking out. If you want to get on base in the field of meaningful, supportive human relationships, this is the one book you can't do without. Buy it and adapt!"

—Marshall Goldsmith, *New York Times* bestselling author of *What Got You Here Won't Get You There*

"Once we've had the honesty to admit we're hooked on our screens, we can make the courageous choice to free ourselves. *Screened In* is a clear, strong, and important book for our times that shines a fascinating and revealing light on our societal addiction, and offers inspiration and practical strategies to reconnect with this creative, vibrant, and precious life."

—Tara Brach, international bestselling author of *Radical Acceptance*

"*Screened In* is a sharp, readable, and savvy guide to making the most of those weapons of mass distraction in our pockets. Silard shows why we are so addicted to screens and—even more important—how we can kick the habit to live richer lives. Put down your phone and read it!"

—Carl Honoré, international bestselling author of *In Praise of Slow*

"Ever since the first iPhone was released in 2007, lamentations, protests, and cries of despair about our increasingly disconnected world have been everywhere and workable solutions have been nowhere—until *Screened In*. It's an essential book for reducing screen time and embracing authentic relationships in the digital age."

—Harriet Lerner, *New York Times* bestselling author of *The Dance of Anger*

"Armed with a prodigious volume of research, *Screened In* invites the reader to question their fundamental assumptions about how much technology and social media usage is safe. Through our device obsessions, we are creating a very lonely world! Dr. Silard provides us with a fascinating and well-researched book that will help us to end this addictive cycle."

—Philip Zimbardo, former President, American Psychological Association, and *New York Times* bestselling author of *The Lucifer Effect*

"Although the Earth is not spinning any faster than a hundred years ago, the world is coming at us faster. We suffer from not just information overload, but emotional overload from never getting a break. Anthony Silard has captured the subversive and damaging aspects of the gift of the technological age. The research is clear—it causes us to be on alert and defensive all of the time. It also fools us into thinking we are more connected when in fact we are more socially isolated. Fortunately, as Tony suggests, the remedies are within your grasp—if you wish to use them. Ignore his message at your peril!"

—Richard Boyatzis, *New York Times* bestselling co-author of *Primal Leadership*

"Silard's book comes at a critical time. Technology has taken over our lives so fast that there hasn't been a moment to deeply contemplate its impact on us. Nor have we learned how to manage it instead of letting it run us. A must-read!"

—Emma Seppälä, Science Director, Center for Compassion and Altruism Research and Education, Stanford University, and author of *The Happiness Track*

"If you aim to change our society in a positive way, it's imperative that you understand how the new digital norms are affecting us. The new book by the world-renowned social entrepreneur, scholar, and leadership trainer Anthony Silard will help you do precisely that. *Screened In* actually caused my facial structure to shift … My eyebrows arched and my jaw dropped while reading this paradigm-shattering book … Silard has provided an undeniable, supremely beautiful gift to our society that we had better heed before it's too late. I offer only one suggestion: accept it and then pay it forward."

—Cheryl Dorsey, President, the Echoing Green Foundation

"As Anthony Silard meticulously documents in his book with the latest research and in-depth interviews with psychologists, pediatricians, and other thought leaders, the digital age has for many become a digital dystopia. If you're looking for well-researched solutions to transcend the mess we've collectively created, this is the book you want to read."

—Roy Baumeister, social psychologist and co-author of *Willpower*

"Anthony Silard is a master of understanding—and explaining—social interactions and the inner qualities that drive them. In this compelling new book he takes aim at our collective addiction to the dazzling devices which are increasing supplanting healthy human relationships. True to form, Silard doesn't just identify the problem; he shows us that the solution lies within each of us. *Screened In* is the book our society needs now."

—Mark Levine, New York City Council Member, 7th District Office

"We are unfortunately seeing an alarming increase in students requiring mental health services over the past few years, and there is increasing evidence that digital addiction is playing a role. Reading *Screened In* is an eye-opening account of how over-attached we have become to our devices and what we can do about it. Silard's book is a well-written and thoroughly researched primer on how to develop high-quality relationships in the digital age. To understand what you can do to reconnect with others through disconnecting from your devices, this is the one book you have to read."

—Michelle Bligh, Dean, School of Social Science,
Policy, and Evaluation, Claremont Graduate University

"Glued to your screen and not experiencing the rich, nurturing relationships you once did? Not sure how to change the direction your life has been going in with your trusty phone by your side? Thanks to Anthony Silard's masterpiece, there is now a workable way out. Rather than being the source of your loneliness, anxiety, and depression, your phone can become your friend. In *Screened In*, Silard shows you how."

—Wendy Smith, professor and co-director, Women's Leadership Initiative,
Alfred Lerner College of Business & Economics, University of Delaware

"Anthony Silard cites a considerable body of compelling research that details the damage being done to us and to our relationships by our attachment to our devices. Screened In offers powerful alternatives to the new heads-down norms that have taken over our society. Silard offers practical strategies to adjust our thinking so we can make positive changes in our lives while we still have the chance."

—Nick Morgan, author of *Can You Hear Me?:*
How to Connect with People in a Virtual World

"Anthony Silard holds a critical position in the global dialogue on screen etiquette. *Screened In* is an extremely important book that will challenge and ultimately change how you approach using your devices so you can experience more happiness, success, and meaning in your life. This book will inspire you to become a better person vis-à-vis your devices and to avoid the loneliness, depression, and anxiety stemming from screen overuse. Our addiction to all of the colors and sounds emanating from our phones, as Silard so well chronicles with a tremendous raft of research to back him up, is currently splitting our society apart. The life you save may be your own ... or the teenager's down the street."

—Thomas Ramsøy, neuroscientist and CEO, Neurons

"Have you experienced moments when everyone around you is staring at their screens instead of interacting with each other directly? Have you cringed at what this fascination with our devices does to our ability to connect on a personal level? At what it implies for our ability to cope with the anxieties that the contemporary world thrusts upon us? After reading Anthony Silard's book, I was relieved to learn that I'm not the only one who feels this way and, most importantly, that there is great hope. Reading *Screened In* felt like completing a master's degree in how to develop high-quality relationships in the digital age. If you are interested in gaining control of how you use your devices, this is a must-read!"

—Alejandro Poiré, Dean, School of Social Sciences
and Government, Monterey Institute of Technology, Mexico

"While we are all busy looking at our smartphones and scrolling through social media, life is passing us by. In this thoroughly-researched book, Anthony Silard teaches us how to break free from the hold that modern media has on our attention. *Screened In* is for all of us who admittedly spend too much time on our devices, and want to have more time for ourselves and for maintaining quality relationships with others."

—Ronald E. Riggio, PhD, Kravis Professor of Leadership and Organizational
Psychology, Kravis Leadership Institute, Claremont McKenna College

Screened In

The Art

of Living Free

in the Digital Age

Anthony Silard

 INNER LEADERSHIP PRESS

Copyright © 2020 by Anthony Silard.

All rights reserved. No part of this publication may be reproduced, stored in a retrieval system, or transmitted in any form or by any means, electronic, mechanical, photocopying, recording, or otherwise, without the prior written permission of the copyright holder, except brief quotations used in a review.

Cover design by Mark Eimer. Interior design by Diana Wade.

Published by Inner Leadership Press.

Manufactured in the United States of America.

ISBN 978-0-9817853-1-8

Published 2020.

For Alex and Chloe, our Digital Natives.
I wish from the deepest recesses of my heart
that you grow up in a healthy world that facilitates
the expression of your essential humanness and freedom.

Contents

PART ONE

DISCONNECTED

1

A History of Praising and Criticizing a New Technology

One night about four years ago, I stood next to the crib of my son, who was about fourteen months old at the time, and watched him sleep. His arms were splayed out, palms toward the sky, in a position of complete innocence and vulnerability. Becoming a father changed me in many unexpected ways: the love a parent has for her or his child stands alone; it's unlike any other feeling I had ever experienced. My love for him transformed at times into feelings of protectiveness and fear. I felt so strongly, in the depths of my soul as I watched him that night, how much I longed for him to live a long, healthy life.

That was when it hit me: if he makes it to the ripe old age of eighty-one, he will live until 2094. My thoughts of the future suddenly became more salient than ever before. My mind began to race; I soon realized that when he is my age (I was forty-seven at the time), it will be 2060. I couldn't believe it: this human being sleeping innocently in front of me will live ten years past 2050 if he makes it to my age. I realized in that moment that I was writing this book for him, and for many others like him who will hopefully occupy our new world long after my departure.

The importance of plunging my heart, mind, and soul into writing this book multiplied exponentially in my thoughts as I realized that the concepts I was writing about—from the effects of the Internet on how we communicate, work, and keep ourselves safe to our need to find balance in and actually enjoy our time on this earth—would affect how he experienced his life. I felt a deep yearning for him to have the privileges I've had—to truly live, to connect with others, to feel relatively safe, and to thrive in this wondrous physical world surrounded by its spectacular, awe-inspiring nature and relatively healthy human beings to interact with and draw meaning from.

That night watching my son asleep in his crib, thinking about the promise and beauty of a new life, was the second critical moment in my life that inspired me to write *Screened In*. The first occurred five years earlier when I watched a man die.

Tragedy in Yosemite

I was driving with a few friends to Yosemite National Park in Northern California. We were in search of a hike, and I proposed that we take what we later discovered was a wrong turn, which propelled us onto a long, winding road headed into the middle of nowhere. After numerous twists and turns, we encountered three cars stopped in the road, one after the other. In front of the first car was the scene of an accident. Bodies and motorcycles were strewn on the tarmac. I stepped out of the car and walked past the cars.

There were two people lying silently on the pavement about seven feet apart. A third, along with his bike, had ended up on the dirt embankment about five feet above the road. The two people on the road, a couple who had been riding on the same bike, were covered with blood. I approached the woman and asked her how she was doing.

"I'm all right," she replied. "How is my husband?"

"He also looks okay," I told her. "Help is on the way."

I slowly poured water into her lips and then her husband's. The third person, lying in the dirt on the embankment, had been riding on his own while listening to music on his headphones and had lost control of his motorcycle and rammed into the couple. He was unable to speak.

A park ranger finally arrived and put an oxygen mask on the man on the embankment. I listened to his breathing; it had an uneven, staccato sound I had never heard before that sent a chill through my body. It sounded as if he had broken a windpipe, lung, or jaw. The paramedics arrived about five minutes later. As I left, he was being rushed into an ambulance. A helicopter flew overhead, trying to locate a place to land and medevac him to the nearest hospital.

A few days later, I was having dinner with friends and told them what had happened. "For some reason, I don't think that man made it," I said, remembering the disconcerting sound of his uneven breathing. "I just had the feeling as soon as I heard him breathe that he was too internally damaged to survive."

"Why don't you Google the accident to find out what happened?" one of my friends asked.

I hadn't thought of that. I went online, and within a few minutes discovered he had not even made it alive into the ambulance. He died within minutes of when I stood up from kneeling next to him to make way for the paramedics.

Cleaning House

The next morning, I decided to clean up my email account, as my old emails were taking up too much space. I deleted about five thousand emails. I had a sinking feeling I was unable to shake, that worsened by the minute, as I went through thousands of emails I had sent or received: they had amounted to absolutely nothing. I felt like most of my long, laborious hours spent dutifully typing away at my desktop had done nothing but raise clouds of dust.

I couldn't shake the image in my mind of the man who died on the embankment. My memory of him was followed by the devastating feeling that so many of my limited breaths in this lifetime had been expelled from my still healthy lungs while I sat hunched over this machine, an exercise in futility at the most primal, deepest existential level. I deleted hundreds upon hundreds of emails I had systematically labeled for various categories of my life—acquaintances, conferences, book sales, foreign rights, dating—that had led to nothing meaningful whatsoever. *Well*, I thought to myself, *for every five hundred or a thousand emails there was the spare message that had led to something positive, perhaps even something beautiful. Was it all worth it for that occasional email?* I couldn't figure out the answer to that question; I still can't.

The mental picture of the man lying on the embankment persisted. It was the first time I had watched a man die right in front of me. I thought about the ways I try to make a difference in the world, to help others, to improve their lives in some way. I realized that each of us has one means of truly making the lives of others better, of discovering the form in which we are called upon to give to others.

For me, that form was to write—to pour the deepest essence of myself into the written word with the objective of making life easier, more understandable, more livable, and more appealing for my brothers and sisters with whom I share this planet.

Diffuse Energy

So much of my energy had been poured not into writing, but other ways to contribute, many of which were probably more manifestations of my insecurities about paying the bills than a genuine desire to help people—in other words, mostly futile emails attempting to drum up new contracts and business. *I've never been a businessman; I'm a writer,* I thought to myself.

I sat there checking "Delete" in the box next to message after message—each virtual missive spawned by my insecurities and fears of not being "good enough" as a writer, each drafted to attract new clients, each falling on deaf ears, or, more aptly, over-weary eyes trained on a screen for much too long.

I also had less altruistic thoughts: I was throwing my breaths away; working until seven every evening; returning home to my wife an unappealing vessel of stress and fatigue; a weary, humorless soul recovering from the day's digitally mediated ups and downs; a robotic automaton deficient in the vitality of life; a deflated, disappointing dinner date. For six years, I had set an alarm on my cell phone to ring at six in the evening to remind me to stop working—and then "snoozed" (ironically, in my case synonymous with "worked") until around seven. I changed the alarm, for the first time ever, to go off at five, with the intention to stop working by half past.

Then I called my guitar teacher and set up my next two lessons. Playing guitar helped me *feel* something deep inside. It helped me bring my life into alignment, albeit temporarily, with the rhythm of an instrument that does not care about any of the glowing screens surrounding me. I would play it as it had been played for centuries (by novices like myself seeking rhythmic respite from the trivialities of life) because that is *its* purpose.

I decided to schedule my guitar lessons at six so I would have no other alternative but to stop working by then, like it or not. I would start doing yoga more. I checked the paper for upcoming concerts and discovered that Maná—both my wife's and my favorite rock band—was playing the following week; I bought tickets on craigslist and thought about how to surprise her.

The Need for Reconnection

Thinking back to the man on the embankment gasping his final breaths, I realized that our time on the only planet (that we know of) that supports organic life is so limited, and that our lives are so fragile. We have no idea whatsoever when it will be over, and it can end just like that, in a matter of seconds, as it did for him. We have to embrace each day, and do our best to truly live and experience life while we still have the opportunity.

We have a limited number of breaths to take. He lost this ability—to use his lungs to breathe in oxygen—and his life flickered out as precipitously as a candle under an open window. I realized that I am not afraid of dying. I imagine there will be some suffering, and then silence. I just want to make the most of the limited time I have left on this earth—to actually experience the *life* within each day that is there to embrace and enlarge or dismiss and miss—and also help others to live with more grace and happiness during the limited time they have left.

This motivation drives the pages that follow. This book is about how each of us can reclaim our essential freedom and humanness in the digital age. Why? Because, as numerous social psychological studies have found, the people you surround yourself with (possibly including you) are now most likely less empathetic, less comfortable with themselves, and more depressed and lonely than they were only a few decades ago. While some of these studies are correlational and note that screen time and these unhealthy variables are both rising (which could point to another variable other than screen time driving these variables upward), others suggest a stronger, predictive relationship. For example, one randomized controlled trial assigned otherwise similar individuals to either spend more or less time on their screens, while another simply monitored screen use over time in a random set of individuals. Both studies found that more screen time causes increased loneliness, depression, and anxiety, and less emotional connection with others.

I've spent the past ten years researching and teaching people about how to manage complex emotions such as loneliness and trauma. After interviewing hundreds of people from all walks of life and listening to their stories about what has precipitated the loneliest moments of their lives, I'm convinced that the recent increases in screen time and loneliness are inextricably linked.

No Two Places at Once

As we will see below, this link is not far-fetched due to a "displacement effect" (think: the water displaced when you drop a bowling ball in a bathtub, which I'm sure you do often) in which more time online equates to less time face-to-face with family and friends. This effect was first observed by social psychologist Robert Kraut and his research team at Carnegie Mellon University in the late '90s when they provided free computers, Internet access, and a phone line to ninety-three families in Pittsburgh. They subsequently tracked the activities and emotional states of every family member over ten years old who was interested in joining the study (169 people in total) for two years.

The researchers found that the more time these individuals spent online, the less time they spent in person with family members and friends—and the lonelier and more depressed they became. Because Kraut and his colleagues surveyed these family members before they received daily access to a computer and the Internet, the research team was able to identify electronic communication as a *cause* of social isolation, depression, and loneliness.

A decade and a half later, nothing has changed. Consider the experience of Hannah, the vice president of a technology company in San Francisco I interviewed last year who recounts how loneliness and time on her digital devices impacted her life after a recent breakup:

> After a six-year relationship ended in 2016, I jumped into another relationship in 2017. Following the most recent breakup, I realized how much I have relied on others to feel happy. I have spent the last eight years of my life relying on someone else for fulfillment. Throughout these experiences, I made it a priority to display my relationships and outings online for others to see. I wanted others to see how happy I was. Scrolling through my Instagram feed has become a bad habit and quite unhealthy because I have the tendency to compare my life with the lives of others. People have never witnessed any authenticity or my true emotion of loneliness because I choose not to upload that part of my life. I choose not to upload when I am struggling emotionally, socially, or financially. This habit has only reinforced the fact that I utilize social media as a drug to temporarily cure my social isolation.

These interviews have convinced me that the reason we're unable to cope with the dysfunctional nature of our lives is that the new technology-induced social norms we unwittingly conform to are dysfunctional. Our smartphone and screen use have propelled us down an unfulfilling path. We have been promised connection. Instead, we have ended up with loneliness and misery.

A grim picture? Yes, when you consider that loneliness is more detrimental to our health than smoking and, in older people, twice as likely as obesity to precipitate death. Yet as you will read in the coming pages, such a scenario is an unfortunately accurate portrait of what our lives have become.

The Internet in Historical Perspective

In order to understand how we've become so hooked by the Internet, let's first put it in historical perspective. After all, it's not the first time that a new technology has come along and upended many previous customs and shaken up our society.

Throughout our collective history, people have either enthusiastically embraced or warily distrusted new technologies. As with any medium that changes the status quo, technology has always attracted flocks of both enthusiasts and detractors. The invention of the typewriter in the 1870s, for instance, quickly divided the public. Newspaper and magazine editorials and articles proliferated, taking sides on whether or not it was polite to use a typewriter.

Many considered the typewriter discourteous and an insinuation that the receiver could not read script. Others disparaged the invention as harmful to eyesight, and cited statistics that more people than ever wore eyeglasses. Still others deemed the typewriter inconsiderate of privacy—sound familiar?—as clerks had presumably read the typed page in addition to the writer. Capturing the ambivalence surrounding the typewriter, the State Department called it a "necessary evil."

The inventions kept coming: the next half-century would revolutionize how people went about their lives. A decade after the invention of the typewriter, the telegraph—from the Greek for "to write from a distance"—was heralded by *Scientific American* in 1881 as having ushered in "a kinship of humanity." Again, sound familiar? The Victorians were not so sanguine, and lamented that the telegraph meant that "the businessman of the present day must be continually on the jump."

Turn It Up

A decade later, the Italian inventor Guglielmo Marconi was thrown into a mental hospital for believing he could "send messages through the air." After his discharge in 1895, he became the first person to transmit long-distance wireless signals (over 1.5 miles) and subsequently invented the radio.

To understand how unusual the radio was at the time of its invention, consider how Albert Einstein helped people understand it: "You see, wire telegraph is a kind of very, very long cat. You pull his tail in New York and his head is meowing in Los Angeles ... Radio operates exactly the same way: you send signals here, they receive them there. The only difference is that there is no cat." In 1920, virtually no American homes owned radios. By the mid-1930s, about two-thirds did.

The radio enjoyed unprecedented popularity. Even during the Great Depression, a huge proportion of rural homeowners in the US purchased radios to stay connected with current news and entertainment such as *Grand Ole Opry*. Other radio shows such as *Amos 'n' Andy* targeted city dwellers. Once again extolling the connective benefits of a new technology, one journalist attributed the radio's role in "achieving the task of making us feel together, think together, live together." A similarly ardent newspaper editor from Albany, New York, wrote in 1928:

> One night last week we ... enjoy[ed] a relaxed evening with friends. For three hours hardly a word was spoken and all ears were strained to catch every word and note coming from the radio loud-speaker. We've heard tell that the motion picture industry is getting panicky because people are staying home with their ears tuned to earphones and loudspeakers instead of going to the movies. I might be sticking my neck out, but I think this new entertainment medium is great and will be around for a long time.

It's for You

Around the same time as the birth of the radio, in 1892, Alexander Graham Bell and Thomas Watson invented the first commercially viable telephone, inaugurating the first long-distance connection between New York and Chicago. After the telephone was introduced, some thought that others could eavesdrop on them even when the receiver was replaced on the hook. The chief engineer of the British postal service, William Preece, said that, unlike in America, the telephone would not find much use in the UK: "Here we have a super-abundance of messengers, errand boys, and things of that kind."

Once again, alongside the diehard proponents of a technological shift were its detractors. While the telephone was deemed by some an "antidote to provincialism," others were not so generous in their estimations, and claimed—with words that could easily be read today in a blog decrying the pitfalls of Internet addiction—that the telephone portended a "general withdrawal into self-pursuit and privatism" and the "destruction of community because they encourage far-flung operations and far-flung relationships." Imagine what they would have thought of Skype!

Others claimed the heightened familiarity with distant others spawned by the telephone promoted incivility and threatened neighborhood solidarity. Many feared that thieves could plan their crimes discreetly without the risk of having to meet in person. Yet, enthusiasts exclaimed, police could also communicate more rapidly to counter lawbreakers. Additionally, medical and other emergencies could be handled much more efficiently thanks to 911 and the ease of reaching a hospital or police station.

Telephones were also criticized for their interruptions of everyday activities. In 1900, the German philosopher Walter Benjamin decried the arrival of the telephone to his home in Berlin with its "alarm signal that menaced not only my parents' midday nap but the historical era that underwrote and enveloped this siesta."

Taken for a Ride

Like the telephone and radio, the automobile—an invention rare in that it was mass-produced by one of its creators—also stirred controversy. In 1899, the employer of a high school dropout offered him a promotion with the condition that he give up his private obsession with designing a gasoline engine that would inexpensively transport people.

Henry Ford refused the offer and quit his job. By the time the Model T gave way to the Model A in 1927, the pioneer of modern assembly-line production had sold 15 million cars worldwide. Both praise and criticism soon followed, igniting a dilemma called the "enigma of automobility" or the "automotive paradox."

On the positive side, street sweepers lauded the automobile for the striking reduction in animal carcasses to dispose of and manure to cart away. The automobile was heralded in 1916 as a great "equalizer" and "liberator" that had succeeded in making "happier the lot of people who led isolated lives in the country and congested lives in the city."

Celebrity home economist Christine Fredrick, for instance, declared in 1912 that "the car has wrought my emancipation, my freedom. I am no longer a country-bound farmer's wife.... The auto ... brings me into frequent touch with the entertainment and life of my neighboring small towns—with joys of bargains, library, and soda water."

Not all were so optimistic. Like the bicycles before them, which were condemned in 1896 by the Presbyterian Assembly for steering parishioners toward other activities on Sunday than church, automobiles were deemed by some—such as Robert and Helen Lynd in their classic book *Middletown* in 1929—to foster promiscuity, as they brought hedonistic influences such as roadhouses and movies within reach.

College administrators and farmers in the 1920s joined the chorus: the former blaming the car for students skipping class and dropping out at higher rates, the latter decrying the new auto drivers for frightening their livestock and destroying their bucolic tranquility. Simply owning a car could cause trauma. Writing two decades earlier in 1902, a Vermont resident observed:

> In my stable, my horses took the arrival of that automobile much
> to heart, and five of them almost died with some form of distemper
> the next month. My hostler did almost as much kicking as his
> four-footed charges. He insisted that he had to hunt for the horses
> in the hay loft, because they invariably went up the feed spout every
> time I started the engine in the stable: and when I asked him to wash
> the automobile, he fainted dead away, and revived only long enough
> to give his notice of departure.

Automobiles were described by one critic as "the greatest consumer
of public and personal space yet created by man," and were soon
blamed for pollution, congestion, suburban sprawl, and the shift of
attention away from, and consequent dilapidation of, central cities.

What's On Next

The next great invention, like all those that preceded it, divided public
sentiment. The television was first available commercially in Germany
in 1934, in France and the UK in 1936, and in America four years later
(only eight thousand TV sets were manufactured in America prior to
World War II—the cheapest with a twelve-inch screen costing $445, the
equivalent of $10,970 in 2018 dollars—before the War Production Board
halted US production in 1942).

Philo T. Farnsworth, who began developing the first image dissector
at age fourteen on his farm and invented the first working version of
the electronic television at age twenty-one, promoted the television as
a harbinger of world peace: "If we were able to see people in other
countries and learn about our differences, why would there be any
misunderstandings? War would be a thing of the past."

Despite such rosy proclamations, fears about the social consequences of the television were widespread. Capitalizing on these fears,

in 1935 Cameo Pictures released a film starring the Hungarian-born actor who had played the original Dracula four years earlier, Bela Lugosi, titled *Murder by Television*. TV was also dismissed by many, such as the *New York Times* in 1939: "The problem with television is that people must sit and keep their eyes glued on a screen; the average American family hasn't time for it."

Want More Time Outdoors? Try Prison

Why this condensed history of the kudos and whining associated with a new technology? Because it's important to be aware that every major new technology creates a division among people based on whether they deem its benefits to their way of life to outweigh its costs or vice versa.

After the introduction of a new technology, it is normal for the histrionics to begin, and for both overly glowing and excessively critical perspectives about its social implications to flourish. The Internet, in this sense, is no different in inducing divergent feelings about how it has affected our lives. As in any marriage, something is gained and something is lost.

To argue against the utility of the Internet would be about as successful a proposition as railing against the existence of any new technology that gained widespread usage quickly, such as the typewriter in the 1870s, the telephone in the 1900s, the automobile in the 1910s, or the television after World War II. In fact, the smartphone has achieved mass societal penetration more rapidly than any of these other (once) new consumer technologies, with only the television a close second. Like these other major technological developments, the Internet and social media are here to stay.

Consequently, this book is not about getting rid of the Internet so we can reconnect with ourselves: that would be a futile endeavor. Instead, it's about learning how to live with it. It's about learning how to spend time online to reap what we need from this unprecedented access-you-name-it extravaganza while also retaining the essence of who we are as human beings.

To launch us on this journey, we must first understand what we're up against. We must deconstruct and better comprehend why the Internet has become associated with addiction. We'd better hurry, for three critical reasons. First, loneliness is not just increasing: it's skyrocketing. On both sides of the Atlantic, loneliness has become a complex, ubiquitous problem.

In the US, a Cigna survey of twenty thousand Americans released in May 2018 found that nearly half of Americans are lonely based on the UCLA Revised Loneliness Scale, a finding that has raised the decibels on siren calls of a "national loneliness epidemic." In this survey, 43 percent of Americans acknowledged that they feel isolated from others and that their relationships are sometimes or always not meaningful. Twenty-seven percent reported that they never or only rarely feel understood. A year later, Cigna conducted another survey of over 10,000 American adults and the findings—and the national trend it uncovers—are even more unsettling: over three in five Americans are now lonely.

The "epidemic" designation has also been invoked in the UK—for example, recently by the Royal College of General Practitioners—which is further ahead of the loneliness curve ever since Prime Minister Theresa May appointed a Minister for Loneliness in 2018. May made this decision on the heels of two studies that found that 9 million British citizens are often or always lonely and that British children spend less time outside than prison inmates. Yes, really.

Is It Worth It?

A recent study led by psychologist Philip Hyland of the Centre for Global Health at Trinity College Dublin sheds light on why loneliness is increasing so dramatically in the digital age. Hyland and his colleagues surveyed 1,839 Irish adults and found that what most induces loneliness is not the quantity of relationships, but the quality. Low-quality relationships—which abound when the people around you are too distracted by their devices to pay sufficient attention to your socioemotional needs—were found to be the primary driver of untenable levels of loneliness.

Viewed in this light, a recent meta-analysis of seventy-two studies conducted between 1979 and 2009 that found that the empathy levels of American college students have dropped 40 percent—which the authors primarily attribute to the rise of social media—can only be seen as a grim portent for the future of our society if the current shift toward texting, emailing, and instant messaging and away from face-to-face interaction continues.

For a more poignant and real example of this phenomenon, imagine a girl sitting on a sofa who tries to talk with her brother about her feelings of being bullied or embarrassed by some of the "popular" kids at school earlier that day. He continues staring at his phone with the television also on in front of him. She feels ignored and so pulls out her phone or also settles down in front of the TV. We are all that disappointed girl today: feeling unimportant to those around us and coping with our rejection with even more screen time—which only exacerbates our loneliness.

The second reason we'd better put understanding the addictive qualities of the Internet on the fast track is related to research by Jean Twenge. The San Diego State University psychologist, among others, has found that self-esteem is plummeting and suicide rates are rising to unprecedented levels.

The third reason is that social connection is at an all-time low. As of 2004, the number of close friends of the average American had decreased from three to two in less than twenty years; it has likely decreased even further since. While the most common response to the survey in 1985 was three close friends, in the 2004 survey the most common response, reported by 25 percent of Americans, was having no close friends whatsoever—not even one person to talk with about important issues.

In short, the current situation is dire. Let's see what we can do about it.

The Road Map

So here's what's coming. This book has three very different parts. In Part One: Disconnected, I explain how we became so disconnected from ourselves and each other. Part One will help you gain a deeper understanding of why smartphones, email, and social media are highly linked to addiction.

Part Two: The New World Order presents the State of the Union: the forces that unite us in our precipitous slide into disconnection. In Part Two, I describe where we are now, individually and as a society, as a consequence of our new digital habits: what we—and our world—have become. Like Part One, it will help you understand how we arrived to our current state: why we are so lonely and depressed, and how we have unwittingly become so disconnected from ourselves and others.

Armed with this understanding, we will be equipped to design strategies to reclaim our essential humanness and freedom. That is precisely what we will do in Part Three: Reconnected, in which I share concrete, specific strategies to become reconnected with yourself and others vis-à-vis the new technologies that have rendered such a goal seemingly impossible. Part Three includes practical strategies you can begin implementing right away for self-renewal—for reconnecting with who you truly are and what you deeply care about.

Jacob Weisberg wrote in his famous *New York Review of Books* article on the addictiveness of the Internet in 2016 that while the problem has been identified, "there aren't many good solutions at the moment." Well, there you have it: that is the goal of this book. Part Three: Reconnected is dedicated to finding solutions to our current plight: strategies to enable new, life-affirming habits that guide how we manage our phones and digital devices. These strategies culminate in the last two chapters with the Heart of Darkness Challenge—a guide to transforming your relationship with your phone in seven weeks.

Please note that the journals of five of my clients who have risen to this seven-week challenge are included in Appendix A (along with their responses to a follow-up email asking them four to six months later to briefly share "how, this long after the challenge, your relationship with your phone has evolved"). I have selected these journals because they are a good cross-section of the challenges my clients are currently confronting with directing the use of—rather than being directed by—their phones. If you do not find yourself relating to at least one of the Heart of Darkness Challenge Journals in Appendix A, this is probably not the right book for you.

The strategies outlined in *Screened In* have evolved from the leadership conferences I have been teaching over the past twenty-five years to thousands of CEOs, senior executives, and employees of Fortune 500 companies, small businesses, and the world's largest nonprofits such as GE, Disney, Nokia, Bank of America, IBM, CARE, Save the Children, the United Way, and the American Red Cross. I have also provided leadership development training to many political leaders, including G-20 cabinet ministers, and thousands of social workers, police officers, school counselors, and child development specialists.

In addition, I have taught leadership courses and lectured at numerous universities, including Harvard, Stanford, Berkeley, Howard, Georgetown, IESE, ESADE, and INCAE business schools, Cal State San Bernardino, Claremont McKenna, the Monterrey Institute of Technology, and Cal Poly Pomona. I spent the last ten years researching and writing this book because my conference participants, clients, and students repeatedly shared the problems they faced in their lives with managing their phones and other screens and I wanted to offer them solutions. On a deeper level, I observed them becoming more and more disconnected from themselves and others as technology surged over the past two decades and I wanted to do something about it.

Throughout the book, I will share excerpts from some of my conference participants, coaching clients, and students who have attempted the Heart of Darkness Challenge. When I do, I will just share their names (I have changed their names to protect their privacy) instead of indicating "one of my conference participants" or "a client." All of their quotes in this book are verbatim, exactly as they expressed them.

Imagine that you ignored your spouse for a decade and she or he finally had the sense to leave you. You realize how much you love your spouse and that your life is devoid of meaning without this person. You go to great lengths to implore her or him to return. She or he resists. You try harder and harder; it's not an easy road—one many would abandon.

Retrieving yourself after ignoring it in order to be available to others 24-7 by hovering over a screen is similar. Relearning the art of living free will not be easy; it will resist until you demonstrate that you're committed and will never again dismiss who you truly are. This is the journey I invite you to take in the coming pages.

To Change Your Actions over the Long-Term, First Change Your Motivations

While the stakes are high and the road long, the benefits are immeasurable. The word confidence comes from *com* (with) and *fidere* (trust) and means "trust with." To build the self-confidence to recover your essential freedom and humanness, you must plumb the depths of the meaning of self-confidence, which is "trust with self," and rebuild this fragile relationship. If you are willing to put your full effort into rising to this challenge, you will rediscover a long-lost friend inside who has been patiently waiting all the while, throughout your innumerable digital meanderings, for your return.

While the loneliness of wanting more connection with those around you will be partially diminished by revitalizing some of these relationships through the strategies that fill these pages, it will be even more reduced by revitalizing your connection with *you*. By making your deepest humanness a priority once again, you will cease to be a casualty of the digital age like most of your compatriots. You will relearn how to realize your potential as the person you always dreamed and knew you could be.

Read this book in any way that works for you. If you grow impatient and start to have I-know-all-this-and-am-getting-depressed-thinking-about-what-we-have-all-become thoughts while reading Part One, then go straight to Part Three. I would think twice about this approach, however. Although it's tempting to read the book backward and begin with the most effective strategies to combat what you will come to know as "the brogrammer brigade"—who cleverly exploit our darkest human motivations and impel us to touch our phones, on average, over twenty-five hundred times per day—making sustainable changes in your life requires more than just being knowledgeable about strategies.

Making lasting changes in your life requires a deep understanding of the motivations that drove you to this untenable state in the first place, which I highlight in Parts One and Two. Why? Because those same motivations will continue to affect your life—inside both you and the people around you—and you will need to identify them to be able to build the inner strength to overcome them.

Can you guess the first step an exorcist took in ancient mythology to help a possessed individual extricate the demon inside? To ask them to name the demon. Similarly, you have to name your demons that keep you hovering, clicking, and tapping your life away, which Parts One and Two will make easier.

If you are ready for this internal journey, let's get started. Let's begin by taking a close look at how the Internet has induced so many of us to hand over the majority of our waking hours to it.

2

The Bait-and-Switch of the Internet

Man wishes to be happy even when he so lives
as to make happiness impossible.
—Saint Augustine

About six years ago, a friend of mine was sitting in a restaurant with his wife in a small town in France and noticed that almost everyone in the restaurant was looking at their smartphone. Then he noticed he and his wife were doing the same. When I told him I was writing this book, he asked, "Are you sure spending less time on the Internet and their smartphones is something people want to do?"

I didn't know how to answer him.

"It's kind of like legal heroin," he continued. "It's really come to this point where people are addicted, and many are happily addicted."

Stanford psychologist Kelly McGonigal begs to differ. "People have a pathological relationship with their devices," she claims. "People feel not just addicted, but trapped." Perhaps most disconcerting about this story is that it occurred in 2011. Only four years earlier, on January 9, 2007, wearing his trademark black turtleneck, Steve Jobs unveiled the first iPhone operated by touch screen at the Macworld convention, cheerfully announcing "Today, Apple is reinventing the phone!" The first iPhone was released six months later on June 29. The first Android-power phones were released the following year.

Today, the story of what happened at the restaurant in France is no longer a story: it's what we witness just about every time we go out. Sharing this story today is like recounting that you went to a baseball game and observed the fans standing up and cheering. What's not new is not news.

Steve Jobs put the computer in our pocket, yet its addiction-enhancing qualities date much further back, to the first time computers became equated with an efficiency and power unprecedented in world history.

Code-Breaking Power

The genesis of the modern computer was the "Turing machine," a digital computer developed at Bletchley Park, England, by Alan Turing during World War II to intercept and break Nazi military codes. In fact, most technological developments have come about through warfare and have been related to either military power or medicine.

By one estimate, in 1943 Turing's computer was breaking a total of eighty-four thousand Nazi codes per month, replete with information ranging from the positions of U-boats about to sink much-needed supply ships heading to Britain to direct orders from Hitler himself. By other estimates, Turing's work ended World War II two years earlier than it would have otherwise and saved 14 million lives.

In exchange for his service, Turing was charged with homosexuality in 1952 and forced to consume estrogen, a chemical castration agent. One year later he committed suicide. In 2009, British Prime Minister Gordon Brown apologized on behalf of the British government for "the appalling way he was treated." Queen Elizabeth II granted Turing a posthumous pardon four years later.

If a computer can help end a war and save the lives of millions, clearly the digital revolution is a force to be reckoned with. Going back to fully analog would be akin to visiting an African game park without a safari vehicle (which I foolishly did in Uganda in my early twenties and, after being chased up a tree by a herd of Cape buffalo, will never do again).

Yet, as my friend experienced in France, the smartphone has transformed the computer for many from a useful tool into an inseparable bodily appendage that fits in our pockets, what some have come to describe as adult pacifiers or comfort objects—yes, like the stuffed animal you clung to until you became more independent—or even an "extended self."

Who, Me? Addicted?

Martin Lindstrom, a branding consultant, tried to identify the sounds that most powerfully affect people. A giggling baby was second to the Intel chime. Third was a vibrating smartphone. Britain's telecommunications regulator, Ofcom, notes that 60 percent of teenagers and 37 percent of adults who use smartphones describe themselves as "highly addicted" to their electronic gadgets.

Researchers at the University of Maryland asked two hundred students to give up all media for twenty-four hours. Many showed signs of anxiety, craving, withdrawal, and an inability to function without access to their online social networks. You can conduct your own experiment: on your next flight, observe the "customary reaction of passengers" who have gone for a few hours without Internet access, as author Teddy Wayne amusingly observes, "quick-drawing their phones upon landing like Wild West gunslingers."

Many of us have become so addicted to our virtual worlds—in 2017, almost half of Americans surveyed by Pew said they couldn't live without their smartphone—that we confuse them with reality. In 2008, a forty-three-year-old Japanese woman was jailed after killing her online husband's avatar after he divorced her. "I was suddenly divorced, without a word of warning. That made me so angry," she said.

Two years later, an Italian woman reported to the police that virtual burglars had stolen $140 worth of virtual furniture from her virtual apartment in the Facebook game *Pet Society*. She claimed it was a real-world crime, saying, "I don't think it matters that the apartment only exists in Facebook. It is real to me, and I have suffered a real loss."

Much more tragically, the parents of a three-month-old girl in South Korea created avatars in *Prius Online*, a program similar to *Second Life*, to raise a "virtual infant," and subsequently left their (real) daughter unattended during a twelve-hour gaming session, causing her to die from starvation. The parents, an unemployed couple, were upset she had been born prematurely.

Addiction Has Become the Norm

Our addiction to what the Internet enables us to effortlessly access can even prevent people who live in areas with beautiful weather from going outside. Craig Smallwood, a man in Hawaii, sued the designers of *Lineage II*, a virtual-world simulation video game, claiming that he should have been warned of its addictive qualities. Smallwood claimed to have spent about twenty thousand hours playing it over a period of five years (that's eleven hours every single day during that period) and that his addiction interfered with his "usual daily activities such as getting up, getting dressed, bathing, or communicating with family and friends."

These stories seem to implicate the Internet for its addictiveness, which has become the conventional wisdom. Early diagnostic criteria for "Internet addiction," which was considered by some a clinical disorder, included "Have you repeatedly made unsuccessful efforts to control, cut back, or stop Internet use?" and "Do you stay online longer than originally intended?" along with "Excessive use of the Internet for periods of time longer than planned" and "Preoccupation with use of the Internet that are experienced as irresistible."

If we were to assess ourselves by these diagnostic criteria, it would be safe to conclude that nearly all of us are now suffering from Internet addiction.

Yet what if the Internet is not addictive at all? What if, contrary to popular wisdom, there really isn't an addiction to the Internet, smartphone apps, or social media sites like Facebook, Twitter, or Snapchat? What if it's not the Internet or social media we're addicted to, but something else?

The Internet Accelerates Other Addictions

The Internet provides a welcome respite and distraction from reality. The less comfortable we are with reality, the more appealing is an alternative. Yet it's not the Internet that is the alternative. Rather, the Internet accelerates our access to the alternative.

Addictions always stem from unmet needs. An "addict" engages repeatedly in an activity in an attempt to meet a basic human need. The last I checked, staring at text, images, and videos on a pixelated screen was not a basic human need. Other rudimentary human needs, however, can be satisfied through this medium.

A recent psychological review of addiction suggests that an addiction emerges when an individual engages in a habit beyond the point where they have control of it; what started as a habit becomes a compulsory behavior the individual is unable to regulate through their own volition. In other words, when an individual compulsively engages in behaviors in the pursuit of rewarding stimuli despite the detrimental consequences of those behaviors, they are addicted.

Consistent with psychological research that has found we focus more on avoiding what we don't want in our lives than seeking what we do, addictions are less about seeking pleasure and more about reducing psychological distress. According to NYU marketing professor Adam Alter, "Addiction is really about soothing a psychological ill and that's true no matter what the addiction is … You only develop an addiction when there is some psychological motive that hasn't been fulfilled for you: loneliness, that you've been bullied, or you can't make good things happen in your life."

The existential psychologist Rollo May referred to anxiety as an emotion without an object. Placating the anxiety of living in our current society by using a smartphone or other digital device is a behavior rather than a chemical drug, which has created a lot of confusion around whether it should be diagnosed as an addiction.

Yet as Alter notes, "It doesn't actually matter what you use to soothe that addiction, whether it's playing a particular game that lulls you into a distracted state or whether it's taking a drug. In terms of soothing those psychological ills, behavior and substance addictions are very, very similar." As with chemical drugs, smartphones may reduce anxiety in the short term—which is why they have been called "adult pacifiers," as we turn to them to soothe us when we feel bored, distressed, or irritable—but then increase it in the long term.

Full Disclosure

I can't write this chapter without making a confession: researching addiction has been eye opening for me because I am Exhibit A of an individual with many addictive qualities. Compulsive behavior to soothe anxiety or psychological distress? Absolutely; probably daily. I've become hardwired, ever since I lived in a village in Kenya as a Peace Corps volunteer thirty years ago, with the inner belief that when I am experiencing troubling emotions, I can prevent them from taking over my life through three primary means: exercise, going for long walks at sunset, and meditation.

I engage in all three of these behaviors almost daily—usually intentionally, yet sometimes compulsively, as in I feel I need to do (at least one or two of) them to function well—and the more I do, the better I am able to manage my emotions and the more robust are my inner feelings of well-being. The only difference between these behaviors and those Alter and other addiction experts classify as addictions is that the behaviors I engage in have (primarily) beneficial rather than detrimental long-term consequences.

There are three truths regarding addiction and technology that we must confront. First, the new reality is that the majority of us are now engaging in addictive behaviors accelerated by our phones and other devices. If you're in doubt, consider that according to a 2013 Kleiner Perkins report, we are now interacting with our phones about 150 times per day.

Second, these phone-, tablet-, and laptop-accelerated behaviors are addictive according to the above definition because they are detrimental to our well-being in the long term (leading to loneliness, depression, and diminished self-esteem, as we will see in the following chapters).

The third truth is that the challenge of this or any book that attempts to help us transcend these digitally mediated addictive behaviors is to enable us to develop other behaviors to replace them with. These other behaviors may also possibly be repetitive and compulsive. Such behaviors, if they lead to beneficial rather than detrimental long-term outcomes in our lives, are often called "habits."

Four Addictions Before and After the Internet

To develop these new habits, it's imperative that we first understand where we are. Let's now take a look at addictions before and after the Internet. Contrary to what many scholarly and popular writers claim, once again I do not believe there is an Internet addiction. Instead, it's an addiction to an external object that the Internet facilitates. To evaluate this hypothesis, let's consider four common addictions: gambling, shopping, seeking an intimate partner, and social approval.

First, suppose a person has an addiction to some of the material things money can buy. This need for material things—whether it's new cars, new clothing, or whatever—could manifest as an addiction to gambling. Alternatively, the addiction may be to winning: "I am worthy because I can play Texas hold 'em or slot machines or bet on horse races well," and so on.

In both cases, gambling, like most addictions, stems from a need to avoid the psychological distress of not feeling worthy enough as one is—naked and vulnerable, without external objects to win and then hide behind that convey the illusion of worthiness. Each gambling win is a dopamine burst that feels damn good because it mollifies that psychological distress. When we don't find our worth inside, we seek it through our work outside. And for an addict, the acquisition of whatever external object they are chasing is rarely pleasure and almost always work.

Before the Internet, a person might spend a lot of time going to casinos. One of the challenges in the pre-Internet era, however, was that it was socially frowned upon to spend a lot of time in casinos. Perhaps that meant the person could go once or twice per week, but not every day; many hid their habit and were careful about how they presented themselves to others, so they placed limits on their casino visits.

Now, they can just open their smartphone or tablet or laptop and, boom, they're gambling. Their addiction has become much more accessible. Also, no one really knows what they're doing behind their screens. Thanks to the Internet, the shame, fear of social unacceptability, and other social costs associated with gambling are greatly reduced.

Till You Drop

Now let's look at an addiction to shopping. Like the other three addictions, the need to go shopping may camouflage a deeper human need for self-esteem. When we can't provide ourselves with a sense of value from within, we try to do so from without—by buying things for ourselves. We attempt to fill this gaping internal hole with material things.

Alternatively, similar to gambling, the dopamine rush may be associated with playing the game well: in the case of shopping, finding a great deal. The need for competence that undergirds the feeling of "I am a great shopper and know how to save money—at least I'm good at something" may be the addiction.

Before the Internet, a person went to shops or the mall looking for bargains. To enable this practice, they had to leave their house, so at least they walked around outside and sometimes met and conversed with people. Now, they just sit at home on their rear end behind a screen. They spend hours upon hours shopping, hunting down the next deal, and other people have no idea what they're doing.

Once again, others are largely unaware. They aren't saying, "Oh, look at Sally. All she does is shop." Before the Internet, Sally may have had family members and friends that she also wanted to see and maybe it didn't look good if every single day she was schlepping around trolling for bargains at the mall. Now, if every single day she's on Amazon and eBay and Facebook marketplace trying to find the Holy Grail of bargains, her family and friends may not have the slightest clue what she's doing. Moreover, her employer may even be unwittingly paying her to do it.

In this sense, the Internet enables much more privacy. It's ironic because it doesn't enable privacy in other ways that are the topic of thousands of media articles every year, such as the protection of personal information, but it does enable privacy in that people (in your physical environment) don't really know what you're doing behind your screens.

People in your virtual environment (especially marketers), on the other hand, know a lot more about what you're doing, and that's where it becomes an invasion of privacy. Yet in your physical world, the Internet can afford more privacy.

Bar Hound No More

Now let's consider a third addiction. Suppose you are lonely and want to meet people. (Imagine that.) Again, according to a Cigna study released in 2020, 61 percent of Americans are now lonely. Before the Internet, you would have to leave the comfort of home and venture out into a lot of social activities. Socializing took a lot of time, energy, and money.

You could go out to the bars and clubs every Thursday, Friday, and Saturday night. On the other nights of the week, however, you may have thought to yourself, "I don't really feel like going out to the bars. I want to relax with a friend or a book (which can also feel like a friend) or watch a movie."

Now, you can be at the bars and clubs of the Internet all day and all of the night (not in the slightest what Ray Davies, the lead singer of the Kinks, had in mind when he wrote that song). You can be on Tinder, Bumble, Hinge, Match, and other dating apps, swiping and viewing one profile after the next. As the comedian Aziz Ansari aptly remarks, "Today, if you own a smartphone, you're carrying a 24-7 singles bar in your pocket. Press a few buttons at any time of the day, and you're instantly immersed in an ocean of romantic possibilities."

Like gambling and shopping, others, once again, usually have little or no idea what you're doing. Before the Internet, if you trolled the bars seven nights per week you earned a stigma: Bar hound. Desperate. Floozy. A drunk. Needy. And so on.

Now, you can go to Match or Tinder seven days and nights per week and no one knows. Once again, the Internet suppresses social costs by affording privacy on the physical—but not virtual—plane. Once again, the cost of your addiction is reduced because it's more difficult for others around you, in real time, to detect.

A Quick Fix with Low Social Costs

In sum, the Internet suppresses social costs (e.g., embarrassment or shame, ridicule or derision from family, friends, and others in society). It provides the necessary anonymity that allows you to pander to your base needs for an efficient escape from reality (seemingly high benefit) without the stigma that has traditionally accompanied such addictions (seemingly low cost).

Take the South Korean couple mentioned earlier. They could efficiently placate their craving for an alternative baby to distract them from the pain of having a premature, "imperfect" baby without their friends and extended family having any idea what they were doing.

We will go to great lengths to distract ourselves from a gaping inner wound. Author Andrew Sullivan writes that it wasn't until he went on a ten-day, leave-your-phone-at-home meditation retreat that he realized the extent to which his phone offered him a distraction from the childhood trauma he experienced growing up with a bipolar mother who was in and out of mental institutions.

After sharing that he "absorbed a lot of her agony," Sullivan reports that at the retreat:

> It was as if, having slowly and progressively removed every distraction from my life, I was suddenly faced with what I had been distracting myself from. Resting for a moment against the trunk of a tree, I stopped, and suddenly found myself bent over, convulsed with the newly present pain, sobbing. And this time, even as I eventually made it back to the meditation hall, there was no relief … I couldn't check my email or refresh my Instagram or text someone who might share the pain.

How You Like Me Now?

A fourth addiction is the need for social approval. While Tinder and Match are attempts to meet the basic need for intimacy, Facebook, Twitter, Instagram, and other social networking sites purport to meet the fundamental human need for social approval and friendship. Before the Internet, you could go to school or work and then return home and call old friends and try to make new friends; you could go meet up with people; you could go to parties. All this socializing took a whole lot of effort.

Once again, you couldn't really do it 24-7. Not only did it require effort, but also just about anything in the physical plane—including going to bars, casinos, or malls—consumes financial resources. It takes money to buy the right clothes and go out to lots of parties. If you are still in school, parents often obstruct all this effort, saying "Hey, you can't be going out all the time. You have to study."

Like the need to find an intimate partner, the need for social approval is a correlate of a deeper fundamental human need for connection with others. (As you will see in William's Heart of

Darkness Challenge in Appendix A, we can seek approval not only for ourselves, but for our children.)

This need can hamper an individual's ability to self-regulate. As the social neuroscientist John Cacioppo found after numerous experiments, "There was only one force that could impair self-regulation enough to disrupt both thinking and behavior. This disturbing, dysregulating force is … the terror of feeling helplessly and dangerously alone."

Unable to regulate this primal need for social connection, you can hole up in your room and log on to Facebook or Instagram or Snapchat and post self-flattering photos with friends and message other friends and spend almost all your waking hours in the relentless, elusive search for the social approval that is one of the lubricants of connection. You can attempt to meet that need all the time—in work meetings, in classes while the teacher's or professor's voice drones on overhead, while lying in bed, or even while on the crapper—and no one knows.

So once again, it's not the Internet to which we're addicted. We're addicted to the same things to which we've always been addicted. The Internet, unlike any prior communication medium in human history, fuels and makes it easier to satisfy that addiction while depressing the associated social costs.

For these reasons, our phones and other devices are like wolves in sheep's clothing: they stealthily weave their way into our lives without our realizing how dependent we are becoming on them to satisfy the addictions they accelerate. In the words of leadership author Simon Sinek, "In the case of alcohol and gambling, we are aware of it. In the case of our love of our devices and social media, we are less aware of the addictive qualities."

Read All About It: Satisfy Your Needs Faster with Less Social Cost

Let's now consider what these four addictions have in common. Before the Internet, a positive outcome of any one of them was that they forced you to get out of the house. Accordingly, they helped you build your social skills. Whether it was gambling, meeting the right person, or winning the good opinions of others to feel better about yourself, you had to go outside and interact with other people to do it. All of these addictions at least required physical movement and social interaction, both of which are often beneficial.

In addition to the social development of engaging in these activities with or at least around other people, even the act of going outside and "getting some air" could offer some measure of physical, emotional, and psychological renewal. Now, you can engage in all of these addictions from the comfort of your own home while barely moving (or exercising) a muscle. It is no wonder we are increasingly becoming like the fat, docile inhabitants of a futuristic earth depicted so well in the film *WALL-E*.

So where does that leave us? In conclusion, the Internet—meaning our smartphones, tablets, and laptops—*accelerates* the appeasement and *reduces* the social costs associated with many addictions. In addition, the Internet diminishes our physical exercise and social interaction and, hence, yes—a positive correlate of some pre-Internet addictions—social skills development.

The significant exception to the Internet-accelerated addictions are physical substances. The Internet doesn't enable you to drink alcohol or smoke cigarettes on a screen without anyone noticing. Yet if your addiction is to gambling, social information, dating, porn … you name it, the Internet will enable you to access it more rapidly and with less social downside than any other means.

Identify the Real Unmet Need

This discovery can help us reduce our time online. Once we become aware of what we're actually pursuing—the satisfaction of a basic human need—we can decrease our dependence on our digital devices. It is no small epiphany to realize that your "digital addiction" is not an addiction to punching letters or numbers on a keypad, or swiping your finger to the left on a small screen. I have yet to hear of someone waking up in the morning, wearily extending their hand onto their nightstand for their phone, and excitedly exclaiming, "I want to hover my finger over some electronic letters! Give me my digital fix, baby!"

Those at the front lines of assisting people with "Internet addiction" are coming to precisely this conclusion: it's not the Internet that drives our addictions, but something else to which the Internet enables easier access. Take David Greenfield, the director of the Center for Internet and Technology Addiction in West Hartford, Connecticut. In a recent interview, David shared with me, "Most of the reasons why people come in [to the center] are because they're having problems managing some specific content. I wouldn't say that they're overusing the Internet in general, but they're having a problem with one specific area of content."

The co-inventor of the iPod, Tony Fadell, concurs: "The devices themselves are not addictive. That's like saying a refrigerator is addictive. No, it's the food inside them. The devices are not addictive, but the things they deliver can be addictive." There is always something beyond the metal, plastic, and glass contraption in the addict's hands they are pursuing, such as intimacy, approval, or self-worth. (Yet as we'll see in Chapter 4, many app developers play an integral role in fostering these addictions.)

Reaching for your phone would rapidly lose its allure if it didn't, with unprecedented efficiency and marginal social costs, create the impression of placating a burning desire inside. That desire may be to find an intimate partner, or to receive social recognition from others, or to make money quickly so you can buy a newer car, or to feel like you are better than others at something in your life—even if it is a video game. If you can identify the underlying need or motivation, you will then be able to envision other, healthier strategies to meet that need.

> **Make It Happen:**
>
> 1) Consider what motivations and impulses cause you to log on and leave the physical world. First identify the activities that are the most alluring to you about online life. Are they Facebook and social media sites, reading the latest news (e.g., Twitter, CNN, BBC), online dating (e.g., Match, Tinder), fantasy football, gaming, email, Internet porn, discount travel, shopping (e.g., Amazon), watching unusual videos (e.g., YouTube, Facebook), reading product reviews (e.g., CNET), or repeatedly checking weather or other local conditions before going out? Whatever the activities are that draw you to your smartphone or tablet or laptop, identify them in the first column.
>
> 2) For each of these activities, at the top of the second column write "Motivation." Determine the underlying motivation that makes this activity so appealing to you. For example, if the activity is "Checking Facebook," the motivation might be "Seeing what my friends have been up to." If the activity is checking email, the motivation might be "Making sure every-thing is OK," or "Staying on top of my work."
>
> 3) At the top of the third column, write "Deeper Motivation." Try to name *the basic human need* underlying the motivation you identified in the second column. For example, if the motivation in the second column is "Seeing what my friends have been up to," the deeper underlying motivation may be "Emotional connection." If the motivation in the second column is "Staying on top of my work," the deeper motivation may be "Be acknowledged for my competence" or "Make a contribution to society."

4) Write down more online activities with associated motivations and deeper underlying motivations. For example, if the online activity is "Make money," the motivation might be "Buy a new car" and the deeper underlying motivation may be "Approval," or "Acceptance," or even "Love." (Your implicit mental script may be "Someone will love me if I have money and a new car.")

The importance of this exercise is that you may have multiple motivations for any single activity, and understanding your rawest, most fundamental human needs associated with any activity you repeatedly engage in online will help you wrest yourself from its control. The more you can identify your own unmet human needs—those that impel you to repeatedly engage in any online activity in the hopes that you can meet them—the more you will reduce the power of this activity over you.

5) Acknowledge how well your online activities meet the basic human needs you have identified: in other words, assess the extent to which your online activities *actually* satisfy the basic human needs you are attempting to meet by engaging in them.

6) Based on what you have written in Steps 1 through 5, design some healthier, offline, real-time strategies to meet the basic human needs that impel you to go online.

Pretty Damn Amazing

At five years old, Saroo Brierley begged for food to survive in Khandwa, India. One day he boarded an empty carriage in a rail station and fell asleep while waiting for his brother, who had promised to return. Unbeknownst to Saroo, his brother was killed by an oncoming train. Later that night, Saroo awoke to find the train moving. The next day, he alighted from the train nine hundred miles away from his family, in Calcutta. After living homeless on the streets for some time, he was taken in by an orphanage and then adopted by an Australian family.

What would you consider the chances of a thirty-year-old Indian man in Australia identifying the village he grew up in among the many thousands of Indian villages, much less finding his family? Enter Google Earth. As is chronicled in his book *A Long Way Home* and the movie *Lion,* Saroo devoted himself for many months to searching satellite images of villages in India for a familiar sight from his childhood. In February 2012, he spotted a small railway station sign with a name phonetically similar to the station he remembered being trapped in as a child before the train continued on to Calcutta.

He followed the images of the railway lines near this station on Google Earth and found a small village, Khandwa, that—although its name was unfamiliar to him—displayed an image of a fountain near the railway tracks that looked similar to a place where he remembered playing as a child. Through a Facebook group, he contacted people in Khandwa who reinforced his hunch that his family might still be there. He boarded a plane and traveled to this tiny village, where local people took him to see his mother, brother, and sister.

Try telling Saroo that the Internet is bad for humanity.

Saroo is unlikely to listen to you, so perhaps you could try Lina or José? Lina was thirty-four with a good job working for an international oil company in Mexico. Yet she was very lonely. Many Mexican men head north for illegal work in the US, resulting in an unfavorable ratio for the women who remain in their hometowns.

José was living in a small town in Ecuador. A sporadically employed thirty-two-year-old musician, José was single and did not have much of a future. Because he had very little money, he had never married. Lina and José met on Facebook. They chatted for a few weeks and then talked by phone for eight months. They then agreed to get married.

Lina came to Quito to meet José, bringing along a wedding dress and eleven family members. José met her at the airport with nine members of his family. Before she hugged him, she first hugged her future mother-in-law. José's cousin, who told me José's remarkable story during a trip to Ecuador, said José and Lina had been married for five years and were living in Mexico. According to his cousin, José drives a BMW that Lina bought for them. "*Un sueño realizado* (A dream come true)," José's cousin told me.

Have Time, Will Go Online

If Saroo, Lina, or José are unwilling to join the Internet-bashing club, try Henry, David, Esther, or Melissa. They are all participants in a program started by FCB Brazil, an advertising agency that connects Brazilian students wishing to practice their English via a Skype-like video-chat platform with residents of Windsor Park Retirement Community in Chicago who are interested in finding new people to talk to.

"I look like I'm only twenty-five, but I'm eighty-eight," Henry, a Windsor Park resident, tells David, his partner in Brazil.

"It's the first time I'm speaking with someone from another country," David shares. Half an hour later he asks Henry, "Have you ever been to Brazil? If you come, you can stay in my house if you want."

Another Windsor Park resident, Esther Barker, patiently tells her video-chat partner, Melissa, a teen from Brazil who has just told Esther about her brother, "Instead of saying 'He has twenty-three years,' you could say, 'He is twenty-three years old.'" After his elderly partner in Chicago shows him some pictures of himself with his wife in their youth, another Brazilian student comments, "You were good-looking when you were young," and then quickly, to qualify his compliment, "and you are still good-looking."

These two demographics—elderly people in the developed world and young people in developing nations—share two important characteristics: time on their hands and a willingness to learn about a new culture. This innovative program simply introduced them to each other. Before the advent of the Internet, such connections would have been difficult to organize and extremely unlikely.

The Bait-and-Switch of the Internet

Bait-and-switch is an old trick primarily used in sales. A product is offered to a potential customer at a low price in order to "bait" them into the store or vendor's location. Once the customer has entered, they discover that the product they came to purchase is not available. Instead, they are offered a more expensive substitute (the "switch"). In some cases, the product they were initially enticed with is available but they are still pressured into buying another product.

Bait-and-switch also occurs outside of sales. If you have ever gone out on what you thought was a date, only to be pawned off on your date's less desirable friend, you have experienced a bait-and-switch. The attractive hitchhiker whose friends are waiting behind a bush for the car to pull over is also well-versed in bait-and-switch.

Experimental research has found that bait-and-switch actually works. When the social psychologist Robert Cialdini invited his students to join an experiment that began at seven in the morning, less than a quarter turned up. When he instead asked them if they would agree to participate, and then, once they had agreed, told them the starting time would be seven, over half showed up.

So what does bait-and-switch have to do with this book? In the next chapter, let's dive deeper into what exactly the Internet, social media, and our phones offer us (the bait) and what they actually deliver (the switch).

3

Social Information Versus Social Connection

*T*he efficiency of information sharing—the miraculous benefits that Saroo or Lina can attest to—is the "bait" the Internet uses to entice you into its virtual realm every time you power up your laptop or pick up your smartphone. Once you are online, it pressures you through pop-up ads and attractive icons to help you make or build friendships.

Yet while using the Internet to share information can truly be a worthwhile use of your time when done in a measured (e.g., limited) way (this is the low-priced/high-value product it offers that attracts you to it), numerous studies have found that using the Internet leads to less face-to-face time with others and more loneliness and depression. The Carnegie Mellon study of Pittsburgh families we reviewed in Chapter 1 is just one example. Robert Kraut, the social psychologist who led the Pittsburgh study, has called this phenomenon the "Internet paradox."

Studies on the Internet's paradoxical effects abound. Take, for example, a study by cancer researchers Paula Klemm and Thomas Hardie that found that 92 percent of the participants in online cancer support groups were depressed as compared to *none* of the participants in face-to-face cancer support groups.

Why would people living with cancer become depressed only if their group meets online? There is a displacement effect: more time online means less time on the phone and in person with family members and friends and more disconnection from one's social environment. This effect was first discovered in a study of over four thousand individuals from across America led by Stanford social scientist Norman Nie.

More Phone Time Means Enjoying In-Person Interactions Less

"This 'displacement effect' does not emerge in my life, oh, over-generalizing author," you may be thinking. "By checking the social media feeds of my close friends, I have more to talk about with them when we see each other in person." In your unique case, that may be true. Yet most people are experiencing the opposite.

Take Paul, a financial analyst I interviewed recently, who told me about a reunion dinner he attended. "Many of these people had already been so involved in my digitally displayed life that we didn't have much conversation," Paul shared. "Most of the people at the table were focused on their cellular devices, not knowing what kind of isolation they were projecting. This behavior has led me to become socially awkward and increasingly lonely."

Recent research supports this displacement effect and offers an even worse prognosis: phone use does not only equate to less face-to-face time with the people we care about, but actually *causes us to enjoy this in-person time less.*

Psychologists from the University of British Columbia and the University of Virginia recruited over three hundred students and community residents and asked them to eat a meal at a restaurant with family or friends. Some participants were asked to keep their phones on the table while others were instructed to put their phones away during the meal. When phones were present during the meal, the students/community members felt distracted and enjoyed spending time with their friends and family less.

A second study, in which participants kept their phones present or absent during interactions with others throughout their day and reported on how they felt five times per day, yielded the same results: when their phones were present, they experienced more distraction and less enjoyment of their face-to-face interactions.

When I asked lead researcher Ryan Dwyer why participants enjoyed speaking with people in person less the more they used their phones, he replied, "The culprit is distraction. Using your phone during an interaction makes it harder to engage with your conversation partner, which may stunt conversation and lead to more boring interactions."

Extending this research, a 2016 study in *Computers in Human Behavior* found that in romantic relationships, this reduced satisfaction of in-person time when a phone is visible is attributable to conflict over when each partner is using their phone.

The Allure of Social Information

Yes, it seems that we've unfortunately arrived at this point as a society: the addictive tendencies more easily accessed and accelerated by our phones have led to our becoming less satisfied with our real-time relationships with the people around us. (I suppose it shouldn't be that surprising: our phones obediently do just about whatever we ask of them; people, as uppity and headstrong as they are, may tend to annoy in comparison.)

This finding is particularly worrisome, as the more isolated we become from others, the more the addiction-accelerating properties of our smartphones, tablets, and laptops thrive. As addiction expert Adam Alter affirms, "People who have a strong social support network, who have a very full life, tend not to develop addiction."

So the Internet attracts people like Paul and, yes, you and me, with promises of efficiency and social connection. Let's now consider the "switch." The Internet turns out to have a higher price tag than advertised: the price is the relationships you would have effectively built offline if you weren't wasting untold hours tapping away on apps that promise social connection but only provide, as Paul grimly recounts, social information. Once the switch occurs, the value of the Internet becomes much more dubious.

It's sobering—and a wake-up call to questioning why we are in contact with so many "friends"—to realize the brevity of our list of social media contacts we would even wish to speak with in real time. I've asked many conference participants to try this exercise, and my sad discovery is that for over 95 percent of our "friends" on Facebook, we have no desire whatsoever to actually talk with them by phone or in person.

This discovery, of course, raises a question: Why are we in contact with most of them at all? What is the purpose of repeatedly viewing profiles of people we didn't really speak that much with in high school or college or at a previous job back when we had the chance? We are most likely in contact with these people because they fulfill our need for social information.

The One Versus the Many

This need, unfortunately, seems to prevent many of us from experiencing social connection. Not a sage choice, considering that while the existence of social information is not a buffer against loneliness, social connection—which we forego by scanning status updates of hundreds of people on social media instead of listening to the status update of one in person—is.

One of the key lessons of this book, which I will highlight in the coming pages, is to utilize the Internet for information sharing, which improves your life, and not for online relationship building, which causes your life to decay. Every time you spend a few hours meticulously curating your social media profiles, what you are really indicating is that refining your digital brand is more important than developing your relationships in real time with the people you care about, or could care about if you were to get to know them better.

To understand the addictiveness of the social information you share with those seeking such information, let's try to answer another relevant question: Why do others seek information about your life? Is it because they care about you deeply and wish for your well-being? For a few, yes.

Yet the reason most of those high school "friends" and other people you haven't seen in years are digesting chunk after chunk of your social information has nothing to do with warm, concerned feelings about you—and everything to do with their own self-esteem. Let's see why.

Social Comparison on Steroids

As it turns out, when our self-evaluations are difficult to measure objectively (e.g., how successful, creative, or happy we are), we seek out similar others (called our "reference group") and then measure ourselves by how we are faring in life relative to them. The phenomenon of social comparison was first identified by the social psychologist Leon Festinger. If we're doing better than similar others in any specific dimension of our lives we feel insecure about, we can raise our self-esteem by comparing ourselves to them.

Conversely, if we are the ones doing worse than others similar to us, our self-esteem can diminish in comparison to the artificially positive social information they project. It is for this reason that students are likely to have a higher academic self-concept if they are attending a high school in which most students are average performers. Once they graduate and go to a more demanding university, their academic self-concept tends to decrease. Yet clearly the answer here is not to put our children in low-performing schools so they can feel good about their relative performance.

As happens in most casinos in the world, you enter social media seeking to enhance your self-esteem, but the cards are stacked against you. The current problem is worse than ever because the casinos have now entered our homes, schools, restaurants, stadiums, and every other place you can access the Internet on your phone. Never before has the social information of similar others been so readily available for you to digest than since the genesis of Facebook and other social media sites where you can bring these folks into your network under the astonishingly ironic title of "friends." Yet, as in the casino, your chances of winning the social comparison game are infinitesimal. And self-esteem seems to me to be the last thing you'd want to gamble.

Hence, you are always making a critical social decision: to either spend time online with people who hunger for your social information in the hopes of boosting their fragile egos if they stack up favorably in comparison with you, or to spend time in the real world strengthening social connections with those seeking meaningful relationships with you.

To help you assess the worthiness of these two options, it may help to recognize that this decision serves two distinct groups of people. The first group is those sitting behind their screens evaluating your social information along with that of former classmates and coworkers. Many such people you see very infrequently, if at all; most of them you will never physically see again, ever.

The second group is those people with whom you maintain a strong emotional connection. These people make their decisions to spend time with you not based on their perception of how successful you are, or how enjoyable your last vacation was, or how amazing the restaurant you went to last week was. Instead, they make their decisions regarding how much value you bring to their lives based on the strength and stability of the emotional connection you share, which fulfills their need for attachment with others.

Most importantly, *your emotional connection with them does not relate strongly to what you share on social media about your life when you are not with them.* As the novelist Maya Angelou once wrote, "At the end of the day people won't remember what you said or did, they will remember how you made them feel."

Don't Be That Person

If the people closest to you couldn't care less about most of the self-image-inflating photos, comments, and videos you post on social media, it means that most of your efforts to develop relationships with the people you truly care about by hurling hours of your life down the black hole of social media are largely futile.

Think about it: How emotionally connected would you feel with a friend who met you at a restaurant, sat down across from you, and said, "I aced my test. My husband was so cute when he brought me flowers afterward. We had such an amazing vacation. Our kids are so funny. We ate lots of seafood." You would probably start looking at the clock. My money says you would hesitate before accepting another invitation from said person.

You on social media *are* said person. The platform of social media encourages said people to boast about themselves. Research has found that this energy allocated to self-aggrandizement has reduced the energy we allocate to listening to and supporting others emotionally. It seems your close friends are wise not to spend much time with said person.

They make this choice because empathy induces the emotional connection Angelou refers to. Hence, if social connection is what you are after, the hours you spend scrupulously updating your social media profile are your personal contribution toward the most colossal waste of time in human history.

If you wish to look back upon your life at age eighty and, while painfully lonely and surrounded by no one whatsoever, be able to say, "I dutifully shared social information with thousands of people whom I rarely, if ever, saw in person," then keep updating those profiles. Facebook is your best friend.

If, alternatively, you would prefer to have a few people around you who actually care, who actually visit, who actually answer the phone, then close Facebook, close your texting app, close your email, put down your screen, and start calling, visiting, inviting, listening, and caring.

Seeking Connection, Will Travel

Viewed in this light, it seems that the Internet may be the most pandemic game of bait-and-switch we've ever collectively experienced as a society. It initially baited us with social information, then pulled a switch by promising us social connection. Yet ninety-nine times out of a hundred, it only delivers social information. It paradoxically tantalizes us into downgrading face-to-face interactions in anticipation of social connection, which remains perpetually elusive.

This bait-and-switch is problematic, as social connection is widely considered one of the most important ingredients of happiness. It is for this reason, among others, that we relentlessly pursue meaningful relationships with others. Yet what the Internet provides—social information—does not increase happiness, as evidenced by an experimental study that found quitting Facebook causes an increase in well-being.

My goal in this book is to overturn common assumptions about the effectiveness of seeking social connection online. It is clear to me that this search is one of our primary motivations for going online at all. As former Skype CEO Josh Silverman put it, "There's no question in my mind about what stands at the heart of the communication revolution—the human desire to connect." Facebook CEO Mark Zuckerberg echoes this sentiment: "Connecting the world is really important, and that is something that we want to do. That is why Facebook is here on this planet."

This desire for connection impels us to take our smartphone out of our pocket and hover our index finger over the Facebook, texting, Instagram, Bumble, Hinge, or Snapchat app. But that finger, warmed by the anticipation of connection, opens a software program that does not provide us with what we are desperately seeking—social connection. Instead, it provides social information.

So is that why the Internet fuels addictive tendencies so easily? It promises meaningful relationships (social connection) but only provides text, photos, and videos about others (social information)? As it turns out, there is also another, much simpler reason.

The Internet Is Always with You

About five years ago, I was having lunch in Barcelona with one of my MBA students, an almost Digital Native who at twenty-seven was two decades younger than myself. I mentioned the argument of this subchapter: that fears over addictions to new technologies are not new, as we experienced similar fears with the television, telephone, and numerous other technologies.

Within seconds, he effortlessly illuminated the unprecedented challenge of smartphones: "Yes, but the difference between the Internet and those technologies is that the Internet is always with you."

There you have it. The television, typewriter, and telephone also accelerated other addictions. They offered new opportunities we never could have fathomed before their emergence, such as being entertained by people all over the world and receiving video imagery of current news events (the TV) and talking with just about anyone, anytime, no matter where in the world they might be (the telephone).

The Internet is different from these previous inventions in two very critical ways. First of all, whether in desktop, laptop, tablet, or smartphone form—*the Internet is all of the above inventions wrapped up in one unbelievably addiction-accelerating little package*. It's a one-stop shop. An all-in-one. It places you one click away from accessing, for the most part, every single communication invention that preceded it. As the *Washington Post* journalist Ellen McCarthy put it, "We can't leave the casino—because it's in our pockets."

Second, as addiction-accelerating as the television, typewriter, and telephone were, the requirements of daily life—going to work or school, buying groceries, meeting up with friends—compelled us to leave them behind for at least as long as it took us to reach the office or a friend's house. This instrumental commute or transport time, for many of us, became a psychological and emotional respite from whatever was transpiring inside our homes. It was an opportunity to walk, drive, or ride a metro or bus or taxi and just … think.

Time walking to or from the mode of transport allowed our thoughts to further deepen. While I am admittedly painting an overly embellished, rose-tinted picture of a mundane daily ritual, this time in transport often awoke within us an awareness of our need for more such time to reflect on where we were in our lives and what was important to us.

Always On

This phenomenon became strikingly clear to me about four years ago, also in Barcelona. As we didn't have a car, I took the metro everywhere. It's a different type of life to have feet on the street, walking and metro-ing around a city; it was grounding to feel connected with my immediate environment.

To buffer the existential shift after moving from Barcelona to southern California, I installed a hands-free phone system in my 2004 Honda Accord (many new cars come with them pre-installed) to help me deal with the long California drives, including the half-hour commute from our home to the university where I was teaching.

About six months later, I was driving to a mindfulness meditation retreat in Escondido—about two hours from our home—and decided that I would not use my smartphone to make calls during the ride. For what seemed like the first time, I noticed the stunning beauty of the area I was driving through: unusually verdant rolling hills (it had rained torrentially that winter after years of drought) beautifully juxtaposed against a crystal blue sky.

During the weekend meditation, I realized that I had inadvertently transformed my driving time—to the university, to meetings, to restaurants—into work or social time. While on the road I was always either calling a family member, friend, or client, or even participating in conference calls with the staff, board members, or collaborative partners of the nonprofit organization I was leading.

Regardless of who was on the other end of the line, I was not spending time with myself. Consequently, my self-relationship had suffered; I didn't feel as connected with myself as I had in Barcelona.

One Text or Call Can Wreck It All

At one point during the retreat, I walked up into the hills above the hermitage. Looking over Escondido, I decided not to talk anymore while driving. A simple, clear resolution. And I haven't, up to this day.

Within weeks of adopting this work-life balance strategy, I realized how much more poised I had become at work meetings and how much more connected I had become with my wife and children, my students, and with the leadership teams of the companies and organizations I was training. I had simply become more calm. All due to the impervious, undivided time to relax that I now experienced behind the wheel.

I also started to wonder how I had ever concentrated on the road while embroiled in often complex phone conversations. In fact, studies have shown that even hands-free cell phone calls increase the risk of driving accidents. In 2016 alone, 3,450 people were killed by distracted drivers.

Considering that two-thirds of drivers admit to having used a cell phone while driving, and that more than half of drivers ages twenty-one to twenty-four report that they text behind the wheel, this number of casualties should not come as a surprise. Driving while talking on the phone, even with a hands-free system, has been found in some studies to be associated with the same level of risk of an accident as driving with the legal maximum blood alcohol level.

It's even worse for texting: a study that placed video cameras in the cabs of long-haul trucks and observed drivers for over eighteen months found that when drivers send or check text messages on their phones, they typically take their eyes off the road for about five seconds—at 55 miles per hour, driving the distance of a football field—and are at twenty-three times the risk of collision compared to when they are not texting.

Despite our proclamations to the contrary, texting compromises our ability to effectively engage in other tasks. As a California electronic road sign once warned me, "One text or call can wreck it all." And not just on the road: if you are in doubt, perhaps you can discuss the matter with the woman who fell into Lake Michigan while writing a text message. If she doesn't convince you, try the man who almost walked into a four-hundred-pound black bear while texting.

Let In-Between Time Be In-Between Time

"Now hold on just a moment," you may be thinking. "This all sounds well and good, but you clearly do not have the responsibilities that I do. If I didn't make calls on my way home from work, I'd have to make them at home, which would be much worse as it would detract from the little time I have each day to spend with my family."

It's true that if you need to have a conversation with someone for work or social reasons, making the call in your car can substitute for time on the phone at home. Yet it's also the case that—subconsciously or consciously—we tend to schedule phone calls during our driving time when we know it's an option. This decision in effect eliminates the regular, periodic time to think, relax, and catch up with ourselves that used to be an everyday feature of our transport time in the pre-smartphone era.

Reminiscent of the proverb "Always put off until tomorrow what you shouldn't be doing at all," when the option of making a call on the road doesn't exist—which is what happened in my life three years ago when I decided at the retreat to take this option off the table—we become compelled to integrate these calls into our daily routine in other ways, or not to make these calls at all. While many of these phone conversations may be a high priority in our lives, we have to ask ourselves whether developing our relationship with ourselves is also a high priority.

We also have to make a quality-quantity distinction. How? By asking ourselves if an "always on" schedule—in which even "in-between time" (e.g., time spent walking, driving, or taking a bus, metro, or taxi to or from meetings or other work activities) is allocated to work or social activities—will net us the minimum amount of self-time necessary to be truly engaged and present with others once we step back onto the grid.

The deeper, burning question is how you will integrate time for yourself into your daily schedule so you have the inner capacity to give time with others the quality of attention it deserves. If you drive home, will you stop making calls from the road? If you take the bus or metro or an Uber or Lyft, will you stop checking your smartphone in transit? Before you return home each evening, will you take some time to go for a walk in a nearby park and reflect on how you feel about your life under an incandescent sunset? When you wake up on Saturday morning, will you start the weekend by going to a farmers market or to the beach? What will you do to develop yourself each day such that when you are doing it, your time will be undisturbed by interactions with others?

You may fear that if you do not use your transit moments efficiently by making calls or texting, you will miss out on social opportunities or be too distracted by these social obligations once you arrive home. Let in-between time be in-between time and you will discover that when you are engaged with others, you are truly present and connected with them. Why? Because you are connected with yourself.

Honor Your Desire for Connection

Accordingly, the next time you think "I need to make a call while I'm driving to this meeting," recognize that while you may be becoming hyper-efficient, an important question to ask yourself is which approach to your day will enable you to become the type of person you want to be? Ask yourself whether you want to look back on your life in your later years and see an "always on" person or an "on for a while punctuated with in-between periods for energy renewal" person.

Allow yourself to just drive, to just cook, to just wash the dishes, to just walk, and you will be amazed at how much stronger and more targeted your energy becomes when you return to your daily interactions with others.

While you are considering making some of these changes and imagining what your life would be like if you carved out time for self-renewal and revitalizing your relationships, give yourself some credit: you engaged in your previous, always-on digital activities because you desire to connect with others. You were rightly aware—even if it was in your subconscious mind—that, as research has confirmed, this social connection is one of the healthiest mechanisms available to stave off cancer, heart disease, and other life-threatening maladies.

Our relentless search for this connection is noble and adaptive. Without this drive for connection, we would certainly perish. Yet we are being deceived by the Internet—more specifically, by unscrupulous technology companies competing for the most valuable commodity in the third millennium: our attention. These companies have hired hordes of psychologists to understand how to exploit our need for social connection and then teach programmers how to churn out the most captivating social information possible, wrung from digital pixels produced by a binary series of 0s and 1s.

So who are these people who have created these technologies, exactly, and what do they think about what they've done to our society?

4

The Brogrammer Brigade

At the highest echelons of our new technologies, the innovators and leaders designing the products that have so deftly hooked us are still mostly men. The Forbes Technology Council, an "invitation-only community for world-class CIOs, CTOs, and technology executives," for instance, in July 2018 asked its members to select "the most influential tech leader of our time" and featured the top eight picks. From Bill Gates and Steve Jobs to Jeff Bezos and Mark Zuckerberg, all eight were men.

In 2009, *Entrepreneur* magazine selected its top twenty-five innovators in technology. Ninety-three percent were men. Nine years later, *Inc.* magazine featured thirty-five US tech startups that reached a $1 billion valuation in 2018, and it displayed pictures of some of the CEOs/founders: once again, 93 percent were Y-chromosome holders.

As apps and software all involve coding, they are biased toward the inclinations and priorities of those who write the code. And the more we use their products, the more we accept their influence in our lives. At Google, for example, most of the C-suite executives (with "chief" in their job title, hence the "C") are men.

Why? Because they are programmers rather than businesspeople. As a senior Google employee once shared, "Part of the issue is who Larry [Page] wants around him, and those are the guys he's most comfortable with because he knows their whole engineering and computer science background." Perhaps for this reason, in the early days of the Internet, one of its rare female programmers, Ellen Ullman, warned that embedded inside the programs we tirelessly imbibe is "the cult of the boy engineer ... alone, out-of-time, disdainful of anyone far from the machine."

While most of the programmers behind the latest technologies are male, female tech workers and engineers are on the rise. In 2017, 20 percent of the tech workers, 25 percent of the leaders, and 31 percent of the overall workforce at Google were women. In the same year, 15 to 30 percent of tech and leadership jobs in the other largest tech companies—including Amazon, Twitter, Apple, Facebook, and Microsoft—were similarly occupied by women.

Brogrammers Are Peaking, Baby

Male coders, however, still rule the roost. We can say what we will about these brogrammers, yet one thing is certain: they have succeeded in capturing our attention beyond their wildest dreams. According to a 2016 study, the average smartphone user touches, swipes, or taps their phone 2,617 times per day. If you are close to this average and sleep eight hours per night, each waking minute of your life you touch your phone about 2.7 times.

A Kleiner Perkins study in 2013 uncovered that the average smartphone user has approximately 150 distinct interactions with their phone per day, primarily between 7 a.m. and 11 p.m., which translate into almost 10 interactions during every waking hour of life. To comprehend the tremendous scope of what the brogrammers have accomplished, consider that before smartphones, people spent an average of eighteen minutes per day on their phones.

Nothing is out of their reach—including our deepest emotions. In 2014, a leaked internal report indicated that Facebook manipulated information on 689,000 users' home pages without their consent in a clandestine experiment in collaboration with two Cornell University researchers. The experiment demonstrated that users' emotional states could be altered through emotion contagion effects: if others in their network reduced positive posts in their news feeds, users followed suit and uploaded less positive posts and more negative posts; in parallel, when their "friends" posted less negative posts, they similarly followed suit.

Other documents leaked in 2017 have shown that Facebook can reveal to advertisers when teenagers are feeling "worthless," "defeated," "useless," "insecure," or "a failure" based on the posts and photos they upload. According to Tristan Harris, a former Google employee and founder of the Center for Humane Technology, the granular information Facebook collects on its users is "a perfect model of what buttons you can push in a particular person."

Nir Eyal, who teaches courses in Silicon Valley on how to manipulate people into habitually using technology products—training for which up-and-coming programmers pay as much as $1,700—agrees: "The technologies we use have turned into compulsions, if not full-fledged addictions. It's the impulse to check a message notification. It's the pull to visit YouTube, Facebook, or Twitter for just a few minutes, only to find yourself still tapping and scrolling an hour later." This is no coincidence, Eyal writes. It's "just as their designers intended."

Not in My House

In his home, Eyal protects his own family from the reach of the brogrammers by installing an outlet timer that cuts off the Internet at a specific time each day. Ironically, many of the top Silicon Valley tech titans—including Bill Gates and the late Steve Jobs—place strict caps on their children's technology use.

Jobs, in fact, did not even allow his children to use an iPad. Gates prohibited his kids from having a cell phone until they were fourteen. According to Chris Weller of *Business Insider*, the behavior of Gates and Jobs should have been a red flag for the rest of us. Given that we're touching our phones over two and a half thousand times per day, it looks like we missed the memo.

Harris is a former Google employee and student of B. J. Fogg, the founder and former director of the Stanford Persuasive Technology

Lab. Fogg is the first social scientist to conduct systematic studies on how computers can influence people. He declared in 2008 that "persuading people through technology is the next social revolution. Facebook demonstrates just how powerful it will be."

What technology is able to do, according to Fogg, is "[make] information relevant to individuals," which "increase[s] their attention and arousal, which can ultimately lead to increased attitude and behavior change." As Fogg predicted and we will see in Chapter 14, it is a specific type of arousal provoked by these apps that keeps us hovering, swiping, and tapping all day long.

Fogg has often been identified as the mastermind of this field of user manipulation. In a recent interview, he shared with me, "The characterization that I have this playbook of techniques and then everyone in Silicon Valley studies it, it's their Bible ... that's just laughable, but it's not accurate   I feel especially mistreated when people characterize me as the bad guy that Tristan broke away from. That's just not an accurate narrative."

Concerned about the ethical challenges of persuasive technology, in 2006 Fogg testified to the Federal Trade Commission about its dangers. "The big picture is this," he told the FTC. "We can now create machines that can change what people think and what people do and the machines can do that autonomously. Persuasive technologies are here and more are coming."

To understand the reach of persuasive technology, keep in mind that addictions are rooted in the desire to alleviate psychological distress. The websites and apps we keep returning to first provoke the distress and then offer a short-term solution. "Feelings of boredom, loneliness, frustration, confusion, and indecisiveness often instigate a slight pain or irritation and prompt an almost instantaneous and often mindless action to quell the negative sensation," Eyal concurs. Then an effective app induces a behavioral loop or "persistent routine" we unwittingly adopt. Advising up-and-coming programmers on how to create the next generation of apps, Eyal shares, "Gradually, these bonds cement into a habit as users turn to your product when experiencing certain internal triggers."

Just One More Hit

Unaware of the greatest bait-and-switch in human history, we substitute the time we could spend outside forging meaningful relationships with time inside pecking away at our keyboards or swiping away on our phones. Why would we make such a stupid choice? Because we anticipate that our tapping and swiping will bring social connection. Yet time and time again, we only experience another tantalizing, but ultimately unfulfilling, sip of social information.

"Now just hold on one gigantic moment, oh, agenda-pushing author," you may be thinking. "If we aren't getting the social connection we came for, then why are we constantly on our phones and other devices?" Hmmm ... let's ask Robert Lustig, a professor of pediatrics and endocrinology at USC. According to Lustig, the Internet "[is] not a drug, but it might as well be. It works the same way [and] has the same results." He has found that the brain responds to technology similarly to how it responds to other addictive substances ranging from sugar to heroin.

Other doctors have joined this refrain on the toxic developmental effects of technology. Jenny Radesky, a developmental-behavioral pediatrician who developed the screen-time guidelines for the American Academy of Pediatrics, believes that screen time interferes with healthy child development. Developmental milestones for babies emphasize "serve-and-return" interactions in which parents respond to moments when babies seek connection and assurance by smiling, making eye contact, and talking with them, which lays the foundation for babies' brains.

Tune In

In one study, eleven- and fourteen-month-old infants of parents who practiced this emotionally attuned, interactive style—what the psychologists Roberta Golinkoff and Kathy Hirsh-Pasek call a "conversational duet"—knew twice as many words at age two as those who weren't exposed to this speech style.

That smartphones do not facilitate this style would be an egregious understatement. According to Hirsh-Pasek, "Toddlers cannot learn when we break the flow of conversations by picking up our cell phones or looking at the text that whizzes by our screens."

For younger children, these critical developmental milestones include when parents listen to their experiences in their imaginary worlds and help them both process these experiences (by immersing themselves in the imaginary world with them) and find ways to relate what they experience to their real lives.

With my children, I am sometimes the one who creates an imaginary world. When my daughter is crying because she wants a lollipop, and we either don't have a lollipop on hand or don't want her to eat one in that moment, I sometimes spread my arms wide, stand up, and, acting like I am carrying something heavy, say, "Here is one of the biggest lollipops in the world, just for you. I went exploring and found it." Sounds ridiculous, but it works: she's not getting a lollipop, granted, but I'm engaging with her at her level and validating that, yes, she wants a lollipop and is entitled to feel that desire.

In High Demand: Your Presence

Parents who practice this continually responsive communication style with their children seem to be heeding the advice of a Buddhist monk who popularized mindfulness in the West. I once saw Thich Nhat Hanh speak at the Warner Theater in Washington, DC. He asked the audience, "What is the greatest gift you can give to the person you love?" Over ten thousand people went silent. "To be fully present," he shared.

Parents foster the development of young children and adolescents by helping them develop their self-regulatory abilities—including and especially their ability to regulate complex emotions—during face-to-face interactions. Many parents short-circuit these developmental needs when they attempt to help their kids calm difficult emotions by allowing them to play a game on a phone or tablet instead of talking with them or giving them a hug.

Building on a model developed by the psychologist Joseph Walther of the University of California at Santa Barbara, I have conducted research with communications professor Mary Beth Watson-Manheim of the University of Illinois at Chicago that suggests email or texting tends to cause us to over- or under-regulate our emotions. When we over-control our emotions, the result is very subdued, emotionally flat, "impersonal" communication. When we don't control our emotions enough, on the other hand, it leads us to overly intense, "hyper-personal" communication, including histrionics and, at times, fits of uninhibited anger and rage.

How does this happen? We are overly intense or not expressive enough in how we display our emotions as a response to the inadequate social cues we receive through the solitary channel (textual messaging) of electronic communication. In the absence of sufficient social cues, our devices strip our communication with others of context, separating the message being sent from both ourselves and our immediate environment.

This is not very surprising given that body movements such as gestures, mimicry, and facial expressions have been estimated to comprise 55 percent of communication. Pitch, volume, and other vocal tone have been estimated at another 38 percent. By this analysis, nonverbal communication is *93 percent* of total communication. (This research has been frequently misinterpreted and has come into question by many, including its originator, Stanford professor Albert Mehrabian.) Email, texting, and social media messaging, which solely involve the writing and reading of typed text, neglect this 93 percent of how two people connect.

Face-to-face communication, on the other hand, helps us regulate our emotions through observing how others react to the ways we express ourselves. We continually receive verbal and nonverbal feedback from others during in-person interactions that help us express deeply felt emotions without overdoing their intensity. Recall a time when you were extremely angry and went to talk with the person you felt had provoked your anger. It is likely that their facial expressions, vocal tone, and empathetic messaging had a calming effect that helped you avoid blowing your top and falling prey to the admonishment of Benjamin Franklin that "a small leak will sink a great ship."

They're Starting Early

At all ages, numerous studies have found that babies, children, and teens who experience significant face-to-face interaction with their parents do much better in life—including higher educational achievement, less risky behavior with drugs or sex, higher self-control, and other healthy life indicators—than those with parents who delegate this responsibility to screens.

Two-and-a-half-year-olds who spend over two hours per day watching TV, for example, are more likely than other children to have social and behavioral problems when they are five and a half, an ominous statistic given that the average age at which children begin to engage in "regular" screen use has been frontloaded from four years in 1970 to just four months at present.

Responding to the detrimental health effects in recent years of the overuse of screens as electronic babysitters, the World Health Organization updated its recommendation on screen use in May 2019, advising that children ages two to four should be exposed to no more than one hour of "sedentary screen time" per day and children under the age of one should have no exposure whatsoever.

The WHO claims that limiting or even eliminating screen time for children under the age of five "will result in healthier adults." According to their director-general, Dr. Tedros Adhanom Ghebreyesus, "Achieving health for all means doing what is best for health right from the beginning of people's lives."

Further, a longitudinal survey (meaning a survey in which data is collected at multiple points over time) of approximately thirteen hundred children at ages one, three, and seven led by pediatrician Dimitri Christakis, MD, of the University of Washington found that each additional hour of exposure to television at ages one and three equates to a 9 percent increase in attentional problems at age seven.

This pediatric study documents how social alienation is created and then grows: we put our kids in front of the TV and they subsequently possess less self-control and are more difficult to manage later. How do we respond as parents? We give them less of our attention because we feel less capable of influencing them and helping them grow healthily. It's a vicious cycle that begins with the electronic babysitter and ends in dysfunction and much worse.

After the Next Episode: Behavioral Problems

I asked Christakis how this vicious spiral emerges. "Unlike most other mammals, including mammals that we're closely related to, we're born with our brains not fully developed," he shared. "Our minds are fine-tuned to the world we inhabit. That's one of the reasons, evolution-arily speaking, humans are incredibly adaptive, not just physically and emotionally but cognitively.… If you expose a developing brain to the fast pace that television can provide early in that critical window, you precondition the mind to expect that very high level of input. And by comparison, reality seems boring. It's underwhelming. It's under-stim-ulating. It doesn't happen quickly enough."

"So it's not just watching TV, but the pace of the shows children are watching, that leads to attentional difficulties later?" I asked.

"Exactly. We looked specifically at what shows children watch to further test the hypothesis that it's the pacing of the programs that really drives the effects and that's exactly what we found. Fast-paced programs increased the risk. Slow-paced programs don't increase the risk ... it's not a conscious decision that children make. It's the wiring of their brain that makes it that way. It's not that they deliberately say, 'This is boring.' It's that their mind has high checkpoints. It's been conditioned to expect very, very rapid inputs, high levels of stimulation that reality can't provide."

Pondering Christakis's words, I set out to better understand this phenomenon. "If fast-paced TV is leading to later attentional and behavioral difficulties, what are the effects of our phones and tablets on children?" I asked Jenny Radesky (who, as I mentioned earlier, developed the children's screen use guidelines for the American Academy of Pediatrics).

"We've done a couple of studies where we followed parents and kids over time because you really can't tell if there's a directionality in the relationship or presume causality until you actually are able to follow the changing patterns of technology use and child development over time," Radesky shared. "We found that when parents use a lot of technology in activities with their young kids, in the course of the next three to six months, those children were more likely to develop more behavioral problems."

If you are still in doubt, consider this study of 1,266 middle-school students led by the applied developmental psychologist Kimberly Schonert-Reichl of the University of British Columbia: the kids who spent most of their time after school on social networks, watching television, or playing video games consistently felt less competent and happy than their classmates. The children who spent more face-to-face time with and felt more emotionally connected with their parents, teachers, and friends, on the other hand, consistently felt happier and more competent.

It must be noted that this study, like many others I cite in this book, is correlational and hence cannot prove causality. Such studies warrant a measure of caution in making causal inferences, for two primary reasons. First, with correlational data we cannot be sure of the direction of the relationship. In this study, for example, it is unclear whether more screen time induces children to feel less happy and competent, or children who feel less happy and competent spend more time on their screens. Second, with all correlational studies it is also possible that other variables are triggering both of the variables in question. In the case of this study, for instance, perhaps bullying is causing kids to both spend more time on their screens and feel less competent and happy. Correlational studies are useful, however, because they flag that there is a relationship between two variables that may merit further research.

Got Dopamine?

Once we are no longer children and become more self-reliant, many of us turn away from refining our ability to regulate our own emotions and instead turn toward technology for a dopamine burst. A neurotransmitter located primarily in the right side of the brain that regulates movement, learning, attention, and emotional responses, dopamine is important for understanding why we act the way we do, as it is associated with "mammalian reward and motivation" and is released from the brain when we are engaged in reward-seeking behavior. In other words, dopamine is a chemical transmitted between the brain's neurons, or nerve cells, that plays a critical role in motivating our interest in taking action to achieve goals.

As Lustig advises, "Technology, like all other 'rewards,' can over-release dopamine, over-excite and kill neurons, and lead to addiction." The USC endocrinologist notes that when the brain becomes accustomed to a higher level of dopamine, it impels us to continue seeking out the addictive habit or substance—whether it's a drug, sex, or a habit mediated by technology.

Why, then, are we constantly on our phones? First of all, it makes us feel important and needed. Second we get a "dopamine squirt"—like an adrenaline rush—when we receive messages.

Toward which goals do these apps activate dopamine-addled, rewards-based behavior? Meeting the right person (Tinder, Hinge, Bumble). Developing our friendships (texting, email, Facebook, Instagram). Becoming more adept in our careers (email, Linkedin). Finding the best deal (Amazon, Hotels.com, Expedia).

Dopamine is not only released when you are pursuing a cognitive goal, such as finding a good travel deal. It is also released when you are pursuing an emotion-laden goal, such as trying to find the right partner. Electrochemical studies in male rats reveal that more dopamine is released in the presence of a female receptive rat than during actual copulation. In other words, dopamine is associated with the *chase*, not the *catch*.

If you've ever spent more time on Netflix searching for a film than actually watching it, you are no stranger to this phenomenon. It's the feeling that we are progressing *toward* a goal, rather than actually *enjoying* the attainment of the goal, that releases dopamine.

Bright, Shiny, and New

Dopamine surges with novelty (the chase for something new) and decreases with familiarity (the catch). The Internet has become such a formidable force in our lives because it provides 24-7 access to a virtual flea market of novelty: there's always something new around the cursor.

Research by Stanford psychologist Philip Zimbardo has found that many men today are experiencing sexual performance problems because they have become accustomed to the novelty of online porn and find real-life partners mundane and boring in comparison.

The psychologists behind the most popular apps today possess a highly refined understanding of how dopamine motivates our behavior. Every swipe, tap, or click can release dopamine. According to Chris Marcellino, an Apple designer, technologies affect the same neurological paths as drug use and gambling. Why? They similarly accentuate reward-based behavior that activates dopamine. "These are the same circuits that make people seek out food, comfort, heat, sex," admonishes Marcellino.

These words would merit attention coming from any individual designing the inner framework of the apps that keep us craning our necks down all day instead of looking forward at real people, nature, and the world. But Marcellino is not just any Apple designer.

Listed on Apple's patent for "managing notification connections and displaying icon badges," Marcellino is one of the two inventors who in 2009 helped develop the structural framework for the push-notification technology that enabled real-time alerts: the precise mechanism embedded into our phones that so many of us allowed to cede our self-control to our screens. (We will learn more about the addiction-accelerating effects of notifications in Chapter 14.)

Simon Sinek puts it well: "If you wake up in the morning and the first thing you crave is a drink, you might be an alcoholic. If you wake up in the morning and the first thing you do is check your phone to read email or scan through your social media before you even get out of bed, you might be an addict."

Referring to dopamine, Sinek continues, "Craving a hit of chemical feel-good, we repeat the behaviors that we know can produce that hit." In a TED talk, the leadership author comically shares how he sometimes completes a task he forgot to write down on his to-do list and then writes it down just so he can cross it off and experience the dopamine release.

Each small task in the pursuit of a larger goal—whether it's replying to the fourth of seven text messages, viewing the eighty-ninth of one-hundred-and-twenty-three profiles in your zip code on Tinder, or scrolling through one more status update on Facebook—can provide you with the desired buzz of this neuropeptide release.

Be Careful How Much Dopamine You Wish For

The dopamine over-release that has become normalized since the mass penetration of email in 1995, the advent of social media in the early 2000s, and then the release of the first iPhone in 2007 may sound innocuous, but it's not—for three primary reasons.

First, as the Stanford social scientist Norman Nie and Canadian psychologist Susan Pinker have noted, all of our time seeking the next dopamine hit on our phones, tablets, and laptops is time not spent connecting in real time with the people we care about.

Second, neither is it time spent reflecting on and refining our values. As we will discover in Chapter 8, the more we feel our time is limited (because there are so many small tasks to complete through swiping, tapping, and clicking in order to seek the next social, personal, or professional reward and experience the next small release of dopamine), the less we are attentive to and honor our higher-order values.

The third reason excessive dopamine seeking is unhealthy is that it can actually alter your brain chemistry. To understand how, bring to your mind someone you know who is always on their phone, tapping and swiping their days away seeking the next dopamine fix. Does their thinking seem to be disorganized and impairing their communication because they are so distracted by multiple stimuli?

As it turns out, such thinking processes are a common symptom of schizophrenia. Further, the brains of schizophrenia patients have been posthumously found to contain excessive dopamine receptors. Consistent with this finding, drugs that obstruct dopamine receptors often reduce the symptoms of schizophrenia.

These studies are correlational and, as I mentioned earlier, do not prove one variable causes another. In this case, they do not mean that overexposing yourself to dopamine will cause you to become schizophrenic. Yet there seems to be a link between dopamine seeking through overexposure to excessive stimuli throughout the day—which your phone, tablet, and laptop accelerate—and less focused thinking that, in extreme cases, can manifest as schizophrenia.

One Small Reason Not to Overstimulate Dopamine: It Destroys Your Brain

I didn't realize until my conversation with Rob Lustig that addiction can lead to cognitive dysfunction. The USC pediatrician and endocrinologist explained this phenomenon to me very incisively:

> It's an excitatory nerve transmitter, dopamine. So, neurons like to be excited. That's why they have receptors in the first place … they like to be stimulated and then they like the stimulus to go away. Chronic overstimulation of any neuron anywhere in the brain will lead to neuronal cell death … So that neuron has a Plan B, a self-defense mechanism, a way to try to mitigate the damage. What it does is it downregulates the number of receptors. Then it's less likely that any given dopamine molecule will find a receptor to bind to.… So, you get a hit, you get a rush, receptors go down. Next time you need a bigger hit to get the same rush when receptors go down. And then a bigger hit and a bigger hit until you need a huge hit to get nothing. That's called "tolerance." And then when the neurons actually do start to die, that's called addiction.

"Doesn't sound like too good an idea for those neurons to die in our brains. How does that affect us in the long term?" I asked.

"The problem is that when those neurons die, they're not coming back," Lustig replied. "Those neurons don't resurrect themselves." In line with his reasoning, students who spend a lot of time on social media and their phones tend to earn a lower GPA.

"Now what you've got is a system that can't generate the same level of amplitude, the same game as before," Lustig continued. "And so, you will never be able to generate as much of a pleasure response as you did before, which is one of the reasons why people who are addicted relax so easily. Because they try to get pleasure and they can't even feel it."

"Wait a moment," you may be thinking. "Is dopamine all bad? Doesn't the expectation of it also keep us focused on important goals?" Yes, this is true. In fact, it could be argued that the wiring of this neurotransmitter into our inner circuitry has enabled us as human beings to become goal oriented and focused on progress. Without dopamine impelling us to accomplish the next task, complete the next project, or achieve the next goal, perhaps we would replace ambition with apathy and prefer to slothfully lounge around throughout our lives in a desultory state of uninhibited contentment.

You could even argue that most of our dopamine-deficient ancestors on the open plains were probably wiped out by ravenous predators targeting such lethargic prey. Even if they were not so unfortunate, those who survived were improbable marriage material and less likely to propagate their genes.

In this sense, dopamine is an evolutionarily adaptive neuropeptide wired into our inner circuitry to help us survive. Whether we survive or even thrive in the third millennium may depend on whether the goals we pursue online, spurred on by dopamine, are actually important.

Are they?

Leverage Dopamine to Your Advantage

Identifying the larger objective underlying each of the fifty messages in your email inbox can help you to decide which messages to respond to or even check at all. Aside from the worthiness of each message, you can use the dopamine-inducing effects of email to your advantage.

How? By checking email after lunch when you're tired and about to hit a lull. That way you can avoid artificial stimulants like sugar or soda or coffee. And the dopamine-releasing effects of seeking the empty inbox will wake you up.

Exhibit A is author Alena Graedon, who attempts "to get up as early as I can and, when possible, I stay off everything but essential digital media until the middle of the day. I accept that I'm pretty useless after lunch anyway, so I feel fine being sucked into the vortex after that."

Yet take into account that it's very hard to shift from these dopamine-inducing effects to high concentration on one task, in relation to which reinforcement and approval only come in the long term, if at all. In whatever form you are taking your self-medication—laptop, cell phone, tablet, or smartphone—receiving even short messages from others literally has some of the same qualities as a drug: it makes you feel better temporarily and creates existential angst and loss of meaning later.

Directing the use of your phone rather than allowing it to direct you means that before you lose any more hours of your precious time craning your neck down in search of feeling wanted and important in this world, you can say with conviction, "I will start making a deeper connection with others and with myself in real time. I will use this electronic apparatus as an efficient tool to occasionally complement my real-time efforts to access social and cognitive information and coordinate meetings, but never again as a substitute for the deeper social connections that infuse my life with meaning."

While you are considering how to leverage your natural, dopamine-mediated inclination to pursue a goal or relationship to your advantage, remind yourself that the challenge of developing meaningful relationships and finding balance along the way is nothing new. As we will see in the coming chapters, what is new is that we as human beings have never dealt with so daunting an obstacle or so attractive a tool to communicate with others and get things done as the modern-day laptop, smartphone, or tablet.

So how will we make this adjustment to our riveting, spectacular new frenemy?

5

You Are the Crash Test Dummy

I've been amazed by the number of CEOs and senior executives I've coached who describe the same problem with finding any semblance of work-life balance. Take Kyle, for example, the vice president of an engineering firm.

"I spend most of my breaks checking personal emails or searching what's on the Internet," Kyle once told me.

"How does that make you feel?" I asked him.

"To tell you the truth, I really don't feel relaxed when I return to work; instead, I feel distracted."

"The reason you feel distracted is you really haven't taken a break from what you've been doing all day," I shared, "which is sitting on your ass looking at your computer."

We sit for hours and hours in the same position hunched over our screens, day after day. We use our bodies, which were designed for a broad range of activities, postures, and positions, in only one—seated at a desk or table—for most of our waking lives.

I want to pose an extremely important question: What will become of our bodies after we spend tens of thousands of our waking hours sitting in front of a screen? We don't have even one living example of a person who has spent fifty or more years of their life in a sedentary position in front of a PC.

How many years of passing our days in this way have we managed so far? The word "email" was first used in 1982 (eleven years after computer engineer Ray Tomlinson sent the first electronic mail message), the first Apple hit the market a year later, and most people did not start using a Mac or PC on a regular basis until the early to mid-1990s.

While the Internet was widely used by academics in the 1980s, it wasn't available to the mainstream until 1995, when the National Science Foundation Network—which restricted its commercial use—was decommissioned. (The IPO of Netscape stock, which also occurred in 1995, would become symbolic of the mass penetration of the Internet and the inception of the digital age.)

We Are Each a Digital Lucy

Back to our question: How long have we been sitting our days away in front of a screen? All the people you see around you have sat hunched over a screen for over six or eight hours per day for, at most, twenty-five or thirty years of their lives (a few may have eked out thirty-five years).

While our ancestors in the fields or on the factory floors were on no cakewalk, and often experienced physical aches and ailments due to the repetitive nature of their work, they were certainly much more mobile and dexterous. Even our more recent forebears in offices had to at least stand up to walk over to the copying machine or meander to the office down the hall to deliver a message.

While the carriage return on the typewriter may not seem like much exercise, it involved more body motion than we typically engage in on our screens these days. We weren't built to work, shop, read the daily news, and even socialize while seated on our *gluteus maximus* in front of a machine for so many hours each day. As we will see, our bodies simply weren't created to be stationary for such extended periods of time.

Perhaps most disconcertingly, we can't point to Joe, who at age seventy has sat hunched over behind a screen for fifty years, and say, "Look at Joe's posture—he still stands and walks so well." We are the first screen-obsessed generation, and most of us haven't even made it through our third decade of everyday screen usage. So the jury is still out on the physical effects of protracted screen use.

Ditto for the social, psychological, emotional, and spiritual effects.

At age seventy, can Joe still effectively listen to others? Can he read emotions and nonverbal cues on others' faces? Does he still even feel empathy? Can he still adequately express himself to others in face-to-face conversations? Does he still have friends whom he's invested enough time and energy in over the years that they call sometimes and even visit once in a while?

There is no Joe, so we cannot yet know the answer to this question.

In other words, each of us is a digital Lucy (the name given to one of our earliest bipedal ancestors, 40 percent of whose skeleton was found in Ethiopia in 1974 by archeologists fond of loudly playing the Beatles' "Lucy in the Sky with Diamonds" each evening at their expedition camp). We are each a digital crash test dummy. We are the predecessors, and will become the ancestors, of a future generation of the human race that will have fully adapted to a digitally mediated environment.

Sitting Is the New Smoking

In today's technology-imbued world, you complete many tasks without even leaving your desk that you used to have to stand up and move around to accomplish. Yet your body wasn't created to be stationary for such prolonged periods of time.

Lie in bed for a few days without standing up and what happens? You get "bedsores"—holes that form in people's bodies from too much time in the same position (usually in bed). What's the equivalent for spending too much time in the same position in front of a screen?

"Yes, but the extremes don't define the norm," you may be saying to yourself. "I don't have any 'chair-sores' as of yet from sitting and staring at a screen. This gloom-and-doom picture you're painting is for people who sit at their desks day and night. I go home at six and am not in that pathetic camp of workaholics."

Dr. James Levine, director of the Mayo Clinic-Arizona State University Obesity Solutions Initiative, begs to differ. He has been studying the detrimental effects of protracted sitting for years and has summed up his findings about our increasingly sedentary habits in two sentences: "Sitting is more dangerous than smoking, kills more people than HIV, and is more treacherous than parachuting. We are sitting ourselves to death."

Another expert on sedentary behavior and a professor of public health at the Pennington Biomedical Research Center in Baton Rouge, Louisiana, found that people who spend more time standing have lower mortality rates than those who only sit. Peter Katzmarzyk's study concurs with another published in the *British Journal of Sports Medicine* led by Per Sjögren, a professor of public health at Uppsala University in Sweden, that placed obese men and women, all age sixty-eight, on an exercise regimen. Some were also advised to sit less, while the others received no such advice and hence were more likely to complement their exercise with their previous sedentary lifestyle.

Six months later, Sjögren and his research team drew white blood cells from both groups to measure their telomeres—tiny caps at the ends of DNA strands that shorten and wither as a cell ages. Obesity and illness have been found to accelerate the shortening of telomeres, causing cells to prematurely age, while healthy lifestyles are more likely to preserve telomere length and delay the aging of cells.

The telomeres of the group that had been advised to spend less of their time during the six months on their rear cushions had lengthened. Their cells, it appeared, had become physiologically younger.

The control group of sixty-eight-year-old Swedes, which had also adopted the same exercise regimen but had not received the advice to sit less, experienced a *decrease* in telomere length. Their aging continued unabated despite the increase in exercise. While the researchers do not know precisely what the less sedentary group did in lieu of sitting, Sjögren suggests that "it's most likely that sitting time was predominantly replaced with low-intensity activities" engaged in while standing.

Sit Now, Pay Later

"You're not alone," I shared with Kyle, toning it down after offering such heavy-handed advice about him spending his breaks in front of a screen. "Like the rest of us, you will become much more productive if you learn how to take breaks to renew your energy. And the only thing that will give you a feeling of taking a break is connection."

"What do you mean?" Kyle asked with a slightly bemused expression.

"A connection with yourself or others. Anything you do that involves leaving your screens behind and getting up from your desk is likely to produce this connection. Taking a walk by yourself. Listening to some jazz. Calling a friend. Talking with your coworker about how you or they *feel* about anything other than work."

These studies on the dangerous effects of sitting are disconcerting as most of us, truth be told, have become protracted sitters like Kyle. According to a recent *Washington Post* article, between replying to emails, making calls, writing documents, eating lunch, and sitting in front of the TV or computer at home, the average office worker sits for about ten hours per day.

In South Korea, the government has had to ban gaming on certain websites after midnight, because youth are sitting and staring at their screens all night instead of sleeping. In 2005, a South Korean man went into cardiac arrest and died after almost continuously playing *StarCraft* in an Internet café for fifty hours.

If we are to avoid sitting for over eight hours per day, does that mean that if we sit at work all day—including sometimes even eating lunch at our desk—we should have a standing dinner? Not at all. The research on sedentary behavior suggests that if you sit for eight hours straight at work, you're already done in. It suggests that if you are interested in living a long, healthy life, eating lunch at your desk—rather than getting up off your behind and walking somewhere to sit and eat—is about as horrible an idea as you can dream up.

A Standing Offer

This research also suggests that you should consider pacing around your office while on the phone, taking a break every hour and walking for five minutes to say hi to a colleague, standing up from your desk to stretch for a few minutes every hour, routinely walking to the other corner of your office building, and so on. Given that most of us will eat our dinner sitting (say, for an hour) and sit for another hour or two in the evening (to watch a movie or talk with our kids, spouse, or a friend), that means we can only afford about five hours of sitting during the workday before we start shaving days from and adding distressing doctor visits to our retirement.

Radical, disruptive advice? Not when you consider that prolonged sitting heightens the risk of heart disease, obesity, diabetes, depression, and cancer, not to mention increasing cholesterol levels, slowing metabolism, and producing severe joint and muscle problems. Corroborating the toxic effects of prolonged sitting, a 2015 meta-analysis of forty-seven studies linking sitting and mortality found that those who engage in protracted sitting, which the study's authors at the University of Toronto identify as over eight hours of rear-end compression per day, are 24 percent more likely to die from health problems than people who sit less.

In addition to an earlier death, those who spend most of their days on their butts incur an increased chance of developing cancer, heart disease, and diabetes. Lead researcher Avi Biswas recommends that you "move as much as you can when you're not exercising." And as the Swedish study demonstrates, if you think that hitting the gym or going for a run after work will compensate for protracted sitting in slowing the aging process, think again.

Exercise Must Help, Right?

I interviewed Biswas to better understand the link between sitting and exercise. "It's not that exercise doesn't have any effect," he shared. "When we factored in the interplay effects of exercise, we found that meeting exercise recommendations reduces the risks for all-cause mortality by thirty percent."

"What if you exercise more than the minimum recommended level?" I asked. "Does that help?"

"We did not look at what higher levels of exercise would do to the risks, but they'll probably keep going down," Biswas shared. He then directed me to another meta-analysis of sixteen studies of over one million men and women from when such data was first collected through 2015. This meta-analysis tested the correlation between sedentary behavior and mortality and factored in the potentially offsetting effects of exercise. It found that over sixty minutes of daily exercise does, in fact, eliminate the link between prolonged sitting and mortality.

Sound good? Not so fast (literally). "Sixty-plus minutes of exercise isn't easy for many people," Biswas told me, "in which case, it's probably best to try to exercise when you can, and if you can't, then keep moving as much as you can."

Given that high-level exercise (at least an hour per day) does offset the effects of prolonged sitting, at the least there is some hope for people who feel they must sit for eight hours per day to do their jobs. The problem is that a very small minority of them are actually exercising that much.

It really is sit now and pay later. Each of us can make a conscious effort to limit our time sitting in front of a screen or food each day. Our bodies were simply not designed to be stationed in chairs all day long. If you refuse to heed these evidence-based studies, you should not be surprised when the health problems they document beset you later in life.

This is no short order, as the recommendations of these researchers are difficult to implement in practice. In our digitally mediated environment, there is no question that, just as limiting smartphone use will cramp your style, limiting time at your desk may reduce your short-term productivity and your need to excel at work and show others what you can do.

Yet it will be even more difficult in the long run to lose your health before you finally break free of the shackles of sedentary-mediated responsibility and have more time to stand up, walk around, and enjoy your life in healthy ways.

Yes, you read that correctly. Retirement, it turns out, isn't what it used to be, at least in comparison to our working lives.

To Retire Is to Rewire

Think back to when you were a student in grade school and high school and contorted your body into various postures and poses throughout the day while you engaged in sports, dancing, art, and other activities. After a period of healthy enjoyment of life, we enter the work force and focus, focus, focus and sit, sit, sit our days away until one day we return once again to experience a physically varied, pleasurable lifestyle, paradoxically called "retirement."

Why paradoxical? Because our bodies are not retiring at all, but reengaging with life. In stark contrast to previous generations, in today's workplace "retiring" can ironically be synonymous with an *increase* in activity.

It doesn't have to be this way. If you take good care of yourself throughout your career, retiring will become *rewiring*—the continuance of an active lifestyle with a shift in energy from workplace-mediated activities to life-mediated activities that bring you joy and fulfillment.

Do you wish to have the physical capacity to enjoy the activities you've worked so hard most of your life for the right to participate in— such as traveling, learning about new cultures, pottery, creating and playing music, painting, you name it—or do you want to be a physical, emotional, and social wreck from overwork, over-screen-staring and over-sitting? Up to you.

Kyle once told me that his wife calls him a "slow processor." I became accustomed to his deliberate, well thought out responses. After silently reflecting on my advice for a few minutes, he said, "That's easy for you to say. My job requires me to be seated all day. I'm not sure what I can do about that."

After slow-processing for another week, Kyle made a commitment in our next session to take a non-digital break every hour and a half for at least ten minutes. Three months later, he shared how much more he enjoyed his work: "The thing is, Tony, I'm more engaged and productive in my work than ever before. I used to wonder why one of the younger guys could get so much more work done than me in less time. Now I know."

Thanks to these studies on the effects of protracted sitting, we now understand that the benefit of getting up from your desk and taking regular breaks is not only emotional and psychological, as it was for Kyle, but also physical.

Transcend the New Normal

There is no question that it's not easy to reduce sedentary time in our technology-mediated workplace, where sitting on our asses in front of a screen is the new normal. Yet it will be even harder in the long run to deal with the corrosive physical effects of our über-sedentary lifestyles. How will you integrate periodic respites from sitting into your daily schedule? Will you find some innovative ways to decrease your daily hours spent languishing on your posterior? Your long-term health lies in the balance.

Make a pact with yourself to limit your sitting time to five or six hours per day. How? Heed the advice of Gavin Bradley, director of Active Working, an international organization aimed at decreasing excessive sitting, and a researcher on the effects of our sedentary lifestyles: "Taking your calls standing. Walking around. Pacing. Holding standing meetings. Walking meetings. Walking over to a colleague's desk instead of sending an email. Using the stairs instead of the elevator. Taking a lunch break. Simple stuff ... the point is to just get off your rear end."

Yes, I know that making good on this commitment will overhaul your schedule and produce a ripple effect that disrupts how you're accustomed to going about your career and life. Yet your long-term productivity will actually *increase* when you stand up and leave your desk regularly throughout the day. Not only will you get *more* work done and earn the potential—as per the studies on sedentary behavior—to live longer, but there is also another compelling reason to work less at your desk and more on your feet, and to take more breaks: you will become a much happier person.

Instead of leaving work with a headache, weary eyes, and a rigid body—short-term symptoms of sitting on your rear end all day—you will step out of your office feeling lithe, flexible, resilient, and content that you have conserved some of your valuable energy to bring home and share with the people you love the most. (Take it from my wife. The people you return home to do not in any way enjoy the opposite: greeting a weary bag of bones who—counterproductively accentuating the toxic long-term effects of prolonged sitting—wishes nothing more than to unify their sloth-like, energy-depleted body with the sofa and forget about their day.)

Give this strategy a try. You will never, not even once, look back and say, "If only I hadn't stopped sitting at my desk all day, who knows where I'd be now. I coulda' been a contender!" Instead, you will be amazed at how quickly you begin to reap the physical, social, psychological, and emotional benefits of taking this first giant, vertical (as in up, out of your chair; yes, you) step toward reclaiming your essential freedom and humanness.

This message is important to heed beginning at the youngest of ages. As World Health Organization childhood obesity expert Juana

Willumsen declared, the April 2019 WHO child screen use guide-lines—limited or no use for children under five—are "about making the shift from sedentary time to playtime."

If we wish to spend less of our lives on our rears, it would help to understand how our screens induced us to descend into this seated, hunched-over position and remain there all day long. Why did we so rapidly buy into this new form of working—sitting in front of a screen—and is there hope for a return to healthier forms of making a living?

The New Technology Adoption Pendulum

After the car was invented, people sought any excuse to go for a drive. It was all the rage to go to drive-in theaters. After a while, people decided they really didn't need to sit in their cars while watching a movie. As the novelty of driving a car subsided, drive-in theaters faded into obscurity.

A few decades later, in the late 1950s, another new technology, the television, was so captivating that it was moved from the living room into the dining room so families could watch their favorite shows during dinner. This practice was soon deemed uncouth and TVs were moved back to the living room.

Perhaps we are currently experiencing a similar pendulum swing of a new technology. At the time of publication, the iPhone is now past its ten-year anniversary. Perhaps soon—mirroring the TV's parabolic trajectory—looking at a smartphone during dinner will also be consid-ered poor manners and the practice will subside. It already has in many homes, including ours—but only after precipitating more than a few marital and family arguments (with children as young as one and a half weighing in).

As with the automobile and television, we are undergoing a similar acculturation with a new technology, and our current obsession is also likely to diminish (although, unlike most drive-in theaters, not disappear). My concern is for our current generation caught in the crosshairs of the current technological revolution whose experience of real life is fading while we sort out this new acculturation process.

As with not just the television and automobile, but also the telephone, telegraph, typewriter, bicycle, and every other once-novel invention that has changed the way we live, in the end it is *we* who decide how to adapt the new technology to our way of life. The Internet—due to the sea change it has ushered in to how we live (or is it a tidal wave?)—may take a bit longer, but we *will* adapt. As MIT professor Sherry Turkle wisely cautions, "Technology challenges us to assert our human values, which means that, first of all, we have to figure out what they are ... We're going to slowly, slowly find our balance, but I think it's going to take time."

One thing is certain: we're up against a lot. The Internet is amazing—let's face it. It offers some damn exciting options. This is why we're on it so much!

If we're going to reclaim our lives, we must first understand what's so appealing about our laptops, tablets, and smartphones. Once we have a better understanding of this gravitational pull, we can envision some goals to guide our use of these enthralling new tools in our lives.

Thirty years ago, we never would have imagined we could see a video on just about anything we want, be in contact with people from all over the globe, think of a book we want to read or a song we want to hear and then—within seconds—read or listen to it. We would have been incredulous were we told that one day we would throw away our encyclopedias and have all the same information they once contained—at our fingertips 24-7, more easily accessible, at no apparent cost whatsoever.

The Internet is so amazing, in fact, that we have each become like a kid who has taken up permanent residence in a candy store. We just can't get enough. My fear is that a whole generation of people will miss out on real life because they can never quench their voracious hunger to consume from the digital trough.

FOMO Versus AMO

"Fear of Missing Out (FOMO)" has often been cited as a reason to spend every waking moment checking email, Facebook, Twitter, and other online updates. Yet what are we actually missing out on when we spend so much of our precious lives online?

The older, analog life still holds deep-rooted benefits that cannot be trumped by technology. You never take a walk in nature for an hour and then exclaim, "I wish I had been checking Facebook." You do, however, say the opposite after wasting countless hours online. Similarly, you never spend a few hours hanging out with a friend and then think, "I wish I had been checking email." Yet you often think the opposite after a multi-hour descent from Email Mountain.

It looks like Fear of Missing Out (on social information, by being offline) becomes Actually Missing Out (on social connection, by being online). The FOMO/AMO irony points to an unsettling truth: *We may need to sub-optimize our Internet use in the short term in order to optimize our values, friendships, and well-being in the long term.*

Pick a situation and ask yourself if you are being reasonable in your use of technology. If you are gaming for a few hours after dinner on your tablet or desktop, could you limit your participation to an hour and use the rest of your time to either talk with some of your family members or read a (non-digital) book to give your eyes a rest and help you relax before going to bed?

If you are taking your kids to the playground, can you turn off your phone so you can be truly present in their lives and—while they are either fully engaged with other kids, self-propelling themselves on a swing, or building a castle in the sandbox—also be fully present with yourself by gazing at the trees and sky and reflecting on what you are most grateful for and where you currently are in your life?

Make a commitment to prioritize connection—with yourself and others—and take a stand today to not become a psychological, emotional, and social casualty of the digital age. No one else can climb into your head and determine how you will relate to the increasingly attractive apps many companies are lining up to offer you "at no cost" in exchange for usurping your most valuable commodity: your attention.

Take action now before you give away any more of what you will one day realize, when you view your life in retrospective, was your most valuable asset.

Take action now because our very survival is at stake. Many of us are still acting like the kid in the candy store, gorging ourselves on unlimited digital entertainment and communication offerings.

Like the child who stays in the candy store too long, at some point we will become sick. Judging from the recent increases in loneliness, depression, and narcissism, we are already experiencing the symptoms of an intractable illness.

Like any illness, ours will serve as a wake-up call to change the way we live. It is one of my deepest hopes that this sickness will not be too dire and our lessons not too far ahead in the distance that we are unable to change now while there is still time. Our collective well-being hangs in the balance and compels us to do so. This is why I've written this book.

Screen Division

A friend of mine is fortunate enough to live in Healdsburg, a beautiful town in Northern California. A few years ago, David invited his aunt and uncle (in their mid-sixties) and his aunt's mother (in her mid-eighties) over for Thanksgiving.

David's uncle and aunt sat on the sofa and immediately turned on their iPads. They each quietly retreated into their own world, lost in their individual virtual pursuits. Neither shared anything about what they were doing with his aunt's mother.

"I can't tell you how sad it was to watch my aunt's mother looking on, watching them, completely silent," David shared. "She traveled all this way to spend time with her family, and no one wanted to talk with her. I could tell she was so bored, and there was nothing she could really do about it." David's aunt's mother had been replaced by more stimulating digital alternatives to her company.

It can also go the other way, with older folks snubbing their grown children. "I'm out surfing like I do every morning and I come in and there are my parents in their eighties, they're sitting there in my living room," the Stanford social scientist B. J. Fogg, who lives half the year on Maui, shared with me. "I walk in and they are on their phone and iPad. I say, 'Hi, I'm back' and they keep looking at their technology. They don't even look up at me. And I thought, 'You've got to be kidding me.' I come in, I see them first thing in the morning ... I haven't seen them at Christmas, I haven't seen them at Thanksgiving and they're just so glued to their screen."

At least with the television, family members or friends sitting on the sofa receive information from and are entertained by the same source. Afterward, each person might share how they interpret what they viewed, creating a bonding experience.

Lonely Together

More common today is that each group member, like David's aunt and uncle or B. J.'s parents, receives customized information from various sources tailored to their individualized preferences. As a consequence, there is usually no common topic to discuss, only a sporadic "Did you hear about ...?" This feeble attempt at connection is often followed by an uncomfortable silence preceding each person's quiet retreat to their private, disparate virtual world. Turkle labeled this phenomenon "alone together."

Loneliness has become the suffering of our generation. Yet it's important to note that loneliness and solitude are not the same. As the Belgian-American poet and novelist May Sarton sagely discerned, "Loneliness is the poverty of self; solitude is the richness of self."

Another way to think about it is that social isolation is *objective:* if you are physically alone, you are isolated. Loneliness and solitude, however, are *subjective*. They are emotional states that emerge from how you perceive your social isolation.

Just as one person's trash is another's treasure, two people can each be physically alone and one can experience a devastating rejection and abandonment by others while the other can feel an ineffable wholeness and oneness with the world independent of—or interdependent with—the other people in their life.

In fact, believe it or not, the same person can feel both in the same day; such is the ephemeral nature of emotions. The existential philosopher and theologian Paul Tillich corroborates that "Language ... has created the word 'loneliness' to express the pain of being alone. And it has created the word 'solitude' to express the glory of being alone."

This distinction between loneliness and solitude is a perennial issue human beings have been managing for centuries. Yet thanks to our phones and other devices, we seem to be edging toward a collective loneliness—subjective, negatively experienced isolation—unlike any we have previously experienced. Given situations like that of David's relatives and the recent Cigna study finding that over three of every five Americans are lonely, it seems that, more and more, we are actually "lonely together."

To Retire Is to De-wire

Loneliness manifests in strange ways. Many older people are now transfixed by their iPads because they offer nonstop, instant entertainment—quite a plus when you are bored and unsure of what to do with yourself after retirement.

Judging from my own parents and their friends, it seems that retiring is now "de-wiring": shifting from a (wired, at least in the sense of being plugged into the wall) desktop or laptop (at work) to a (wireless) iPad or tablet (at home). Without an iPad, retirement now seems incomplete.

Working people spend so much time at their desktops or laptops that an iPad or tablet often doesn't appeal to them because they are pixelated out by the time they return home. They would rather do something else with their free time.

Retired people, on the other hand, often have less need for a desktop or laptop, which are really machines for workers, and turn to iPads, tablets, and smartphones to numb themselves from their new reality: attempting to find purpose in their post-work lives.

Tablets are also easier to figure out how to use than desktops or laptops. AOL initially tapped this market of older people who didn't understand technology very well by making email easy, with constant phone support.

For this reason, AOL retained a sense of loyalty from the older generation long after their product added much value (many older people continued to pay for an AOL account rather than open a free email account). With their premium support plans, Apple is now doing much the same with its iPads for this older generation, which is less comfortable with technology.

It's not only older people: there are many differences in how we use technology rooted in when we were born and the technology available to us while we were growing up. Each of us adapts our lives to these new technologies based on how old we were when we began this acculturation process. Through developing a better understanding of how technology has uniquely affected our generation, we can each turn this process around and start adapting these new technologies so we can once again live our desired lives.

Let's now take a look at our generational differences, and how they influence the challenges each of us faces in mastering the art of living free in the digital age.

6

Your Digital Identity

*N*o matter our age, old habits die hard.

A Pew study asked various generations—"Millennials" (born between 1981 and the present), "Gen Xers" (born between 1965 and 1980), "Baby Boomers" (born between 1946 and 1964, like David's aunt and uncle from the previous chapter), and "the Silent Generation" (born between 1928 and 1945, such as David's aunt's mother, and named for their conformist and civic instincts)—what makes their generation distinctive and unique.

While one of every four Millennials replied "technology," only half as many Gen Xers cited technology as a distinguishing trait of their generation, and much less of the two older generations listed technology; they instead identified "work ethic" (Baby Boomers) and the Depression and World War II (Silents). While 75 percent of Millennials attested to having created a profile on a social networking site, only 50 percent of Gen Xers, 30 percent of Baby Boomers, and 6 percent of Silents had done the same.

A recent Pew study found that one-third of seniors over sixty-five don't use the Internet at all. The same study found that while 81 percent of adults ages thirty-one to forty-nine and 75 percent of adults ages fifty to sixty-four have high-speed broadband access at home, only half of seniors over sixty-five have purchased a high-speed connection. Clearly, there are generational differences in how each of us relates to and uses technology.

To capture some of these differences, the term "digital native" was first coined in 2001 in a publication by writer and educator Marc Prensky. I will share the definition of this term and then add some others to our lexicon that I have created to help us discern how various people identify with and use the Internet:

Digital Native = A person born after the advent of the Internet. Digital Natives typically do not question technology and face few, if any, existential issues related to its use. Many have been using Google and YouTube for longer than they have known how to read or write. The smartphone or iPad has become the toy of choice for many toddlers. A friend's daughter knew how to find the icon for Google on his smartphone, then the tab for YouTube, and then the icon for her favorite cartoon before reaching her second birthday. The third word learned by another friend's two-year-old son was "iPad." At three years old, our son learned how to use Google Voice to bring up any image he wanted and soon became fascinated with pictures of the solar system.

Digital Settler = A person born before the advent of the Internet. Many Digital Settlers, like myself, experience existential angst and are generally unsettled about the role of technology in their lives. They remember the way things were. They wax nostalgic about the analog life. Many once owned record players and miss the richer, deeper sound of albums. Most have left their old way of living behind, yet relish memories of the unmediated life. Some look back, some don't. Many vividly remember and have internalized a history of struggling with the Internet and mobile phones: waiting until 9 p.m. or the weekend to make cell phone calls or pay over a dollar per minute; listening to a sound not unlike a radio without an antenna indicating that their dial-up modem was connecting and usurping their land line and that the emails in their outbox would now send and the messages they'd been patiently waiting for would arrive in their inbox. They resent Digital Natives for having it so easy. In about eighty years there will be no more Digital Settlers left; we will all be Digital Natives.

Digital Colonialist = A person who outwardly states they are against technology while exploiting it when it suits their needs (e.g., they use online bill pay, GPS, and Amazon; buy concert tickets online; and have a smartphone they love to complain about). This person could also be called a Digital Opportunist or Digital Hypocrite. I also fall into this category. Digital Colonialists experience an inexorable, ongoing identity crisis stemming from their use of technology that they are unable to bring to resolution despite their best efforts. Most of them sigh and adopt a resigned "If you can't beat 'em, join 'em" attitude. Some of them still think change is possible; for this reason, one of them has written this book.

Digital Conscientious Objector = A person who does not have an email, social media, or any other digital account *by choice*. As the social and material costs of lacking Internet access have risen along with the ever-increasing reach of the Internet, Digital Conscientious Objectors have been decimated; there are very few left.

Digitally Disadvantaged = A person who does not have an email, social media, or any other digital account because they cannot afford it or live in one of the few regions of the world still untouched by the Internet. Aishtan Shakarian was a card-carrying member of the Digitally Disadvantaged. In April 2011, she was scavenging for scrap metal to sell in Georgia (the former Soviet Black Sea nation known for its wine, not to be confused with the US southern state) and cut into a fiber-optic cable. The seventy-five-year old woman didn't realize it, but she had effectively shut down the Internet in Georgia, Armenia, and other parts of Central Asia. She was arrested amid global outrage (shared—surprise—on the Internet) that she should go to jail for her mistake. "I have no idea what the Internet is," she told reporters.

Digital Exhibitionist = A person who uses online technology (e.g., email, sexts, social media) to broadcast any part of themselves they deem worthy enough. Digital Exhibitionists are likely to only respond to your messages if their response can be viewed by the public (e.g., on Twitter or their Facebook wall) for self-presentation purposes.

Digital Voyeur = A person who keeps Digital Exhibitionists in business. Digital Voyeurs like nothing more than to peer into the lives of others to convince themselves that their life is either better or worse than the lives they are viewing.

Digital Scholar = A person whose primary use of the Internet is to research or learn about new ideas or information and increase their knowledge base.

Digital Mercenary = A person whose primary objective on the Internet is to earn money from its users.

Digital Bargain Hunter = A person whose primary use of the Internet is to find the last great deal. They keep Digital Mercenaries in business. For Digital Bargain Hunters, it's all about the chase. The catch is secondary and brings only ephemeral joy, quickly superseded by anticipation of the next pursuit. Research by University of Virginia and Harvard social psychologists Timothy Wilson and Daniel Gilbert has found that the joy we anticipate we will feel once we achieve a goal tends to overshadow the fleeting joy we actually experience. Lottery winners, for instance, are usually much less happy with their new affluence than they thought they would be. Unaware of this phenomenon and fueled by the everlasting quest for the next dopamine hit, Digital Bargain Hunters have little reservation about spending their entire evening or weekend firmly planted behind a screen in the pursuit of saving a few dollars, euros, or yen.

Digital Coward = A person who hides their emotions behind their screens. Digital Cowards send emails, texts, or IMs to circumvent the messiness of face-to-face communication. As a result, their real-time relationships suffer and they experience fewer benefits and higher costs associated with real-time interactions. Consequently, they instead opt for more technology-enabled communication. This decision causes both their competence at expressing their emotions and the quality of their relationships to further atrophy, precipitating a vicious spiral that often culminates in a desolate, bitter loneliness that is toxic to themselves and others.

You may find that more than one of these definitions describes you. I am always a Digital Settler as I was born in the '60s; I try (sometimes unsuccessfully) to be a Digital Colonialist and use technology in ways that are aligned with my larger objectives without letting it take over my life; and I have, at different times in my life, been a Digital Exhibitionist, a Digital Voyeur, a Digital Mercenary, a Digital Bargain Hunter, and, yes, a Digital Coward. I would like to say that I spent a few years as a Digital Conscientious Objector, but I never had the courage.

Now that we have some terms to identify some of the differences in our digital habits, let's take a closer look at the most salient difference—generational—and how Digital Natives and Digital Settlers differentially use the Internet. Doing so will help us better understand its effects on our society.

The Technology Habits of Digital Natives Versus Digital Settlers

The ways in which Digital Natives use technology can be very surprising, at least to Digital Settlers like myself. In 2012, two twelve-year old girls in Adelaide, Australia, fell down a stormwater drain late on a Sunday night. Instead of calling a family member or friend, they changed their Facebook status. A friend was fortunately online and called the police to rescue them. Glenn Benham of the Australian Metropolitan Fire Service, a Digital Settler, was baffled:

> It is a worry for us because it causes a delay on us being able to rescue the girls … If they were able to access Facebook from their mobile phones, they could have called 000 [the Australian equivalent of 911 in the U.S.], so the point being they could have called us directly and we could have got there quicker than relying on someone being online and replying to them and eventually having to call us anyway.

Rifts between Digital Settlers and Digital Natives are common. When the CEO of Facebook, Mark Zuckerberg, testified before Congress in April 2018, Senator Orrin Hatch asked him, "How do you sustain a business model in which users don't pay for your service?" With a slightly veiled smirk, Zuckerberg replied "Senator, we run ads."

Highlighting these generational differences in how we use technology, Angela Ahrendts, the CEO of the British fashion giant Burberry—where 70 percent of employees are under thirty—once said about Digital Natives, "I grew up in a physical world, speaking English. They grew up in a digital world, speaking social."

Popular art and media reinforce this notion: in the 2012 movie *LOL*, which chronicles the coming of age of the lead character—a Digital Native named Lola—every major relationship conversation (e.g., between Lola and her mother, boyfriend, or school friends) takes place through email or instant messaging.

The Effects of Screens on Our Digital Natives

Children now receive instant gratification from online diversions at a speed impossible to replicate in the real world. As a result, they become used to the former and possess less patience for the latter. They link their effort to the instant feedback an online environment provides.

Imagine the effects on a three-year-old's mind of two toy experiences. First, envision that they attempt to build a castle on a Lego set through trial and error for hours. Second, they press a button on an iPad and a castle immediately appears.

In which situation do you think the toddler will begin to learn important lessons about how to manage frustration? What do you think the effect of this second scenario replacing the first might be on the emotion regulation abilities of our youngest generation? It should be no surprise that our children are losing their tolerance for the delayed gratification of real-world pursuits.

Doesn't sound too healthy, does it? Recall what we learned about the effects of technology-accelerated addictions on our brains from Rob Lustig in Chapter 4. As it turns out, "Kids are the most susceptible to [screen-based addictions] because the area of the brain that is the most vulnerable is called the prefrontal cortex. It's the area last to develop in children," the USC pediatrician shared with me. "And so, children are just particularly susceptible to addictive stimuli, including your phones … We have a very potent stimulus and we have a very vulnerable population. And we have no rules or regulations in between them."

There is another difference in the life experiences of Digital Natives that may portend a bleak future for humanity unless we recognize and address it now while we still can.

The Power of Conformity

After watching rank-and-file Nazis in the Nuremberg trials claim they were just "doing their jobs," a Yale social psychologist was curious how people could so easily obey orders to commit such heinous crimes. A former writer of theater screenplays, Stanley Milgram inventively choreographed an experiment in which participants were ordered by an austere researcher in a lab coat to administer increasingly dangerous electric shocks to a man (a confederate in the experiment, meaning a person hired by Milgram) sitting in an adjacent room attempting to learn a series of words.

Participants delivered what they thought were electric shocks to the man for wrong answers in 15-volt increments. The switches had labels such as "Slight Shock," "Very Strong Shock," "Danger: Severe Shock," and, at 435 and 450 volts, "XXX." The (confederate) word learner grunts at the 75-, 90-, and 105-volt levels; shouts that the shocks are too painful at 120 volts; and at 150 volts screams, "Experimenter, get me out of here! I won't be in the experiment anymore! I refuse to go on!"

The learner's protests continue until 300 and 315 volts, at which point he refuses to answer any more questions and falls silent. Meanwhile, the stern researcher continues to insist that the participant continue in 15-volt increments for either a wrong response or no response, with prods such as "The experiment requires that you continue" and "You have no other choice; you must go on."

How far do you think people would go? Milgram asked this question to over a hundred psychiatrists and middle-class adults, and they predicted that almost no one would go as high as 300 volts, and that one in a thousand (the spare sociopath) would go as high as 450 volts.

Milgram's experiments shocked the world (no pun intended) when *65 percent of participants continued administering the shocks to the full, 450-volt level.* All 65 percent also continued with more shocks at 450 volts until the researcher called a halt to the experiment. While this experiment—which will (hopefully) never again be fully replicated due to the American Psychological Association experimental ethics it precipitated, as participants are essentially being induced to kill someone—portends a dreary outlook on human nature, one ancillary finding offers a glimmer of hope.

Let Me Get a Good Look Atcha

When the victim of the electric shock was placed in close proximity to the participant, the percentage of participants willing to deliver shocks up to the maximum 450 volts dropped by over 50 percent. Shockingly (pun intended this time), 40 percent of participants still delivered shocks up to the full 450 volts; in another version of the experiment in which participants had to force the actor's hand onto the shock plate, an astonishing 30 percent still continued up to the highest voltage.

It seems that co-presence—being physically colocated with another person—increases empathy and compassion. When in combat with an enemy they can see, it is not uncommon for soldiers to refuse to fire; such acts of civil disobedience are rare when soldiers are given kill orders with aircraft or more distant weapons.

Indeed, an individual's empathetic accuracy has been shown to be higher when the individual has a close relationship with the other person. As the writer and painter Guy Davenport remarked, "Distance negates responsibility."

The Nazis learned this lesson firsthand in World War II. At the beginning of the Holocaust, German soldiers were given orders to use machine guns to kill men, women, and children standing defenseless in front of them. Some Germans could not bring themselves to fire; others were traumatized by the experience.

Seeking to avoid such disruptive inconveniences, Heinrich Himmler became known as the "architect of genocide" when he came up with the solution of physically separating the soldiers from their victims by constructing gas chambers in which the victims' horrific suffering would not be seen or heard by their killers.

So why is co-presence so important to understanding Digital Natives?

Out of Sight, Out of Mind

Very few Digital Natives have had direct experience with the horrific effects of warfare. Most of their experience of war and government-sponsored killing is confined to brief news blurbs narrating who the president has ordered killed via drone strike in the Tuesday meetings where he decides who to point-and-click-and-eradicate.

Our society currently comprises two generations of Digital Settlers, the Silents (World War II) and Baby Boomers (Vietnam), many of whom have personally experienced the emotional tragedies of war. Since most Digital Natives have not directly experienced or seen the horrific effects of war, the danger is that as they take over—like the Milgram participants separated by a wall from the learner or the Nazi soldiers physically and emotionally distanced from the gas chambers—they will not understand the human consequences of war. The strategic and rational reasons for waging war (e.g., land, oil, perceived aggressiveness of the other side) will likely no longer be tempered with a realistic comprehension of the devastating damage to humanity that military strikes exact.

While technology can prevent us from understanding the horrors of war and make it easier to point-click-and-execute people we've never seen before in person through drone strikes, including women and children (one of the primary reasons Westerners have cited for traveling to Afghanistan or Syria to join the jihadist cause), it can also do the opposite—for example, when someone sends a war documentary to their thousands of Facebook "friends" or Twitter followers.

A more poignant example occurred a decade ago in Point Lookout, Missouri. A former World War II U.S. Army medic, Buster Simmons, first met Micha Tomkiewicz, then six years old, on a train packed with three thousand prisoners coming from a Nazi concentration camp. Thanks to a blog to reunite soldiers and Holocaust survivors, they reconnected over sixty years later, and recently addressed students together at the College of the Ozarks.

Simmons, eighty-seven, tried to help the younger generation understand freedom: "We've never been anything but free here. Their total freedom was gone." Tomkiewicz, seventy, a physics professor, shared that he vowed to never let the war define him: "It was denial on purpose. I just wanted to grow up like a normal kid."

Perhaps the greatest lesson of this reunion is that it is not technology that obfuscates our focus on human tragedies so they do not repeat; it is ourselves and how we decide to use technology. It is this decision, rather than the technology itself, that will determine our future. If we do not wish for history to repeat, we can use the technology available to accelerate our understanding of the lessons history contains.

Understanding Your Digital Identity

While I am a Digital Settler, I have little nostalgia for the times when bullies ran rampant on the playground without a care for the consequences because there were no smartphones with which to record their aggressions on innocent children. Nor do I miss waiting in public for someone to show up for a lunch meeting and then finding out later that something came up and they had no way to contact me.

I do, however, wax nostalgic for the times when friends came over unannounced, when I spent uninterrupted hours talking about life either in person or on the phone with someone I cared about, going deeper and deeper as we went along (which I still do sometimes, although less frequently than before). Life seemed a more meaningful journey back then.

Consider your own experience with technology. At this point in your life, which of the above digital nomenclature most accurately describes you? Are you a Digital Native or a Digital Settler? A Digital Colonialist like myself who decries the role of technology while begrudgingly using it to make your life more efficient?

Have you been a Digital Mercenary, or a Digital Exhibitionist, or even a Digital Coward at various times in your life? Have you experienced any watershed moments that led to your making significant changes in how you adopt any of these digital identities? Most importantly, how would you like your relationship with technology to evolve in the future? Take some time to reflect on your vision for how you will use technology in your life.

If you find yourself losing too many evening and weekend hours on your phone, acknowledge the deeper, underlying reasons you cling to it—a deep loneliness and craving for connection is a common one—and then design some real-life alternatives to serve those very basic human needs. If you spend untold hours refining your social media profiles, ask yourself why how you are perceived by others is so important to you.

Perhaps you have a strong need for recognition, or to prove your worth to others because you doubt it yourself? Find some healthier, real-life means of satisfying these needs, such as exercising, or learning how to play the piano, or volunteering to help others, or other ways of spending your time that will help you feel stronger and better about yourself.

If you can have a no-holds-barred, searingly honest conversation with yourself about your basic human needs that undergird how you use technology—such as the need for connection, belonging, contribution, respect, intimacy, and recognition—then you can also discover real-life, healthier alternatives that more sustainably serve these needs.

Embark on these challenging conversations and you will be pleasantly surprised by how, just as quickly as technology took over your life, it loses its grip on you. The only obstacle standing between you and your desired life is to learn how to call technology by its true name: to realistically identify what it can and cannot do for you. I'm confident you can take this bold cognitive leap and begin to feel whole, resolute, and human again.

Taking this leap will require your self-control when the need for a dopamine burst is rearing its ugly head. Let's take a look at how we develop our capacity for self-control throughout the course of our lives.

The Maturity Principle

In the late 1960s and early 1970s, Stanford University psychologist Walter Mischel and his colleagues conducted a clever test with preschoolers at Stanford's Bing Nursery School. The test was simple: they placed a marshmallow in front of four-year-olds (children of Stanford faculty and graduate students) and told them they could either eat it right away or wait for five minutes and then enjoy two marshmallows. Mischel was measuring an individual's capacity to delay gratification, a form of self-regulation.

The marshmallow test has since been replicated in many other settings and with older children. As Mischel and his colleagues scrambled to track down the original participants (a task made easier because their parents all had ties to Stanford), what began as a one-point-in-time (in research terms, cross-sectional) test evolved into a longitudinal study.

Over forty years later, with the five hundred original preschoolers now in their forties, Mischel's team was able to assess many life indicators and link them to their earlier munch-or-wait decisions. Consistent with subsequent research, they found that the ability to delay gratification and wait for another marshmallow leads to a whole host of positive life outcomes later on, including higher self-worth and educational achievement, lower obesity, and better coping in adolescence.

There is widespread agreement among developmental and cognitive psychologists that early self-regulation ability is linked to one's capacity for self-regulation later in life, that individuals differ in this ability, and that this ability tends to strengthen over a person's life span.

The younger generation tends to possess a less solid sense of self as they are in the throes of puberty, adolescence, and growing up—a time when, almost by definition, they are focused on developing their personal identity. Older folks have had more time to build their skills in the complex task of self-regulation: they've simply had more practice at it.

For this reason, psychological research has found that people become less moody and prone to experiencing negative emotions as adults, at least through their late middle age. They also become more comfortable with themselves, responsible, caring, and emotionally stable. In personality psychology, this phenomenon has been referred to as the "maturity principle."

If it is true that our ability to self-regulate increases over the life span, an important question is what are young people who have not yet developed a strong sense of self and the self-regulatory ability that accompanies it doing with their time today?

Screened and Confused

Two things: First, texting.

A study of "hyper-texting" among four thousand students at twenty high schools conducted by the Case Western Reserve School of Medicine found that 19.8 percent of the students sent more than 120 texts per day. Shoring up the link between low self-regulatory ability and the overuse of smartphones, Scott Frank, MD, and his colleagues found that the texting habits of these students are associated with some common characteristics: they are 40 percent more likely than their less hyper-networked peers to have smoked cigarettes, twice as likely to have tried alcohol, 43 percent more likely to be binge drinkers, 41 percent more likely to have used illicit drugs, 55 percent more likely to have been in a physical fight, nearly 350 percent more likely to have had sex, and 90 percent more likely to have had sex with four or more partners.

Second, spending time on social media. 11.5 percent of the students engaged in "hyper-networking," defined as spending more than three hours per school day on social networking websites. These students' social media habits are also associated with some common characteristics: they are 62 percent more likely than their peers who spend less than three hours per day on social media to have tried cigarettes, 79 percent more likely to have drunk alcohol, 69 percent more likely to be binge drinkers, 84 percent more likely to have used illicit drugs, 94 percent more likely to have been in a physical fight, 69 percent more likely to have had sex, and 60 percent more likely to have had sex with four or more partners.

The hyper-networkers also have higher odds ratios for stress, depression, suicide, poor sleep, substandard academic results, and high levels of television watching and parental permissiveness. According to Frank, "The startling results of this study suggest that when left unchecked, texting and other widely popular methods of staying connected can have dangerous health effects on teenagers." (Note that this study incorporates cross-sectional regression models, and hence provides some support for causal inferences about the link between hyper-texting/hyper-networking and these outcomes.) Other research, linking high levels of phone and social media use among colleges students to lower GPAs, supports these results.

These findings are ominous considering that 75 percent of teenagers have unlimited texting plans. According to a national study, teens with such plans send and receive seven times more texts than those with limited texting plans, and fourteen times more texts than teenagers who pay per message.

Actually, the young people in this study are reflections of ourselves. When we lose control of our capacity to set limits on our digital habits, we also lose control of how we behave in other areas of our lives.

Have Screen, Will Travel

Keep in mind that Digital Natives grew up digital—some even flicking through iPad windows from their first year of life. These Digital Natives have no recollection whatsoever of a world without Internet-ready digital devices.

If you are a Digital Settler like myself, you most likely have memories of spending your summers playing outside with friends, swimming in a nearby lake, sitting in a friend's room for hours on end listening to and talking about a new album, and taking long walks alone without continually updating social information in your pocket. Perhaps you can even remember your parents telling you after lunch to "be home in time for dinner" as you stepped outside.

Most Digital Natives have no such memories. Nor any recollection whatsoever of the contentedness you might associate with these analog memories. When their digitally circumscribed lives feel overwhelming, frustrating, or anxiety provoking, they have no stage of their lives to recall in which they weren't circumscribed by technology. They can't think back to a time when they hung out with friends without digital mediation and remind themselves of the importance of regulating the use of their pixelated screens.

Self-regulation often involves a difficult choice between an emotion and a value: a decision to permit your actions to be determined by either a momentary impulse or a larger vision of what you know your life can become. Although this choice is always there, if you haven't grown up with a connection to deeper, life-affirming values—or with the necessary inner strength to brave extended periods of solitude and develop such values fostered by (but not requiring) secure relation-ships with loving, attentive parents—then the perception of such a decision may be faint: more likely, your emotion or impulse *du jour* will dictate your behavior.

For these reasons, Digital Natives may be the most vulnerable to the psychological manipulation that enables social media companies to thrive by keeping us hovering, pushing, swiping, and clicking while the waves of our lives hasten to the shore. A study of 598 Turkish students in a public university in Ankara that found the students with the lowest self-regulation abilities spend the most time on their phones exhibits how these companies find and exploit their prey.

They Are Our Future

One of my favorite stories, which I heard from meditation practitioner Tara Brach, is of a stockbroker who comes home one night at half past eight. He's talking on his smartphone trying to close a large deal. His eight-year-old daughter has been waiting for him to come home all day so she can tell him about something she learned in show-and-tell that day.

> When he enters the house she screams, "Daddy, Daddy, I want to show you something!"
>
> He says, "Not now, I'm on the phone."
>
> She knows her bedtime is nine, so she keeps jumping around him because she knows she won't be able to go to sleep unless she is able to talk with him. At eight forty-five, he's still busily talking on the phone.
>
> She starts tugging on his trousers, saying, "Daddy, Daddy, it'll just take a few minutes."
>
> Finally, he looks down at her and says, "What are you doing down there?"
>
> She replies, "I live down here, Daddy."

We must protect our Digital Natives. For three principal reasons.

First, they are our physical and figurative children. They have resorted to smartphones and social media because we were too busy with our careers and lives to take care of them when they most needed us. When women flocked to the workplace, no one flocked to the home. There was no response to the weekday migration of women to the office by anyone who picked up the slack and placed value on their children.

As a consequence, children received—and continue to receive— short shrift. With no other recourse, they learned to fend for themselves. They found only one counterpart in their socially isolated, latchkey existence: their pixelated screens cum electronic babysitter.

"So are you saying that women shouldn't work?" you may be thinking. Not at all. Women have just as much right to work as men. I am saying, however, that all of us—independent of our gender—need to man and woman up and recognize that women bore the responsibility of child care for untold centuries. They were often taken advantage of by men in the process due to the nonexistent or lower wages they earned while prioritizing their children, and have rightfully exercised their right to also pursue a career.

While this perennial inequality did not often benefit women, it did frequently benefit children. Now that no gender is prioritizing children, our society as we know it is disintegrating. Farming out child care to nannies and day care centers is not enough. Both men and women need to step up to the plate and cultivate our next generation— in person, and certainly not with the option that most shortchanges kids, an electronic babysitter—before there is too little left to cultivate. The current reality fills me with sadness and remorse. We must change it, one parent at a time.

Critical Interactions

A 2014 observational study led by pediatrician Jenny Radesky, MD, of the Boston Medical Center found that when parents are sharing a meal with their children at a restaurant, they exhibit a high degree of absorption in their smartphones, often spending more time on their phones than interacting with their children.

Even more disconcerting in terms of how we are allowing our

phones to shape our parenting, the children often escalate their bids for attention from their distracted caretakers, which are often met with harsh responses. Reading Radesky's study broke my heart. A few months later, I asked her how the effects of screens on increasingly distracted parents are affecting children. Here's what she told me:

> Starting from the moment of birth, kids are really wired to be looking for other human faces and other human voices in real time to be learning from. They also have these really expansive minds with attentional systems that are just drawn to whatever is novel so that they can look at whatever looks interesting and start to learn about it and start to categorize things and figure out the world by themselves. They do it through their senses, through touching … and they really rely on adults … consistent, reliable adults that they have attachments with to be able to learn about the world

Her words helped me realize how important it is to slow down, listen to, and engage with my children in conversation. My son Alex, for example, used to talk about (the fictional cartoon characters) PJ Masks. Now he talks about the planets. Or whatever it is he wants to talk about. I am more attentive to these serve-and-return moments so crucial to his development, and ask questions about Pluto and Maki Maki and Gekko and Cat Boy (for those out of the loop of what creates "Daddy Brain," the last two are *PJ Masks* characters) so he can further distill his thoughts on what, to him, is a very important subject.

Thanks to the Digital Limiting Strategies I will share with you in Part Three, I'm (usually, but not always) not distracted and really listen to him. When he asks all those "Why" questions—why aren't there any dinosaurs around anywhere and why does the sun shut off at night and why is this that way and why are all these things happening the way they do—I'm taking the time to explain it all to him. I'm not counting the minutes to return to my electronic exchanges. I can't express in words how much more meaningful this change has enabled my life to become. "The more that parents and kids have reciprocal language interactions, meaning the parent says one thing, the child says something that kind of feeds off of that and then the parent feeds off of that. That is how language ... and attentional systems ... are laid down in the child's brain," Radesky continued.

Parental Responsibility Is Advised

As an emotions researcher, I couldn't resist the next question: "How do these interactions influence the child's capacity to regulate their emotions?"

"When you see that parent look back at you and make a facial expression that helps you understand what you're feeling inside, that's how that infant starts to learn about their own emotions and they start to learn how to handle and how to soothe their emotions internally," Radesky explained.

Whether you are a mother, father, or concerned adult, we must all man or woman up and take responsibility for the guidance and healthy growth of our children, which requires our frequent, continual, digitally unmediated presence.

The second reason we must protect them is, as George Benson, Whitney Houston, and others have reminded us, they are our future. We have not led well, and they unwittingly (and, one could argue, involuntarily) followed, ending up in their current predicament.

Now—like it or not—where they lead, we will follow. The person you will rely on to visit you in your old age and buffer you from the ever-encroaching tentacles of loneliness: a Digital Native. The people who will govern our society and usher it into the future: Digital Natives. If their youth is any indicator, unless we make some significant and transformational changes—rapidly, decisively, soon—an uninviting future awaits all of us.

It's Just Unfair

There is a third reason we must protect our Digital Natives, starting with those who are too young to own a smartphone. It is plain and simply unfair.

I thought about the restaurant in Radesky's study and the children escalating their bids for attention from their parents who were too busy on their phones to be present. Then I remembered a family we recently sat next to at a restaurant near our home. Both parents were on their phones for the entire meal. Their three children were each on a tablet. Once in a while, I watched their daughter put her tablet down, put her chin in her hands, look around the table sadly, and then pick the tablet back up.

I wanted to shake the father and shout, "What's the matter with you?! This is your one chance, and you're blowing it. You'll never have this time with your kids again. You're squandering your inheritance, the most beautiful gift you'll ever receive in this life. If the transcendent reasons don't convince you, consider that the less time and energy you invest in them now, the less they'll invest in you later."

Well, I didn't shout anything. (Incidentally, that would have been a lot to shout in any context, and especially at a restaurant.) He did, however—the only words he directed toward his son during the entire meal. After he paid the bill, everyone stood up. Except one of his sons, about seven years old, who was nervously shutting off his fast-paced cartoon. "Let's go. Now!" the father tersely barked.

Listening to Radesky articulate what I had observed at that restaurant—something I didn't know what to do about in the moment and that left me frustrated for days—I started to become angry. I finally found my way to channel my frustration from the restaurant, in a rant I shared with Radesky: "It's kind of like if you and I were to go and have lunch in that restaurant together and I was to spend half an hour on my phone, you'd never want to eat with me again.

"Children are a captive audience," I continued. "The only people forced to connect with you, forced to talk with you are your children who sit there with eyes glazed over looking at their distracted parents. Parents carry with them everywhere this external object to soothe their anxiety, which they use all the time, and children don't have one. We as parents have to really take stock of that and just recognize the unjustness in all this."

"Right," Radesky agreed. "Devices are boredom relief objects … or soothing objects … it is important for parents to realize that. Your children are going to learn from role modeling that way. It's not the learning we're saying out loud to them: 'Don't use your phone. Here's your screen time rules.' It's the learning that they're doing by watching."

Alone with Their Anxiety

I couldn't stop thinking about it. There is a lot of anxiety in this world. Adults tote their pacifier around 24-7 and turn to it for comfort when the world around them seems uncertain—in other words, all the time. Children also experience anxiety—arguably much more, as they are experiencing novel, uncertain situations for the first time in their lives. If they are strengthened by emotionally attuned parents who help them manage this anxiety, they are able to become more emotionally stable over time.

At this early stage of attempting to understand how to navigate this complex, confusing world, children look to us for reassurance and help so they can grow healthily, and we are on our phones. They have no such pacifier. The solution is not to buy them a phone, but to use ours less and to reinstate the hard work of device-free parenting. There is no other way.

Women used to carry out the vital responsibility of facilitating the serve-and-return conversational duets that buffer the psychological and social complexities of growing up in an anxiety-filled world from which new life thrives. When women entered the workplace en masse, as I mentioned earlier, no one filled in for them to carry out this critical role. No one except the screens, and they clearly don't do a very good job.

Unfortunately, for many that's the new childhood. Let's now take a look at what our Digital Natives are experiencing as they grow into their teens.

7

The Kids Are Not Alright

Not surprisingly, the younger generation is the most hard-hit by smartphones. First of all, almost all of them own one (92 percent, compared to 74 percent of adults ages fifty to sixty-four and 42 percent of seniors over sixty-five) and a whopping 100 percent of them own a cell phone (the only generation that can boast this claim). Almost half of eighteen- to thirty-four-year-olds check Facebook within minutes of waking up, and over one in four before even getting out of bed.

It would be all well and good that Digital Natives are using phones and social media more than Digital Settlers if it weren't for one small catch: they are becoming more and more depressed each year. The Monitoring the Future Survey, for instance, which the Institute for Social Research at the University of Michigan has used to poll approximately 1.4 million eighth, tenth, and twelfth graders in the United States since 1976, shows an unsettling spike in depression since the release of the first iPhone in 2007.

The increase in depression has coincided with a sudden, precipitous decline in self-esteem, life satisfaction, and well-being, starting in 2012, just after the mass penetration of smartphones in the US a year earlier. Adolescents only experienced this decline in well-being during the years in which they spent more time on their screens; in years during which they spent less time on their screens, their psychological well-being increased.

It's a global phenomenon: a recent study of almost eleven thousand fourteen-year-olds based on data from the UK Millennium Cohort Study found that social media use is linked to poor sleep, low self-esteem, poor body image, and online harassment, all of which are in turn linked to depression.

In fact, for the first time in history the majority of American students entering college report that their mental health is below average. According to San Diego State University social psychologist Jean Twenge, who chronicles these societal changes in numerous articles and her book *iGen*, "The sudden, sharp rise in depressive symptoms occurred at almost exactly the same time that smartphones became ubiquitous and in-person interaction plummeted."

… Especially the Girls

The toxic effects of phone overuse tend to be worst for teenage girls/ young women, who report using social media more than boys. For the British fourteen year olds who spend over five hours on social media per day, girls exhibited a 50 percent increase in depression as compared to 35 percent for boys.

Corroborating the UK study, in the Monitoring the Future Survey in the US, the link between social media and depressive symptoms was worse for girls than boys, with depression increasing 21 percent for boys between 2012 and 2015 and more than double—over 50 percent—for girls.

To understand why the link between social media and depression is higher for girls, consider that girls (in general, but not for any specific individual) tend to form tighter-knit social groups and exclude others more often from these groups. While girls often become addicted to social media, boys are frequently addicted to gaming.

This phenomenon can be understood through the lens of evolutionary psychology, by envisioning our ancestors on the open plains trying to propagate their genes. Males attempted to demonstrate their competence in order to attract the most fertile females in the group. Females, on the other hand, relied on their ability to form and be included in a cohesive group of other females in order to raise the children.

Thousands of years later, boys are still attempting to satisfy their need for competence through gaming. "What percentage of the people that come to see you about gaming addiction are men versus women?" I asked the director of the Center for Internet and Technology Addiction.

"Virtually 100 percent," David Greenfield replied. "If you look at what a man's job is in life, it's to find competence. Competence within himself, competence within his family, among his peers, and the sense of mastery. And the normal ways that men do that in our culture have really evaporated...Gaming really has become almost a substitute for that manner in which we find mastery."

Girls, on the other hand, are still attempting to satisfy their need for inclusion in strong, cohesive groups, primarily through social media. Given this hyper-competition for group membership, girls experience social ostracism more often than boys, a practice that has been accelerated by social media.

A series of earlier experiments led by Twenge and another social psychologist, Roy Baumeister, found that even a brief experience of social rejection can propel someone into a downward spiral that includes feelings of hopelessness, increased aggression, binge eating, and irrational, risky behaviors. This toxic digital cocktail has disturbingly negative effects on all teens (and especially girls and young women) in their most vulnerable stages of socialization and identity formation, such as increased risk of depression and suicide.

The Need to Belong

Roy Baumeister is a reserved and extremely intelligent man who, for good reason, has become one of the most cited social psychologists alive. I first met Roy for lunch in Barcelona about seven years ago. More recently, I asked him why social ostracism or rejection, which now comes fast and furious through electronic communication, so easily sends us into a tailspin.

Baumeister's answer reminded me why his work has inspired my research on loneliness and disconnection. "It thwarts one of the most basic and powerful drives in the human mind," he shared. "We evolved with a strong need to belong, so that we connect with others. Rejection and ostracism mean that one has failed to satisfy that need."

The importance of this need has not escaped others intent on damaging an individual. In traditional societies, social ostracism was often used as the most severe form of punishment. This effect is more pronounced in younger than older people, as the rapidly developing brains of younger people are more highly sensitized to detect social exclusion.

It is perhaps for this reason that the Cigna study released in 2020 counterintuitively found that it's not the elderly, as most anticipate, who are the loneliest in US society, but children and teens. Almost eight of every ten Gen Zers (79 percent) and over seven in ten Millennials (71 percent) are now lonely, compared to half of Baby Boomers (50 percent). This finding is extremely disconcerting, not only because of the suffering of our youngest generations, but also because they gradually replace the oldest and *become* our new society.

Yet social media-accentuated ostracism continues to surge unchecked while we blithely log on to Facebook, Twitter, and Instagram. A recent study by Baumeister and his colleagues has found that ostracism even disables some facets of psychological functioning, including a sense of meaningfulness in life. Believe it or not, even feeling rejected by a social group one despises—in another study, participants were manipulated into believing they were being ostracized by the KKK—can be hurtful.

This unmet need to belong—again, especially critical in the lives of young people, who often lack a history of feeling like they belong to anything at all and can feel distraught when satiating this need appears out of reach—can lead to tragic consequences. The numbers are deeply disturbing and point to a common culprit: *46 percent more teens in the US killed themselves in 2015 than in 2007, the year the first iPhone was released.*

In 2011, the year smartphones achieved 40 percent penetration in the United States at the fastest rate of any consumer technology in history, for the first time in twenty-four years *the teen suicide rate surpassed the teen homicide rate.*

Three years later, in 2014—a year before 73 percent of teens had access to a smartphone—*the teen suicide rate was already 32 percent higher than the teen homicide rate, the largest gap since these statistics were recorded.* In short, teens are now killing each other less and killing themselves more.

When teens spend most of their time alone behind their screens rather than interacting with others, the natural anger and disillusionment with society that teens (and some adults, such as this one) often experience—which can be easily piqued by the social ostracism many experience from their efforts to socialize on the Internet—can be more easily turned inward, toward themselves, than toward others.

Not Just the Teens: It's Not Looking Good for the Rest of Us Either

It's not only teens who are adversely affected by their devices. A national study of American adults based on longitudinal data from the Gallup Panel Social Network Study survey in 2013, 2014, and 2015 published in the *American Journal of Epidemiology* comes to precisely the same conclusion: real-world social networks are positively linked—and virtual social networks (e.g., Facebook) are negatively linked—to overall well-being.

The advantage of this study is that it is longitudinal rather than cross-sectional, so it can examine how behaviors one year influence the way individuals feel in a subsequent year. Study authors Holly Shakya of the University of California at San Diego School of Medicine and Nicholas Christakis, Director of the Human Nature Lab at Yale University, consistently found that liking others' content or clicking on links on Facebook in one year predicted a subsequent decline in physical health, mental health, and life satisfaction in a future year. It's literally click now and pay later.

Shakya and Christakis wrote in a recent *Harvard Business Review* article that "the tricky thing about social media is that while we are using it, we get the impression that we are engaging in meaningful social interaction. Our results suggest that the nature and quality of this sort of connection is no substitute for the real world interaction we need for a healthy life."

In other words, as we have discussed before, we go online thinking we are experiencing social connection, when in fact we are only receiving social information. While the first is a natural buffer against the future physical and mental detriments associated with loneliness, the second isn't. This bait-and-switch is costing many of us our experience of a rich, vital, and meaningful life. It's costing some people life itself.

These national studies corroborate the already well-understood link between strong, positive relationships with others and psychological well-being (and the lack of such relationships with stress, psychological distress, anxiety, and depressive symptoms). In short, we need other human beings to play a vital, socioemotionally supportive role in our lives. Anything—including phones and other devices—that prevents the development and flourishing of such roles is a major hazard to our mental health.

"Everything bad does not happen because of smartphones and the Internet, Mr. Jump-to-Conclusions Author," you may be thinking. "With the rising disparities between haves and have-nots, there have been fewer economic opportunities available to our next generation, which could be the cause of increasing depression and suicide."

You are making an excellent point. Jean Twenge, the San Diego State psychologist who led this national study, however, already thought of it. She matched the unemployment rate and the Dow Jones index to teen depressive symptoms and suicide rates from 2010 to 2015 and found no correlation.

… And Once Again, Especially Not for the Girls

If this phenomenon is indeed occurring, it should not only be teen suicide that is on the rise, but inwardly directed teen violence, especially among young women. This is precisely what's happening.

Consider this recently released *Journal of the American Medical Association* study of 43,138 self-inflicted injury visits to sixty-six hospital emergency rooms across the US from 2001 to 2015 by young people ages ten to twenty-four. For boys and young men, there was no statistically significant trend in these visits throughout the fifteen-year study. From 2001 to 2008, neither was there a statistically significant trend in these visits for girls and young women in the same age group.

Then, in 2009, two years after the release of the first iPhone, something surprising happened: there was an 8.4 percent increase in nonfatal, self-inflicted injuries such as poisoning, cutting, and striking oneself with a blunt object for the girls and young women in the study. Even more surprising, among girls ages ten to fourteen, there was an 18.8 percent increase in such self-inflicted injuries in 2009.

"Well, 2009 may have been a fluke," you may be thinking. Yes, it might have been. It wasn't. From 2009 to 2015, the last year of the study, there was an average 8.4 percent increase in self-inflicted injuries among all girls/young women and an average 18.8 percent increase among girls ages ten to fourteen *in each and every year of the study*.

Such a consistent increase in acts of self-harm among girls and young women—believed by the Boston University psychiatrist and trauma expert Bessel van der Kolk to be actions taken to reduce feelings of numbness, or to feel something different from what one is currently feeling to seek relief from it—*over seven consecutive years subsequent to the release of smartphones* is clearly no coincidence. Worse, it provides a deeply disturbing portrait of a current transformation occurring in our society. The critical question is what is driving these troubling changes?

Pick on Someone Your Own Size, In Person

The study authors speculate that some of the culprits may be social isolation, cyberbullying, and the lack of sleep associated with excessive smartphone use. Self-harm techniques may also be spread among young women through social media itself. As lead author Dr. Melissa Mercado of the Centers for Disease Control and Prevention in Atlanta warns, these techniques are a primary risk factor for and can often lead to suicide.

The cyberbullying can be nasty and very difficult to handle for a young person attempting for the first time to make their way in the world. Twenge shares an Instagram comment Sierra, a fifteen-year-old girl, received for one or her uploaded photos: "You have no ass girl, stop trying to take pictures like you have one, it's not cute, you look like a ho. You look stupid … that outfit makes you look like a cheap prostitute that stands on the corner."

Young teenage women feel pressured to make themselves look attractive on their Facebook and Instagram pages; yet when they do, they are often slut-shamed by envious competitors for attention.

It's happening to boys too. David Molak, a high school sophomore in San Antonio, Texas, received relentless text messages from classmates insulting him and his physical appearance. He committed suicide on January 4, 2016. His older brother Cliff wrote on Facebook: "I saw the pain in David's eyes three nights ago as he was added to a group text only to be made fun of and kicked out two minutes later. He stared off into the distance for what seemed like an hour. I could feel his pain."

The New Costs of Socialization

Can you remember the enduring pain of being ostracized from a social group as a teenager? I certainly can. I remember as vividly as if it were yesterday the day that Charles, who I thought was my best friend when I was a senior in high school, told me that the group of five guys with whom I was planning to create a yearbook page said to him, "I'm just not sure I want to be remembered as being friends with Tony Silard."

I retreated into myself after that conversation and stopped making so much effort to be their friends. Instead, I started hanging out with some students from Holland, India, and Iran who went to a nearby international school.

Surprising to me at the time, the international students didn't seem to care about the common labels I had been tagged with at my high school (e.g., "geek" and "nerd") and were more interested in who I was as a person. I managed to cope with the ostracism and use it as fuel for growth and intrigue with other cultures that have become self-defining over the years and have led me to spend about half of my life overseas and to marry a Mexican woman.

Let's now fast-forward a few decades to the digital era: Try to picture the accelerated ostracism young people like David Molak are now experiencing at the hands of peers they thought were their friends through the medium of texting, email, or social media. Imagine that subsequent to being insulted and told you are nothing and not desired as a friend, you are sitting at home alone rather than ensconced in a social milieu of other teens, as I was, some of whom are actually friendly toward you.

These small acts of human kindness may be all it takes to provide the buffer you need to move past the toxic emotions associated with feeling ostracized and once again feel some semblance of self-confidence and inner strength. It is for this reason that a National Institutes of Health study found that victims of cyberbullying subsequently become more clinically depressed than those of in-person bullying.

These are some of the social costs teenagers are paying for their socialization in the digital era. We have to remember that it hasn't been their choice: we've unquestioningly accepted the rise of a few social media companies and the associated consequences for how our children grow up. We must remember that when we point the finger at anyone— including Facebook or Instagram—three fingers are pointed back at ourselves.

Marshmallow Test 2.0

Consider the social plight of Maria, a twenty-something accounts manager who once attended one of my leadership conferences:

> If you were to ask me, "how many of your two hundred sixty-one Instagram followers do you still talk to on a monthly basis?" I would answer ten. That includes my two siblings, close friends, and a few coworkers. I have used social media to share my personal life and experiences with others—with people I no longer socialize with anymore. This habit has stuck around because I feel like I need social media to stay alive in the social world. It feels like I need these outlets to keep up with everyone else. I believe that due to the amount of time I spend on social media, I have experienced growing feelings of isolation.

It seems that Maria does not feel like she has a better option than allocating untold hours to her phone and digital devices in the hopes of creating a healthy social life. We have to ask ourselves how we allowed such a situation to so rapidly become the norm in our society.

Yet not every person becomes circumscribed by the norm, and we must also remind ourselves that managing a smartphone is a marshmallow test—a form of self-regulation. Based on the collective frustration people are currently experiencing, I will speculate that the use of one's phone and other devices has become one of the most challenging self-regulatory tasks facing the twenty-first-century citizen today.

How we fare at this daunting task depends on our track record with self-regulation. As Walter Mischel's maturity principle elucidates, younger people simply don't have sufficient experience regulating their behavior to manage the Herculean challenge of living a healthy, functional life when they have rapid access to anyone perpetually available in their pockets.

"Yes, but not all young people are the same," you may be saying to yourself. "Doesn't it depend on the self-confidence they are raised with and construct for themselves?" You are absolutely right: let's take a look.

Feeling Bad About Yourself? Just Go Online

In agreement with your statement, University of California at Irvine professor Melissa Mazmanian found in an empirical study that people higher in self-confidence are less likely to overuse their smartphones than those lower in self-esteem. The reason? There are three, actually.

First, the lower our self-esteem, the more we feel we must "prove" our worth to others—by quickly replying to their emails and social media messages. Does this mean that the most confident people in your office or home are the ones who least often check their smartphones? In general (meaning on average, but not for every single person), this is exactly what it means.

Take Elaine, an administrative assistant in Pittsburgh, Pennsylvania, who described her relationship with work emails in the first week of the Heart of Darkness Challenge:

> I would ALWAYS constantly check my work emails to see if my boss has messaged me or if I am missing any important information at work, even checking emails when I would wake up at 2 a.m. I did not know that my addiction to my work emails was that extreme. For some reason, having unread messages in my inbox gives me anxiety.

Second, when our self-esteem is low we also continually try to prove our worth to ourselves—by frequently checking who has liked a recent social media post or replied to a text or email message.

The third reason people low in self-esteem overuse their digital devices dates back over sixty years to an interesting theory developed by the social psychologist Leon Festinger. Chess players don't compare themselves with chess masters but with other players of similar ability, Festinger found. Why? Because when our self-esteem is low, we tend to look for similar others to compare ourselves to in an attempt to feel worthy.

It's no coincidence that Festinger developed his theory of social comparison just after the introduction of the only other technology adopted with a speed comparable to the smartphone: the television. As with the smartphone, the rapid adoption of the television led to some surprising behaviors. Let's take a look.

Screen-Induced Envy: Nothing New

After the popularization in the US of the television in the early 1950s, an innovative study led by USC social psychologist Karen Hennigan (conducted three decades later) examined the larceny theft rate following its mass penetration. What made this study so compelling was its natural control group: citizens were prohibited from owning televisions until four years later in some US cities due to a government freeze on TVs in those cities by local city councils.

In total, the study compared the rate of small crimes such as bicycle theft and pickpocketing in thirty-four cities immediately after the television became widely available in 1951 and another thirty-four cities in which televisions were banned until a federal ruling overturned the ban four years later.

The results of the study were astonishing: there was a marked increase in the larceny rate in the first group of cities in 1951, due primarily to an escalation in small crimes such as bicycle theft and pickpocketing. The second group of cities in which televisions were not on sale, however, did not experience any increase in the larceny rate whatsoever.

Petty crime rates did not increase in these second thirty-four cities until four years later, in 1955, when televisions were finally legalized there. The study authors attributed the increased crime to individuals' enhanced feelings of deprivation relative to the economically better positioned others they observed on the silver screen.

Everyone Glistens On Screen

Imagine you are living in a small town in Oklahoma where most of the people around you are similar to you in terms of what they own. All of a sudden, you have a screen in your living room on which you observe that some people, in fact, have much more than you do. You may experience an envy unlike anything you have ever felt before, and faster than you can say "I want it," you begin stealing from others so you can have what they have.

Social media has taken this rudimentary human drive—the need to compare oneself favorably with similar others in order to feel worthy—and placed it on steroids. As with other Internet-accelerated addictions, we can while away our days looking through the social media profiles of others like us and then assess how they are faring in their lives with very little apparent social or material costs. If we are faring better, we preserve our fragile sense of self. If they are doing better, our self-esteem plummets.

Thanks to Facebook, Instagram, and other social media sites, we are now playing in a house of mirrors that renders the whole social comparison process meaningless. Social media users now routinely inflate images of their lives while hiding the flab and unhappiness.

Hell bent on optimizing self-presentation, they sift through hundreds of photos from a recent family vacation to find the one moment of the entire week in which everyone was smiling. In fact, some young women even go so far now as to post selfies doctored with shrinking software to curry favor in the social comparison game.

When You're Down, Social Media Doesn't Pick You Up

Leanne described the greatest ordeal of her life in one of my leadership conferences. A twenty-eight-year-old woman from a rural Mexican-American family, she hadn't experienced an easy life. Her parents crossed the border into California illegally in the trunk of a car a few decades ago.

Leanne's mother, through domestic work, and her father, by starting from the ground up on a farm, struggled to keep food on the table for her and her three brothers. Her father is now managing forty people as the foreman of an industrial parts company in Riverside, California. His hard-won success became her motivation to make something of her life, which brought her to my conference.

"One of the more vivid events in my life was the time that my daughter, at two years old, was diagnosed with central diabetes insipidus (a rare disorder)," she said, looking down at the floor. "Individuals with diabetes insipidus experience extreme thirst and urination. Before being diagnosed and treated my daughter was drinking a sixteen-point-nine-ounce water bottle within the time span of an hour, significantly affecting her life."

Being a parent myself of a two-year-old at the time, I could only fathom the depth of suffering her daughter's rare disease had caused Leanne. I asked her how she had been able to handle it.

Embarrassed but wanting to share what she had been through, Leanne replied: "When my daughter was diagnosed with diabetes insipidus, my three hundred sixty followers on Instagram and seven hundred and one Facebook friends never became an outlet to feel better. Not once did I feel the need to post how I was feeling or reach out to any of my 'social media friends.'"

Only the Good Times Roll on Social Media

Leanne's experience with social media is unfortunately relatively common: she was reluctant to share social information that would generate a downward social comparison in which others' impressions of her life would be lowered. After exclusively sharing her positive life moments for years, when she went through one of the most difficult experiences of her life she had to go through it alone. The alternative would be to risk the loss of the upward social comparison she had invested years of her life cultivating.

"I admit," Leanne said finally, "that in our digitally mediated society where everyone decides to highlight the best parts of their lives, I felt afraid to post and acknowledge my feelings of loneliness."

A sophomore at Cornell University learned a similar lesson. In her freshman year, Emery Bergmann shared that she "had to minimize my time on social media. It became a platform for comparison. I evaluated every picture my friends posted, determining whether their college looked like more fun than mine, if they had made more friends than I had, just meaningless justifications for my unhappiness."

Bergmann created a video describing her experience that went viral and led to her first *New York Times* article. She was surprised when the same high school friends she assumed were so happy in college because of their glistening social media posts contacted her to let her know how much they related to what she was experiencing. Social media, she discovered, "reinforces the notion that you should always be enjoying yourself, that it's strange to not be happy and that life is a constant stream of good experiences and photo-worthy moments. I taught myself that everyone's college experience is different, and slowly, I started to embrace the uniqueness of my own."

The Insidious Face(book) of Envy

Experiences like Leanne's and Emery's are consistent with a recent study of 584 Facebook users led by Hanna Krasnova of Humboldt University in Berlin that found—in an eerie ode to Hennigan's earlier finding of an increase in petty crimes attributable to the other most rapidly adopted technology in history, the television—that the number one emotion reported by Facebook users is envy.

Moreover, Krasnova and her team found that the envy people experience on Facebook decreases their life satisfaction, especially when they primarily engage in "passive following," or using Facebook to view the lives of people they know rather than as a medium for active socializing. Recent studies that have found we are more motivated by envy than admiration help explain why we waste so many of our precious hours in passive following on Facebook: we're not admiring others (a positive emotion), but envying them (a negative one)—hence the decline in life satisfaction.

If the emotion people experience on Facebook is primarily envy, it would be helpful to understand what motivates Facebook users that provokes this emotion in others. A number of psychologists set out to do exactly that.

The psychiatrist Ashwini Nadkarni of the Boston Medical Center and the psychologist Stefan Hofmann of the Center for Anxiety and Related Disorders at Boston University reviewed forty-two evidence-based studies on the motives of Facebook users and discovered they are motivated by two primary needs: the need to belong and the need for self-presentation. Further, they found that the need of Facebook users to present themselves favorably to others is driven by narcissism, low self-esteem, and emotional instability.

Defined from Outside

The experience of Nancy, a marketing director who attended one of my leadership conferences in Mexico City, is illustrative of how the users of Facebook and other social media apps stoke envy in others, especially after a tragedy that causes someone to believe that the complex emotions they are experiencing no longer enable them to authentically present themselves online without incurring the dreaded downward social comparison:

> Eight months ago, my father died unexpectedly. Following his death, I felt separated from the rest of my social connections by my complicated feelings of grief. I seemed to become disconnected from a world where life had not stopped for everyone else, while I was stuck on the loss of someone with whom I had always had a difficult relationship. I felt isolated by my extreme emotions, which

was further compounded by a desire for social support while feeling incapable of reaching out for help or human connection. Additionally, I felt overwhelmed by the presence of social media. While I tried to avoid social media websites, occasional visits left me discouraged, as everyone else appeared to be posting life events and experiences that were so much more fulfilling than my own.

All three of the motivations described above that are associated with low self-esteem—proving our worth to others, proving our worth to ourselves, and desiring positive (upward) social comparisons with others—converge to induce one cardinal time-consuming behavior: checking a phone or laptop or tablet for social media or email or text messages over, and over, and over again. The less an individual has constructed a sense of self, the more frequently they will crane their neck to glance at a digital screen in their quest for self-assurance.

In other words, the less we rise to the lifelong, arduous challenge of developing substance within, the more we seek it from without.

Ask yourself how you would experience your life if you were to develop meaningful ways to provide yourself the daily reassurance you need rather than seek it from other people who are also camouflaging their deeper feelings of insecurity behind their screens. What would you be able to create if you stopped posting on social media in hope of gaining the approval of others?

What would be possible in your life if you were to instead devote your creative energies to developing projects less for short-term recognition and more for long-term impact? Imagine how your feelings about yourself would grow and propel you toward other long-term projects—whether they were creating a book, a new business, or a meaningful relationship.

Seeking approval from outside is but one of the reasons we lose sight of who we are when we go online. In the next chapter, let's go deeper and better understand why once we turn on a screen, we lose our way under its luminous thrall.

8

Digital Drift

*Computers make it easier to do a lot of things, but most of
the things they make it easier to do don't need to be done.*
—Andy Rooney

About four years ago, I was visiting family in the city I grew up
in, Washington, DC, and came down with the flu. A few days
later, I was starting to feel better and slept through the night for the
first time. The next day, I really didn't feel like writing this book; I just
didn't feel like thinking much.

I was still in a little bit of a funk and ended up checking emails for a
couple of hours. I realized that checking email is relatively painless, an
easy way to fire the mind back up and become active again. In short,
checking email helped my mind emerge from its groggy state and
become more alert. It was like a reassimilation into work.

Email can do that: reintegrate us into what we think we ought to be
doing. Sifting through a queue of brief electronic messages can help
us mindlessly and facilely become efficient again; it gives us a sense of
"Okay, I'm not wasting time and am accomplishing something again."

This is how I felt when I hopped onto my laptop and didn't really get
anything important done that day. Checking email made me feel like I
was accomplishing something anyway.

Am I describing how you often experience your days at work? Many
of us spend immeasurable hours daily climbing Email Mountain, never
achieving anything really significant. If we just log on and see what
strikes our fancy rather than developing a vision for how we want to

use our digital devices, we lose ourselves along the way.

We succumb to our baser instincts as have been adeptly identified and manipulated by the continually reproducing web and app developers—not unlike the continuously regenerating FBI agents in *Men in Black*—who have made their fortunes by paying closer attention than we have to the sage words of the German philosopher Friedrich Nietzsche, "To forget one's purpose is the commonest form of stupidity."

The alternative is to allow your life vision to guide how you navigate the Internet and social media. They are merely mechanisms—as is the automobile—that will help you get to where you want to go if you know how to utilize them correctly.

The Greatest Obstacle to Focus Today

Exhibit A of a person succumbing to Nietzsche's commonest form of stupidity? Me. Just to disabuse you of the notion that I have this all figured out and that's why I can write about it, I'll share one of the countless incidences of Digital Drift in my own life.

I had just watched one of the Liam Neeson career-resurgence action films, *The Grey*. After arriving home, I logged on to the Internet to read what animal rights groups had to say about the depiction of Alaskan wolves in the movie.

Was checking up on this information the problem? Not exactly— although perhaps it was indirectly, as it led me into the lion's den. The problem was I then remained on the Internet for another two hours— until three in the morning. Was this a net benefit to my life? I obtained more information about wolves, but felt like a mind-deadened zombie and lost a few hours of the next day that I never saw again after pathetically treading the walk of shame from the digital multiplex to bed.

As it turns out, I'm not alone. Exhibits B, C, D, and on and on and on are all around us. In a survey of 2,260 adults conducted by the Pew Internet and American Life Project, 58 percent of people ages eighteen to twenty-nine indicated that, on any given day, they use the Internet for no real purpose other than to pass the time.

While we used to be bored from information underload, we have now become bored from information overload. The difference with "mediated boredom," as the Belarusian writer Evgeny Morozov calls it, is that it camouflages itself "in the rhetoric of nowness and newness" and induces a craving for more information to suppress it.

Mad magazine adeptly described this phenomenon when it stated that one of the worst things about Facebook is the "Bermuda Triangle-esque vortex of time-wasting, where you sign in just to check your latest updates, and suddenly it's eight hours later and you've seen every picture taken of your friends since they were 12."

Digital Drift is the greatest obstacle to focus today. It's what you experience when you plan to go online for ten minutes to research something and the next thing you know it's three hours later and you've been looking at a friend's spring break pictures and sneaking excessively long glances at the photos of their scantily clad friends, or checking five travel websites for the best deal on a trip you are not even sure you will take, or checking the status updates of people five concentric circles removed from your closest friends.

Online with Purpose

Henry Ford brought personal (physical) mobility to the masses over a century ago with the invention of the Model T. Sergey Brin, Mark Zuckerberg, and Steve Jobs have brought virtual mobility (or the mobility of ideas) to the masses over the last two decades. It was once a privilege to own a car so you could travel much farther than ever before. Today, it's a privilege to own a laptop, smartphone, or tablet so your ideas can travel much farther than ever before.

Yet we don't get into a car just to drive. We initially set a destination in our minds and then map out our journey. We must do the same with our screens.

Every time you make the decision to look at your phone or laptop, imagine you are on a shopping trip. There are two primary forms of shopping: the first, the shopping walkabout, is to go see as much of the merchandise as possible so you know what's on sale and have a full awareness of the plethora of purchasing options available. The second, the shopping incursion, is to know exactly what you want, go in, find it, buy it, leave, done.

If you take the simple step of reorienting your mind and viewing the Internet as it rightfully is—an unprecedentedly enormous, interactive digital shopping mall—and only enter for a rapid in-and-out shopping incursion during which you retain your focus on finding precisely what you're looking for and then leaving; if you can bypass the massive candy-colored distractions lining your path at every moment that the human brain has never been biologically prepared to bypass; if you can overcome the best efforts of tens of thousands of software developers who have created every minute facet of that virtual shopping mall to ensnare you and never allow you to find the exit door so you spend every last dime of your most valuable currency in life—your time— before you saunter out and ashamedly schlep your way home, less of a person than when you entered; if you can do that, you will have just availed yourself of the most ubiquitous flea market in history without allowing it to spit out whatever is left of your life.

Yes, but how?

Your Shopping Style

To achieve this Herculean goal, imagine there are only two types of stores in this grandest of all shopping malls. You walk through the large atrium and are immediately confronted with one or another of these two stores. The first type of store, of which there are thousands, has a sign above the door that reads, CRAP YOU DON'T NEED.

The second type, of which there are only a few, maybe even only one, has a sign above the entrance that reads, THE REASON YOU CAME

HERE. You can make the decision to consider every email or text, every Twitter, Facebook, Instagram, or WhatsApp message, photo, or video as either a priority—the reason you went shopping—or a distraction—another unnecessary, immaculately choreographed impulse-buy opportunity inconsistent with your values that you, quite plain and simply: Do. Not. Need. The ability to make this distinction is one of the most evolutionarily adaptive skills of the twenty-first century.

To help yourself make this distinction, ask yourself how you feel after spending a few hours climbing Email or Facebook Mountain, or entertaining yourself looking at photos of the children of old classmates you no longer speak with, or reading about an obscure '60s rock band. How do you experience the aftermath of spending so much of your day online?

Do you feel recharged, renewed, happy to be alive, like you are grabbing life by the horns? Or alternatively, do you feel lonely, anxious, and like you are missing out on something deeper, something more important to you, such as time in nature or connecting with the people you care about?

Now ask yourself how you experience spending only a few minutes searching for an email or text from a good friend and then exiting the app to go meet her or him in person, or going on Amazon to buy a power cord and effortlessly turning off your screen afterward and spending time with your family or going to a ball game, museum, or karaoke bar?

In which situation do you feel that you maintain a healthy semblance of control in your life? That you are living on purpose? That you are content with the meaningful social relationships in your life?

Gaining the upper hand in your use of technology means that before you turn on any screen whatsoever, you can declare to yourself, "I know for what purpose I am using this digital tool. Once I have completed this activity that's aligned with my greater vision for how I wish to live my life, I'll quickly shut off the screen and return to my non–digitally mediated (read: real) life. In so doing, I increase my confidence in using my digital devices to enhance rather than diminish my life."

I Don't Mean to Do It

The attractions of the digital megaplex are many. They assail your psychological defenses one after the other until you succumb. You become another psychological, emotional, and social casualty in the war waged by adept brogrammers who have learned—very, very well, my dear—how to control you.

If you are in doubt, consider these ominous words from the former Google strategist who constructed the metrics system for the company's global search advertising business. James Williams describes the current technology industry as the "largest, most standardized and most centralized form of attentional control in human history."

Williams came to this realization when, a few years later, he found himself circumscribed by technology and having difficulty concentrating on what was most important to him. One day, he stopped in his tracks in front of one of Google's internal dashboards exhibiting how much of people's attention it had appropriated for advertisers.

"I realized: this is literally a million people that we've sort of nudged or persuaded to do this thing that they weren't going to otherwise do," Williams observed. In a statement of regret stemming from a disturbed conscience, he then queried, "Isn't technology supposed to be doing the opposite of this?"

Given that most of us usually turn on our screens with a clear goal consistent with our higher-order values, how is it that, as our time online progresses, we become more susceptible to the myriad distractions provided by our virtual environment and lose sight of why we went online in the first place?

Why We Don't Walk Our Talk

A social psychology experiment from almost half a century ago will help us understand the answer to this question. In the early 1970s, Princeton social psychologists John Darley and Daniel Batson designed a clever experiment in which sixty-seven Princeton Theological Seminary students were asked to walk to a recording studio to record a talk about the Good Samaritan, a parable about someone who helps an ailing man on the street.

In perhaps the shrewdest twist ever conceived in a psychological experiment, Darley and Batson placed an actor in the street on the way to the recording studio and asked him to slump in a doorway with his head down and cough and groan.

Participants were divided into different groups, each of which was given different instructions to go to the adjacent building to record their talk. For the "low hurry" group, the researchers advised "It'll be a few minutes before they're ready for you, but you might as well head on over. If you have to wait over there, it shouldn't be long." About 63 percent of these students actually helped the ailing man.

For another group placed in the condition of "high hurry," the researchers said, "Oh, you're late. They were expecting you a few minutes ago … The assistant should be waiting for you so you'd better hurry." Only 10 percent of these students stopped to help the man on the street asking for help. Some of these students even stepped over the ailing man to get to the building.

Consider the ramifications of this experiment: when in a hurry, 90 percent of Princeton theology students *were unwilling to help an ailing man on the street while on their way to give a talk about helping an ailing man on the street.* If this is the outcome for this group of generally conscientious individuals, what is the fate of the rest of us?

Joining the One in Ten

We now have so many demands on our time that "high hurry" has become the new norm. We all have a never-ending queue of emails and texts to respond to, not to mention many other non–digitally mediated tasks and responsibilities. Given these pressures, the likelihood of over 10 percent of us actually honoring our values and living our life vision throughout our daily interactions in our technologically accelerated society may be smaller than we think.

The reason for this downward slide from what the psychologist Icek Ajzen refers to as "attitude-behavior consistency" is that the more time we remain online, the more likely we are to complete the initial goal for which we initially logged on and feel the attractive pull of other, lesser goals that we can also accomplish online.

In fact, a 2017 study led by Adrian Ward of the University of Texas at Austin found that merely having a smartphone near you—whether it's on the table next to you during a meal or sitting on your desk while you are working—damages cognitive capacity, even if it is turned off.

Alternatively, we crave the quick jolt of adrenaline from engaging in other online activities that allow our brains to rest from more focused activity, such as checking what others have written about a photo we posted on Facebook or having a quick look to see how a stock or airline ticket price has changed. An individual without a clear goal is more likely to take cues from their environment about the available goals afforded by the current situation, of which the Internet offers many.

Consider the prescient words written by the German philosophical fiction author Hermann Hesse in one of his masterpieces, *Siddhartha*: "Most people ... are like a falling leaf that drifts and turns in the air, flutters, and falls to the ground. But a few others are like stars which travel one defined path ... they have within themselves their guide."

The question we need to answer in this book, then, is what mechanisms can you put into place in your life so you will become your own guide? In so doing, you will become one of the Princeton theology 10 percent (a small minority that will expand the more we are conscious of it) and align your actions with your values despite the myriad temptations placed in your path—many by the brogrammer brigade—to do otherwise.

The Most Critical Skill in the Digital Age

The enemy of well-being and work-life balance is automatic behavior. Usually, it's not the initial, often purpose-driven glance at your phone that is the problem. The effectiveness of the algorithmic features of your phone, meticulously programmed by astute designers to detect your preferences and attract your attention, is the problem. The subordination of your larger life purpose—which likely centers around the connections you forge with yourself and other people—to the allure of these features is the problem.

Writing down a concrete goal helps you stay focused on what you want to create. This skill—maintaining your focus on a specific objective—has never been more critical in the history of humankind. With the advent of email, Facebook, and smartphones, never before have we had so many options, and distractions, at our fingertips.

The next time you are about to glance down at your phone, ask yourself, "Why am I choosing this action? What higher-order purpose am I pursuing?" Then ask yourself, "How else could I spend my time to better achieve this purpose?"

The simple act of asking this question will bring the realization to the forefront of your mind that *you are making a choice.* For unknown reasons, you've been fortunate enough to have received this gift of life. It belongs only to you, and not to anyone else, and whether you make the most or least of it is up to you.

In the early days, many heralded the Internet as "leveling the playing field" between the haves and have-nots. That illusion rapidly melted. How about Digital Drift? Does it affect all of us equally, or does it chafe the wounds of inequality and widen the disparity between the privileged and the disadvantaged? Let's take a look.

The Digital Drift Divide

At the turn of the millennium about two decades ago, I embarked on a one-week hike to Tengboche Monastery near the base camp of Mount Everest. (You know a mountain is large when you walk all day long for a week and do not even reach a place called the "base camp.") I spent much of this hike conversing with Krishna, my Nepalese guide, about his decision to agree to an arranged marriage versus a "love marriage."

Krishna has a Hotmail account, and we have been in touch a few times per year. (He opted to follow his heart and marry his sweetheart, and now runs a trekking agency in Kathmandu. His friendly emails usually have a subject such as "Hello from mountain.") We shared a week together, three meals a day, talking about everything under the sun.

On a social level, Krishna and I both have the same access to email and the Internet. There is no hierarchy. Free email and Facebook accounts may not have leveled the playing field, but at least they have expanded the number of players who can walk onto it.

While there is still somewhat of a digital divide (e.g., while 65 percent of Americans have broadband access at home, only 40 percent of families that earn $20,000 or less have such access), even more striking may be a widening "digital drift divide." According to a recent Kaiser Family Foundation study of over two thousand children and teens ages eight to eighteen, in 1999 children and teenagers with parents who do not have a college degree spent sixteen minutes more per day exposed to media in various forms (e.g., social media, TV, other electronic gadgets) than those with parents with a college degree. In 2010, this difference had increased to an hour and a half.

Worse still, in 2010 African American and Hispanic children spent almost four and a half more hours per day watching television and playing video games than white children. It should be no surprise, then, that despite the strong sense of community associated with their cultures, the recently released Cigna study found that the two loneliest ethnic groups in the US today are Hispanics and African Americans. Independent of ethnicity, children and teens who spend the most time on their screens receive the lowest grades in school.

This widening time-wasting gap is largely attributed by the study authors to more-educated mothers and fathers monitoring their children's use of their digital devices more closely than less-educated parents. In poorer families, it is not uncommon for parents to be working more than one job and to have less time for child rearing. For this new latchkey generation, Facebook has become the go-to babysitter.

If you are in doubt about the toxic effects the web is having on the social fabric of our society, ask its inventor. Surprising the world in March 2019 at the thirty-year anniversary of his invention, Sir Tim Berners-Lee declared that the World Wide Web—the information system through which websites and documents are locatable on the Internet via a specific Uniform Resource Locator, or URL—has become "anti-human" and an "engine of inequity and division" that has led to "a lot of dysfunction in society."

Time for Dinner

What are children missing out on when they spend so much time on their digital devices? Vital time to connect with their parents. According to a study from The National Center on Addiction and Substance Abuse at Columbia University, teenagers who participate in fewer than three family dinners each week are likelier to experience a future life of self-medication: they are four times more likely to use drugs, over twice as likely to drink alcohol, and four times more likely to smoke tobacco.

These findings are ominous, as they suggest that technology-mediated addictions, which naturally decrease face-to-face time with family, can subsequently lead to substance addictions. Another disturbing trend from the Kaiser study is that the baseline (children from families of higher socioeconomic status) is ten hours of electronic media per day, largely for entertainment purposes, with children of lower socioeconomic status racking up eleven and a half hours per day.

Let's take a deeper look at this disparity: if you sleep for eight hours per night and spend an hour preparing for school and another hour getting ready for bed, that leaves fourteen hours in a day for other activities. Children and teenagers are now fastened to their smartphones, televisions, desktops, or laptops all but two and a half or four hours of this time, depending on their socioeconomic status.

Even if we count all awake time in a day (about sixteen hours), poorer children are spending 72 percent and more affluent children are spending 63 percent of their waking hours embedded in an electronic version of reality. Most poignantly, all children and teens are spending more of their waking hours in a digitally mediated environment than interacting with real people in the physical universe.

The Electronic Babysitter

The eight-hour-sleep assumption may be faulty, however. Consider Markiy Cook, a resident of Oakland, California, who was twelve at the time of the Kaiser study. His family has an Xbox 360, a Nintendo Wii, and two laptops, and Markiy has his own smartphone. He uses all of these electronic gadgets primarily for YouTube, texting, Facebook, and video games. Markiy confesses that "I stay up all night, until like seven in the morning. It's why I'm so tired on Monday."

At Markiy's school, Elmhurst Community Prep, there is a tribute hanging in a hallway to a fifteen-year-old girl who was stabbed to death by her baby's father. Most of the students at Elmhurst are Latino; about 35 percent, like Markiy, are African American. Parents frequently complain to the school principal about being unable to stop their children from using their digital devices; such attempts are often met by tantrums and screaming fits.

Are you no stranger to the electronic babysitter? Have you used your smartphone or tablet to "cover for you" so you can access some breathing room from your kids? I certainly have. The temptation is always there, an ever-available ticket to free time that is usually just a few feet away. It becomes even more appealing when we realize that, at least in the short term, our kids would prefer to spend time on a screen rather than with us.

It only becomes a problem in excess. A small amount of smartphone or tablet use—an hour or a half hour (better) per day—is considered relatively healthy for children, especially if they are using their digital devices to do something even remotely educational.

Everybody's Doing It

On average, Americans of all ages now spend sixty hours each week— between eight and nine hours daily—across four digital devices: smartphones, computers, tablets, and televisions. Leading this trend are Hispanics, who have adopted smartphones at a higher rate and watch more hours of video on their digital devices than the rest of Americans.

Further, the assumption that more time on the Internet equates to less time watching TV has been found to be a myth. Children and teens spend over eight hours per day, seven days per week, in front of a screen—more time than the average adult spends at a full-time job.

Screens are part of our lives now. They will increasingly become part of our children's lives. As an occasional educational or entertainment tool with adequate oversight, they will not disappoint. They will not erode socioemotional abilities, self-esteem, and relationship development. Like fantasy novels, alcohol, TV series, shopping, eating, and just about anything else, digital devices only become toxic when you over-engage in them.

"I get all this," you may be thinking. "But based on your own historical argument, couldn't you have made the same argument before about other technologies such as the telephone and the automobile? We recovered our self-esteem then, and we can do it now. It will only take time for us to acculturate to smartphones."

On the whole, I agree with you. In many ways, I am simply trying to accelerate this process of acculturation. Yet as you will see in Part Two, there are critical differences between our current screens and all of the technologies that preceded them that go beyond their portability (which we explored in Chapter 3). These differences could slow down this acculturation process, enabling smartphones and other devices to wreak untold damage on our self-esteem and well-being for the foreseeable future.

Let's consider the ways in which our smartphones, tablets, and laptops are different from any technology we've previously assimilated into our lives.

PART TWO

THE NEW WORLD ORDER

9

The Meta-Democratization

*I*n the late nineteenth century, years after his application for a grant from the Municipal Council of Le Havre was rejected due to his "natural inclinations," keeping "the young artist away from the more serious but less rewarding studies which alone deserve municipal generosity," Claude Monet stood at the forefront of a movement of painters. Due to the invention of oil paints, they were able to take paint with them in small containers to the countryside and etch rustic, bucolic settings.

Previously, painters needed to have their water-based paints in large, unwieldy buckets by their sides. Because of this constraint, painting was an occupation only engaged in indoors, in studios where painters depicted still objects or models. In the salons of Paris, these norms defined "serious" painting, while the artistic forays into the countryside of Monet and other "Impressionists" were considered an absurd waste of time.

The Impressionists painted a landscape based on their temporary perception of it—which could change depending on the time of day, the winds, the confluence of sun and clouds, the temperature, and, just as importantly, the mood of the painter. Monet created "series" of paintings of exactly the same landscape, each depending on his momentary *impression*. "For me," Monet shared, "a landscape does not exist as a landscape, since its appearance changes at every moment; but it lives according to its surroundings, by the air and light, which constantly change."

While studio-based, water-mixed painting evoked permanence, Impressionism—a mostly outdoor activity (hence Monet's meticulously tended garden at Giverny, which offered him a continuous supply of natural objects for his pictures)—evoked *the moment.* As Monet's biographer William Seitz described it, Monet was "shucking off the image of the world perceived by memory in favor of a world perceived momentarily by the senses."

If You Can't Make a Picture, Take a Picture

The photograph proved to be an even more momentary artistic process than the often itinerant painting of the Impressionists. In many ways, the photo legitimized the capricious pastime of the Impressionists by enabling a more scientific rendition of instantaneity.

Taking the first photographs took twenty minutes or longer (requiring models to be still), using a large, bulky, stationary camera propped up on the floor. The word *camera,* in fact, comes from the early-eighteenth-century term for a dark chamber or room, *camera obscura.*

The term "photograph," derived from the Greek term for "writing by light," was first used in 1839 by Sir John Herschel. A friend of William Talbot—who invented two-step photography, coming upon his discovery after accepting that he wouldn't sustain his career as an artist—Herschel also added to the photography lexicon the terms "negative" for an original and "positive" for its copy. Eventually, once wet slides gave way to dry slides, a photograph could be taken in seconds.

Until the photograph, art was reserved for painters and others who often spent their lifetimes honing their craft. After the invention of the photo, art was revolutionized: anyone could buy a "handheld" (mobile) camera and snap away. Instead of *making pictures,* photography heralded a landmark shift toward *taking pictures*—and anyone with much less developed artistic skills could participate.

As the historian Daniel Boorstin notes, photography marked a "democratic revolution, after which images of experience could be made instantly by everybody, and could be diffused to the millions."

Democratization is the process through which an object initially only available to a select elite becomes accessible to the masses. Seen (figuratively) through this light, the photograph first democratized art. Then, handheld cameras—followed by smartphones—democratized the photograph.

Hold Still

Consider the patience of painters, and then early photographers, as they elaborated their ethereal art forms. New technologies are almost always first exclusively used by the economic elite and then later adopted by everyone else. Now, most of us can participate in the art of photography. We don't even need to buy a special device anymore to do so—our smartphones include increasingly high-quality cameras.

From water-based to oil-based paints, from wet slides to dry slides, and then from floor-based to handheld cameras to camera-ready smartphones of spectacular quality, technology has democratized the art of capturing an individual's unique interpretation of their surroundings and the people, animals, and objects that populate it.

Yet most of us allocate only seconds of our precious time to this art form. We then move on to the other realms of our lives to which we also allocate similarly brief chunks of time. We take advantage of our new, digitally mediated capabilities to do more and more and then so much more that we don't have the time or mental focus to truly develop a deep talent in any one activity.

Our interests—like the adage about journalists—span a mile in length and an inch in depth. Democratization has produced unprecedented opportunities, fragmentation, limited attention spans, increased activity, reduced down time, and more stress. Good? Bad? Both, depending on whom you ask.

Introducing the Meta-Democratization

Just as the photograph democratized artistic mobility, the automobile democratized physical mobility. Before the early twentieth century, you had to be able to afford to travel by horse-drawn wagon, train, or ship if you wanted to move around by any means other than your own legs.

Then, in 1908, Ford developed an automobile "the common man" could afford. Ford's invention enabled the masses to purchase their own mode of transport, enabling anyone with enough money to buy one to travel independently.

Widespread access to automobiles galvanized the nationwide development of not only highways and suburbs, but bed and breakfasts and amusement parks (both industries spawned by city dwellers' new capability to drive to more tranquil rural areas for weekend respite or large-scale entertainment not possible in more expensive urban areas), drive-thru restaurants, and other amenities for the recently mobile.

Along similar lines, the television democratized entertainment. Before the TV, to see a series of pictures that give the appearance of motion (hence the term, "motion picture") you had to be financially capable of buying a movie ticket.

Another technological invention, the telephone, democratized long-distance communication. In the pre-phone era, you had to be able to afford to travel and make a personal visit if you wanted to communicate by voice with another person outside your immediate area.

Just as Ford's development of the automobile expanded the nation's development to the traditionally underserved, computers have now reached mass saturation and have also generated a new way of living. Yet the computer is different from these once-revolutionary technologies in that it has democratized all of the above democratizations.

The computer is a technology that makes countless previous technologies more accessible and affordable in one centralized location: your smartphone, laptop, or tablet. Try to beat that.

Got Democratization?

The car? Democratized. If you can't afford your own, numerous websites will now help you book one, or even just a seat in one, for as little as a few hours. There are already computer-driven cars on the roads, and this industry will most likely supplant human-driven cars within our generation.

Similarly, while the camera democratized the artistic rendering of one's environment, the computer democratized photography and turned it into an inexpensive collective effort via photo-sharing social networking sites such as Facebook and Instagram.

Art has also been democratized: anyone can write, design, sketch, sing, play an instrument, or dance and then easily and rapidly broadcast their art form to the world as long as they can reproduce it in a digital format. That is, as long as they heed the cautionary advice of author Jonathan Franzen, who once claimed, "It's doubtful that anyone with an Internet connection at his workplace is writing good fiction," and enact Digital Limiting Strategies (see Chapter 16) that enable them to retain their focus.

We can anticipate that soon almost every facet of our lives will be digitally mediated: refrigerators, microwaves, exercise machines—almost everything you use will be connected to the Internet. Apps such as WhatsApp, Facebook, and Skype will continue to proliferate and offer you free services that facilitate your daily habits in exchange for the right to market and sell your private information. As our youngest generation has so well demonstrated, we will likely care even less over time, or at least not covet our privacy enough to prevent companies from intruding into every nook and crevice of our daily activities.

The irony of this meta-democratization is that by democratizing access to the products we crave and wish to use daily—automobiles, cameras, television, and more—a few companies have begun to control our every move. This irony has not been lost upon Sir Tim Berners-Lee (once again, the inventor of the web), who has become "increasingly distressed" by the Big Tech oligarchy. (More than half of all traffic to websites since 2014 has come from only two sources: Google and Facebook.) He believes we need to "return ownership of data to the users who generate it."

Similarly, the researcher who developed the technical infrastructure of the Internet in the 1970s intended for it to be "not controlled by any group." Vint Cerf recently expressed his regret that the "Internet has become the opposite of what it was intended to be."

Ain't Goin' Nowhere Soon

These misgivings notwithstanding, computers, the Internet, and social media are here to stay. To argue against their utility would be as futile as railing against the existence of any new technology that has rapidly gained widespread usage, such as the typewriter in the 1870s or the telephone or television in the 1920s.

Almost a century later, each of our screens, whether in desktop, laptop, tablet, or smartphone form, is all of the above inventions wrapped up into one neat, easy-to-use little package: a democratization of democratizations. Let's give our screens their true name and call them out: a meta-democratization.

Our screens have also democratized many other activities, such as higher education, encyclopedias, and libraries: where you live need no longer be an impediment to learning, as you can access all of the above now at any time, even if you reside in a remote rural area or a developing country with few real-time educational alternatives.

I became impressionably aware of this phenomenon a few years ago, when I participated in a free online course in social psychology on Coursera offered by Wesleyan University—along with over 200,000 people from all over the world. While the program was very well designed, less than 10 percent of participants completed it. This "graduation rate," it turns out, is more or less the norm for MOOCs (massive open online courses); in fact, only 3 percent of students who participate in MOOCs are satisfied with the experience.

Without the affective element of sharing a real classroom with real people and being able to interact directly with a teacher who cares and provides encouragement, student engagement and learning founder. Yet due to the low costs of online education—professors basically just record their lectures and then reuse them year after year—efficiency and convenience trump the enjoyment of genuine learning. (For more on convenience versus enjoyment, see Chapter 11.)

"It can be overwhelming," you may be thinking. "There are just so many options in front of me twenty-four-seven that technology has made available." Yes, it's true that the pixelated screen you hold in your hand or that sits on your desk offers myriad opportunities that people—most likely including you—couldn't have dreamed of only one generation ago. Yet it's also true that our generation is spending thousands more hours sitting or hunched over a machine than those previous generations.

What did people used to do with all that time? Walk outside. Play. Go camping. Socialize in real time. Um, let me see—*live*? Well, okay, it wasn't perfect. At times, it was stunningly inefficient by today's standards: waiting in long lines, lugging around bulky books and records ... more on that later.

Access the Megaplex and Leave Intact

The critical question today is whether you can take the best that technology has to offer to improve your life without overdoing it and losing your humanity in the process. Each and every day of (what remains of) your life, you have the choice to spend it perched in front of a screen or interacting with nature and the real people you care about.

Make the decision to put your real-life connections with others and the aesthetic beauty of the great outdoors (which is really just a conduit for developing your connection with yourself) first and you will become more centered, grounded, secure, and stable—in other words, the type of person who attracts others, which translates into less loneliness and more high-quality people surrounding you.

If, on the other hand, you are unwilling to integrate some checks and balances into how you use your devices, you should not be surprised if, during those periodic moments when you step out of the digital realm, you experience a foreboding sense of existential crisis. You become what you give your attention to, and I can speculate that as you progress in age you will want to look back on your life and see more than a rapid texter and emailer who kept all of their contacts up to date with their latest activities.

So why would you (or anyone) move your life in such a questionable direction? Why would you electronic message now and suffer later? Why would you fill your later years with regret at having expended so many of your precious days with a screen acting as a barrier between you and the people you most care about?

You may fear that if you don't check your phone during the evenings you'll miss out on what's going on with your friends. Dedicate your evenings to offline pursuits and you'll be pleasantly surprised to find that your friendships begin to feel real, genuine, and vital again.

Yes, it will take more effort, especially in the beginning when your friends don't call you back because they're so deeply embedded in their virtual socializing. (We'll discover some strategies on how to handle this issue in Part Three.) Yet just about anything of value in your life has not come easily, and reclaiming your most important relationships is worth the challenges that lie ahead.

As it turns out, there's a reason many of us have not just become glued to our screens, but subconsciously treat it like a bodily appendage: the way we develop our own identity has become inextricably linked to our screens. In the next chapter, we'll try to understand how this has happened and what we can do about it so we can each reclaim who we truly are.

10

The Brand Is You

*A*bout fifteen years ago, I was struggling in my career. I had left my position as the CEO of a large international organization and started off as a consultant while I continued to work on my first book. Contracts were few and far between. It was the early years of Facebook and Twitter, and I committed the common modern error of allowing my self-worth to hinge on the number of followers I had on these and other social media sites.

I took a break one evening from raising clouds of dust in my career and went out to dinner with a childhood friend and his family. His twelve-year-old son, a practicing magician, asked me how many followers I had on YouTube. He then boasted that he had more YouTube followers than I did.

Perhaps even sadder is that later that evening, I checked. He was right. In fact, he had three times as many followers as I did.

In the same way that technology has ushered in the democratization of transport, entertainment, and art, Steve Jobs, Bill Gates, and the titans of technology have democratized the brand. Today, everyone is a brand. This is why we keep logging onto social media—we're checking up on our brand. We want to know how we stack up against others. Yet despite our efforts, as my friend's son taught me, there are always others higher up the hill.

A commercial brand is an attempt to systematically link—through repetitive promotion—a specific image or feeling to a product. The image or feeling is not the product, but that's not the point: as long as people widely associate a positive image or feeling with the product, they will buy it.

Take Coca-Cola. Thanks to aggressive lobbying, the soft drink company successfully edged out Pepsi to be awarded the contract from the US government to supply soft drinks to American soldiers during World War II. Coca-Cola owed its war presence to General Dwight Eisenhower, who—in an extreme slight to Pepsi—requested that (only) Coca-Cola set up ten bottling plants and supply six million bottles to the troops. Eisenhower even forced Italian prisoners of war to work in Coca-Cola plants in Morocco and Algeria.

The resulting images of hot, tired soldiers drinking a cold bottle of the sugary concoction in between battles with the Nazis became emblazoned on the covers of newspapers, magazines, and posters all over the United States. This strategy, along with heavy advertising at sporting events, helped Coca-Cola achieve its goal of permanently embedding its soft drink—despite its staggeringly unhealthy contents—into the American psyche as a symbol of patriotism.

The Atomization of the Brand

The Internet and social media have enabled the atomization of branding to the individual level: any individual can now, with relative ease, attempt to pull off the same achievement that Coca-Cola and many other companies have accomplished for centuries—*to systematically link, through repetitive promotion, a specific image or feeling to themselves.* Many unwittingly also attempt to become this false persona in the way they socialize with others, through the continual promotion of their personal brand.

This approach to life tends to induce existential angst and unhappiness, as people begin to feel as artificial as the constraining image they have linked to their personality. They promote an unrealistic ideal of themselves, confuse the ideal with reality, and then deprecate themselves when they come up short in the physical world. As a result, they embrace a schema of thinking characterized by scarcity— never living up to this desired image—rather than one of abundance, acceptance, and appreciation of their unique attributes.

It's fine for Coca-Cola to refuse to alter its soft drink recipe—in fact, its attempt to do so (with New Coke) was one of the largest marketing failures in corporate history. Why? Americans' emotional attachment to the classic recipe far outweighed their preference for the taste of the new, sweeter concoction (which blindfolded participants preferred in over 190,000 taste tests).

However, when a human being links their *self* to an image they later outgrow, the image becomes a prison cell; a continual reminder of the person they (once) wanted to be but never really were and certainly are not now.

Great Brand, More Social Distance

Our inexorable drive to create a personal brand causes us to become disconnected from who we really are. We think we are innocuously checking social media, but in fact we are nervously checking to see if our status has grown or is under attack, as nothing is more feared in the digital age than a threat to our personal brand.

We live in a perpetual state of fear: we create a personal brand, attach our self-worth to its success, and then fear its loss—fear is always associated with loss—and desperately search for reassurance, every time we log on, that we are not losing our brand.

It is for this reason that many people are now more likely to reply to you if you leave a message on their Facebook wall than if you send them a personal Facebook message: they are building their personal brand. To reply to you privately is (primarily) a (relatively ineffective) relationship-building activity; to reply publicly is a branding activity. A public reply is often a reaction to feelings of insecurity about a personal brand and the need to reinforce it.

We relentlessly seek praise from others to reassure ourselves that the demand for our personal brand remains strong. For this reason, we must be online at all times, up to our dying breath, to ward off attacks on the image we erroneously confuse with ourselves.

It is for this reason that the addictions fueled by the Internet are primarily social. Woe be it to log on and have no emails, texts, or social media messages ... such an outcome would mean we are dreadfully inadequate and alone in our virtually rendered reality, a glorified term for the amalgam of cables and pixels we have confused with the real world.

The result: We have commercialized ourselves. We've shifted from a meritocracy to a marketocracy. The Internet has expanded capitalism from the (broader) commercial level to the (atomistic) personal level. We now frequently assess our daily online tally sheet—permanently etched into the cyber-universe—and lose ourselves in the process.

Many of us have unwittingly transformed ourselves into a product—a set of images people associate with us—and have forgotten that we are not the images; that we are something much deeper than the public persona; that we are much more profound as individuals than the virtual brand we have spent so many of our waking hours cultivating. In short, we have forgotten our essential humanness.

Seeking Relevance

Your brand is enhanced in a number of ways: by the number of "friends" you have on Facebook; by the ratio of your followers to the people you follow on Twitter, which has been referred to as "Page-Ranking for people." I have noticed that the times in my life when I've been the most insecure about my career—such as just before the publication of my first book, when my friend's twelve-year-old son so gloriously upstaged me—are the times when I've been the most glued to social media.

The hours upon hours I've poured into the Internet during these dark moments have come from a grasping, craving mentality: desperate attempts to assert my *relevance* in the world. When I have been more confident, I've cared less about other people's image of me and have felt less of a need to while away hours online distilling my personal brand. Apparently, I'm not alone: people check emails more often when their confidence is shaken.

If you are engaged in this competition to be the most looked at, to have the most comments on your wall, the most followers, the most "likes," the most impressive status update, ask yourself whether you are aiming at the right target, or even playing in the right stadium. Whatever we express should come from the heart, and we should express it because we feel it needs to be shared, not because we seek the recognition of others.

The first African American to win the Best Actor Oscar (but not the first to deserve it), Denzel Washington, incisively remarked: "My mother used to tell me man gives the award, God gives the reward. I don't need another plaque." The only source of approval that will make a difference in your life in the long run comes from within.

Yet most of us, like me fifteen years ago (but not now, never—no likes, thank you very much; really, not at all … okay, it never completely fades; the craving for approval, as William James once shared, is one of the deepest human desires), still seek the (external) award and have lost sight of the (internal) reward.

If many of us now use social media to hinge our self-concept to the good opinion of others, what is the collective result? How does this add up socially? What kind of society does it create?

The Unlimited Billboard

Let's take a look at how society has functioned for centuries. There was always a very small group of celebrities; the rest watched them and read from and about them. The masses focused on the lives and work of this select group of luminaries—which included writers, politicians, movie directors, athletes, entertainers, and so on—who captured the public's attention.

While this small minority still receives top billing, the public now also captures the public's attention. Technology has enabled a much wider swath of society to gain a following through Twitter, YouTube, Facebook, Instagram, and other social media sites. The select minority I refer to above—the A-level celebrities—now share billboard space with the public, yet still attract the most eyeballs.

A whole new culture has emerged that includes B-, C-, and D-level "influencers" in the look-at-me food chain: self-promoting individuals who would have received scant attention before. Now, thanks to social media sites, there is a whole universe of also-rans who cannot reach millions but can build followings of hundreds or even thousands.

In other words, social media has democratized fame. It has brought all of us much closer to the adulation of others. Yet it is an emptier and more illusory prestige. It is much more likely now than ever before in human history that you or someone you know well is one of these minor-league celebs.

Who would have known that the mild-mannered engineer you sit next to in your office has such a mellifluous voice and has eight hundred people following him as he belts out tunes at night on an online karaoke site? You never would have imagined the withdrawn librarian next door is a cause célèbre to hundreds in the world of online chess. And so on. Fame now has a democratized pecking order.

Everyone Has a Dream

Many of us crave the technologically extended limelight. We've become Digital Exhibitionists to obtain our small piece of the expanded pie. The dream of stardom is now Everyman's dream.

On one level, the wider spotlight is positive. It enables broader self-expression among the multitudes. It's probably a good thing that the mild-mannered engineer down the hall is channeling his inner Bruce Springsteen at night. Also, before we curse this democratization of art forms, let me remind you that—like salmon swimming upstream as a sloth of bears ravenously awaits them—only a few magically rise to the highest echelons of the artistic professions.

One such individual is Arnel Pineda. A Phillipine cover-band singer from humble beginnings, Arnel uploaded a few covers of Journey songs on YouTube. In June 2007, he was discovered by the band's founding lead guitarist, Neal Schon, and received an email invitation to fly to Marin County, California, for an audition.

Pineda dismissed it as a hoax until his manager convinced him to reply. Schon called him ten minutes later. Fast-forward two months and he becomes the band's lead singer. Within less than a year, Arnel led Journey to one of the top grossing concert tours of 2008, generating over $35 million in revenues.

While Pineda offers a breathtakingly amazing story, there is a negative side. Just as millions of inner-city youth skip school or downplay their studies and head to the basketball courts in the hopes of becoming the next Magic Johnson, millions of people now choose not to spend time outside so they can craft their global screen-based takeover. Instead of strumming or singing at a local concert with their friends, many strum and sing alone in their rooms in the hopes of becoming the next digital rags-to-riches poster child.

Yet just as there was only one Magic, there is only one Arnel. At least the youth on the basketball courts are learning important, transferable skills, such as physical conditioning, resilience, and socioemotional abilities that enable them to navigate complex environments in real life.

The transferable skills of spending the majority of one's waking hours indoors behind a screen certainly also exist, yet are more nebulous and difficult to link to real-world success or well-being. "A lot of parents take great pride in the fact that their child is so ensconced in the iPad," the University of Washington pediatrician Dimitri Christakis told me recently. "They view it as evidence that they're developing computer literacy skills. That's not what's happening. In fact, we know that most of the skills that children learn at a very young age on these touchscreen devices don't transfer to the real world."

Too Much Supply Kills the Value

Like any scarce resource that suddenly becomes cheap and abundant, unlimited billboard space destroys the value of the billboard. When everyone feels their voice must be heard, each voice loses some of its significance.

In many ways, the pandemic search for meaning through social media ironically renders social media meaningless. Its unrivaled inclusivity produces a club with disconnected, disloyal members who, over time, will no longer be able to remember the club's name or their reason for joining.

As elitist as it sounds, when any club shifts its focus from an exclusive clientele to the general public, in the minds of many it loses its distinction. Eventually, to them, it begins to bear a striking resemblance to a dilapidated, poorly tended, unhygienic public swimming pool. Residents walk past without intrigue, uninterested in stepping into its murky depths; it becomes an invisible neighborhood fixture to many, a vestigial reminder of glory days past.

Until we learn how to temper our insatiable lust for social recognition—which social media companies capitalize on—technology will continue to erode our experience of the real world. We will continue to experience less face-to-face interaction and a growing elusive inner craving for real people in our lives.

In-person relationships are already becoming a nostalgic concept; many are unwilling to cede the convenience and cool detachment of their digital personas to recapture them. Yet the craving remains.

Watching the People We Once Were

It is no coincidence that "reality shows" became popular after the advent of social media. Before the Internet, many would have responded to the concept of a reality TV show with "Why would I want to watch someone like me?" Now we watch because we are not viewing people like ourselves; rather, we are viewing people like who we once were.

There is now a huge demand to know what's transpiring in the lives of real, everyday people who interact with others in real time (which reality shows supply) because these real, everyday people are gradually removing themselves from our lives—lock, stock, and barrel, but not Facebook page.

Capitalizing on our social isolation, reality shows tend to feature highly social characters with extended families and friendship networks. We want to know what real people are doing, but unlike the characters we binge-watch, craving what they have, we're not prepared to step away from our screen to walk or drive over to see them. Instead, we follow them virtually and watch them on TV.

Social media has, strangely, created its own demand. By isolating you from your friends, your loneliness becomes greater and you feel more motivated by what the British psychologist Pamela Qualter calls the "reaffiliation motive" to check your social media and see what your friends are doing.

It doesn't work. In some ways, social media is like calling the delivery number of a pizza franchise in your neighborhood. The more frequently you order, the fatter and less capable of walking outside to a grocery store or restaurant you become.

So what do you do? You call the delivery number more often to save yourself from an increasingly challenging walk (to real, face-to-face connection). Perceptively summarizing this phenomenon, the Italian novelist Umberto Eco once wrote:

> The Internet is one thing and its opposite. It could remedy the loneliness of many, but it turns out it has multiplied it; the Internet has allowed many to work from home, and that has increased their isolation. And it generates its own remedies to eliminate this isolation, Twitter, Facebook, which end up increasing it.

Immobilized Without Connection

By putting you in contact with the many who matter little to you (e.g., former classmates, friends of friends), social media diminishes your ability to connect in real time with the few who matter a lot. Again, research identified this paradoxical effect of the Internet. So we know what's happening, yet seem helpless to change our habits.

Even worse, the more time you spend on your phone, the less enjoyment you derive from real-time conversations with the people who have truly been there for you in your life. You begin to perceive them, with all of their time-consuming idiosyncrasies, as requiring too much effort.

Yet you still crave the intimate connection that only real-time interaction produces, which expands your demand for what seems the easiest, most effortless way to tap into it—ironically, the technology that's stamped it out of your life—social media.

So, like the pizza chain gleefully delivering delicious, non-nutritious food to your home, social media throws you overboard and then dangles a life preserver in front of your flailing, desperately lonely, sputtering body. You never quite make it back into the boat of human connection, but neither do you have the capability to swim away.

In Part Three, I will share concrete strategies you can implement to pursue social connection where it abundantly resides—in the physical universe—and to vastly pare down your time interacting with others through email, texting, and social media to a fraction of what it is now. Let's first consider how our social lives became so distorted by these new technologies. We'll begin by understanding what truly guides our behavior in the digital age.

11

Convenience over Enjoyment

The price of anything is the amount of life you exchange for it.
—Henry David Thoreau

When I was a Peace Corps volunteer in Kenya over twenty-five years ago, I lived in a small town of a few thousand people about a three-hour bus ride inland from Mombasa. I knew most of the residents of Wundanyi by name or at least by sight. My gregariousness was not entirely by choice. To develop a relatively functional life in a small town like Wundanyi back then, you had to know everyone.

There was a central marketplace I frequented after working all day with the local schools, where I knew by name the "mamas" selling vegetables. We traded stories over tomatoes, hand-ground maize flour, and mangoes. They sustained me with fresh vegetables of many varieties. The selection wasn't democratic like at Whole Foods Market: the mamas decided what to offer you based on how much they liked you.

I knew the bakers well, and they went out of their way to help me by baking special bread without sugar for me. I also spent many an afternoon talking with the Indian shopkeeper who brought me imported foodstuffs such as baking powder from Mombasa and Nairobi. And so on.

Without the friendliness and social interaction, many core elements of village life would not have been possible. For example, the factory-made maize flour was not nearly as healthy or delicious as the locally produced variety. To acquire the latter, it was necessary to know someone in the local women's cooperative that operated the "*posho* mill" (where maize stalks were ground into flour). Economic interdependence produced social interdependence.

Screened In

Today, I sometimes feel guilty and tinged with shame as I drive past (what's left of) the mom-and-pop bookstores and instead order a book on Amazon. As our physical marketplace continues to dissipate, the jury is out as to how we will create the social interdependence necessary to access the socioemotional support we all need, especially when something goes counter to our life goals (e.g., an intimate partner leaves, a job is lost, a family member passes away).

When we experience such challenging life moments, it becomes very salient to us that *we need each other.* Yet we find ourselves woefully lonely and deficient in social skills because we didn't take the time to build meaningful connections with others when times were better.

Moments such as the large snowstorms I used to experience growing up in Washington, DC: when we and our neighbors spent long days inside our homes unable to access the usual amenities, we met outside in the snow and joined together to commiserate and help each other.

I can't speak for anyone else, but I know I would not have experienced the same growth as a human being without getting to know so many people in Wundanyi, which led to my feeling a sense of belonging and inner harmony with the community around me. Stepping outside each day to interact with people was one of the drivers of my integration into the community. It led me to many social, emotional, and psychological benefits that enabled me to have some of the most indelible experiences of my life—experiences that irrevocably transformed who I am.

In most Western countries today, you don't have to go out and interact with others in real time to meet most of your material needs. As a result, many of us have become Screened In.

Affluent Pakistani Women and Us

A work colleague from Pakistan once told me there are many well-heeled Pakistani women now who are able to hire one servant for each of their children. They often spend the day going to the spa, shopping, and having lunch with their friends. Meanwhile, their children grow up with their nannies, many of whom are from the Philippines.

Sound familiar? It certainly does to me: I grew up with a Bolivian nanny raising me and my siblings. My marrying a Mexican woman is likely related to my early association of Latin culture with affection.

How do living in an African village and affluent Pakistani women fundamentally differ? In African village life, little is convenient—you must painstakingly carve out a role for yourself in a complex social web just to meet your basic material and social needs. While the responsibilities you assume in order to do so are tremendous, so can be the long-term enjoyment enabled by such a rich social network.

For wealthy Pakistani mothers, and for many of the developing country elite all over the world, it's the opposite: having money in an otherwise poor country renders life stunningly convenient. Yet, as many mothers who hired nannies to raise their children—some of whose kids are now less close with their parents than to these women, who were there for them through thick and thin—can attest, long-term enjoyment is elusive, again as a consequence of (in this case) a shrinking social network.

As the women in Pakistan my friend referred to exemplify, convenience and the maximizing of individual preferences are quite alluring. ("Should I go to the spa and get a massage or stay at home feeding my child to mollify his sixth tantrum for the day?") If we have no limit to how much we can focus on these preferences (for instance, let's say we can have a nanny for each child because nannies are so inexpensive due to poverty in a neighboring country and a lack of minimum-wage controls), we are likely to opt for convenience.

The False Illusion of Independence

Most of us have become like these well-off Pakistani women: convenience seekers who experience less long-term enjoyment and fulfillment. Convenience is king and available in unprecedented quantities. Without leaving not just our homes, but our Internet-ready-devices-equipped rooms, many of us can satisfy most of our material needs, creating the false illusion of economic and social independence from others.

The true, unmeasured cost of prioritizing convenience is social, emotional, and psychological development. In the case of the elite Pakistani mothers, it's not only themselves, but even more so their children who suffer these losses.

I cannot tell you how happy I am that there was no Amazon delivery, Facebook, or email in that small Kenyan town over twenty-five years ago. I had to fulfill my material needs and seek social and emotional support outside the house, which was trying at times but, in the end, much more meaningful and enduring.

Pick a situation and ask yourself whether you're building your social interdependence in your community or increasing your isolation. When you need to buy groceries, are you ordering them online or making a phone-free trip to a local market where you might strike up a conversation with someone? If you are feeling anxious and want to exercise, are you working out on a home machine or going to a gym where, over time, you are likely to start seeing the same people and talking with them, especially if you join an exercise class?

Many people are unwilling to prioritize their long-term development over short-term convenience. They consciously or subconsciously say to themselves, "I'm living in the here and now," and make their life choices accordingly. The problem is that, in the long term, they cease to recognize who they've become. They feel disconnected from their values and what they most care about.

You can make the decision today to question what and how you consume from the digital spigot. You can have a heart-to-heart with yourself about what you truly enjoy, and whether the easily accessed digital options are a sufficient substitute.

If you enjoy going to the supermarket and touching, smelling, feeling, seeing the food your family is going to consume and conversing with the checkout person and even sometimes other shoppers, you can decide to forego online supermarkets, where you often receive food closer to the expiration date anyway. If you enjoy going out with friends and socializing, you can stop engaging in laconic text exchanges and instead call a friend or two, go out, and leave the evening to chance.

Whatever you love to do, ask yourself whether you will do it in real time in the real world. Alternatively, consider whether you will allow yourself to habituate to yet another questionable digital alternative that keeps your neck in place bent over your phone for yet even more of your limited time on this earth.

They Want Your Presence, Not Your Presents

"Now hang on a moment, partner," you may be thinking. "I'm a lover of convenience and not ashamed of it in the least." Well, it is true that our phones have made our lives easier and safer in countless ways. Yet let's not forget that the quality of a mobile call is a fraction of the quality of a call made with a landline. Two mobiles connecting often sound like two-way radios.

Working has also become more convenient: you can work from virtually anywhere as long as you have a permissive boss. (For this reason, many people have chosen to work for themselves—considered by many the badge of freedom in the digital age.) The downside of a world filled with "digital nomads" is a lack of connection.

Sure, you can join a phone conference while waiting in the doctor's office for your teenager to finish her appointment or while you're on a beach in the Caribbean—but so can everyone else. As a result, your sense of friendship and community is likely to diminish along with your physical colocation.

Productivity also suffers. Ninety percent of knowledge workers in a 2014 survey admitted to doing other things during work phone conferences that distracted them from the topic at hand. Only 44 percent found virtual communication as productive as face-to-face communication.

Not Just African

Lest you think community is a distinctly African phenomenon, a few years after living in a rural town in Kenya for three years, I returned to the San Francisco Bay Area, where I became an honorary member of the Kenyan expat community. While we had wonderful parties with about forty regulars with whom I practiced my Swahili—some still close friends to this day—each person was working two or three jobs to survive, and their community was becoming increasingly fractured due to the scheduling challenges of bringing everyone together.

We focus on giving others our *presents*, when what they truly want from us is our *presence*. In many families, the first has become a poor substitute for the second. And even the first has taken a hit: many of us no longer spend any significant amount of time choosing gifts for others, and instead email gift certificates—which are useful but lack soul.

These words—useful but lacking soul—could be a mantra for this phenomenon of convenience trumping enjoyment in the digital age. Since you can buy just about anything with it—the purpose of legal tender, after all—an Amazon gift certificate is one shade short of giving cash.

There is a reason we give gifts to the people we love: a gift signals that you actually took some time out of your busy life to think about the other person because you care about them. That feeling—that the other person put a lot of time and energy into searching for a gift for you—has, for many, become an evanescent memory.

Convenience Is Peaking, Baby

Dating is also more "convenient" now. When you are cycling through hundreds of possible mates on Tinder, there is no denying that it is a *convenient* way to meet people. Yet are you meeting *quality* people? If you are lucky, you are. Most of the time, though, people's virtual personas are markedly different from who they are in person.

The son of one of my best friends, Arvind, met his girlfriend online. At one of the delicious seven-course Indian dinners his parents invite us over for regularly, he told me about one of his coworkers: "He has five pictures in his profile. One picture is with a beard and one is without a beard because he tells me that if a woman likes a guy with a beard, she might like that picture and if not, she might like this picture. He has a picture where he's riding a horse in a polo match in case someone is into sports. He has one of him rock climbing for outdoors enthusiasts, and another with a dog to show his emotional side."

It took a lot of courage twenty years ago to walk up to someone in a store or on the street and introduce yourself. Today, you can introduce yourself to twenty people within half an hour on Tinder or Match. Walking up to that stranger, however, wasn't only an instrumental act to find the right person: it was also an act of self-development that taught us how to confront our fears. Moreover, if the stranger was receptive, it could lead to the development of a different kind of relationship than you might have with someone you've pinged online.

Every relationship has a mythology: popular stories and myths that define its culture. Just as collectively shared myths and stories define the culture of a nation, group, or organization, they also define the culture of a relationship. The moment he proposed; the time she spoke up to her parents and protected the relationship. "He pinged me on Tinder" may be less likely to lead to as strong of a culture to embed and guide the relationship and protect it from hostile, potentially destructive influences.

Perhaps with some mutual creativity, it will. It's certainly okay to meet people online, yet it's also okay to face your fears and say hello to a real-life person who is attracting your attention.

Actually, research shows that the Internet can be useful for meeting people for the first time. But after that, relationships develop much more meaningfully through face time (not to be confused with FaceTime, the iPhone videoconferencing app) or at least phone time. So if you meet someone on Tinder, ditch the protracted texting sessions and suggest a phone call or date.

Similarly, convenience can derail quality while you're growing a business. Are you more likely to develop the kind of quality participants—board members, employees, investors, collaborators—for your enterprise by emailing twenty people, or by having an in-depth, high-quality conversation with two people?

Before the Internet, the latter was, most of the time, your only option. Now that you can message people all day, it takes a concerted effort to get up from your desk and go out and meet with people.

The Elusive Balance of Convenience and Enjoyment

"But can't I have convenience *and* enjoyment?" you may be asking yourself. Absolutely. I'm not suggesting that you uninstall Spotify, Waze, and Match. Sure, I experience more enjoyment picking out and listening to an album on a turntable than thumbing to and tapping it on Spotify, but I can't remember the last time I did the former. I don't even own a turntable anymore.

As for Tinder, Bumble, and Match, again, many people meet their soulmate online. Yet how do you use a dating app? Are you simultaneously engaging in chats with dozens of eligible partners as a means of escaping the real world, or do you use these dating apps to meet someone and then quickly shift to developing a relationship offline?

For many Digital Natives, texting has become the new courtship. In her Heart of Darkness Challenge Journal in Appendix A, Krystle shares how texting has become the new form of getting to know someone new and attempting to not become vulnerable in the early stages of dating, and how it ultimately fails to accomplish either objective.

If you profess to wanting a serious relationship but in practice partake of the former in a relentless search for approval from the opposite sex to fortify your fragile ego, you can run but you can't hide: I'm no stranger to such behavior and am calling you out. There were times in my life when I had online conversations going with many women in faraway places as a kind of buffer to deflect my feeling hurt over a previous relationship and to keep my fear of commitment at bay. I suspect I'm not the only one.

Whether it's an intimate relationship, making friends, listening to music, watching movies, going shopping, or even seeing a therapist (in person or, yes, by Whatsapp or Skype, which some people are doing now to save money), we can ask ourselves how we can integrate short-term convenience and long-term enjoyment in our lives. With a little ingenuity, we can find creative ways to foster our social, psychological, and emotional development, the lifestyle we desire now, and our capacity to become the person we desire to be in the future.

Toward the Shore

While eating his mother's delicious *saag paneer*, my thoughts returned to Arvind's friend who meticulously curated his profile with five photos, each strategically placed to attract a different type of woman. "Isn't your friend worried that he may attract a woman for the wrong reasons?" I asked Arvind. "Is there a unified version of himself he could present in one photo?"

"It's a numbers game," Arvind replied. "He figures that, between his five photos, he will expand the number of people he can potentially attract, so hopefully he'll meet the right woman."

Listening to Arvind, the irony was not lost upon me that his family provided my home away from home during my years of being single and going on dates with women I met on the Internet. I remembered how self-conscious I felt during some of those dinners. The instability and unpredictability of my life always seemed in stark juxtaposition with the regularity, caring, and warmth of their family life.

I always considered Arvind's father, Narendra, to be the mentoring older brother I never had, a lighthouse guiding me through a tumultuous single life toward the shore of commitment and lasting love. It's why I asked him to marry my wife and me and officiate over our wedding in Mexico.

Discover your own healthy equilibrium between convenience and enjoyment and you will be pleasantly surprised to feel more like the master of your life. Why? Because you will learn to use technology as a helpful tool without becoming its servant.

If you desire to meet the right person and wish to use online dating sites, don't become a deer caught in the headlights of innumerable glossy profiles. Recognize that these meticulously curated images and words take self-presentation to new, stunning levels yet camouflage much deeper insecurities. Don't fall prey to yet another opportunity to throw hours of your life into a text-addled cesspool only to earn the right to sit across the table from someone who bears little resemblance to their virtual persona.

Enjoyment and Quality Before Convenience

Jenna, a nurse in Seattle in her early thirties, shared with me how she met her boyfriend:

> I went on a date with a man who, upon first exchanging numbers, apologized that I would have to keep texts simple, as he does not have a smartphone. He also requested, sheepishly, that longer conversations be had by phone or in person, because texting on an old text pad is ten times more exhausting and time consuming than on my iPhone. I totally understood and was secretly envious/in awe of how

he manages a life without this incredibly powerful device. He isn't a complete technophobe; he has a laptop, catches up on Netflix, online dates, watches YouTube videos, and streams music. But he doesn't have these conveniences in his pocket. And he doesn't miss what he has never had! When I first arrived for our date, I found him sitting at a table by himself waiting patiently. All the other tables were filled with patrons with hunched backs and screens in their faces. It was an inspiring (and, frankly, very attractive) sight.

In the same way that you can slow down and derive more enjoyment from dating or your intimate relationship, instead of playing the let-me-see-how-many-cards-I-can-collect game the next time you go to a conference, when you meet someone with whom you connect well, pause and really talk with them for a while. Prioritize enjoyment and quality in your life and you will experience a sea change as your progression toward your personal and career goals becomes infused with values and meaning.

"Okay, I'm with you, fair author," you may be thinking. "But you can't deny the benefits of convenience in the digital age when it comes to shopping. I can get just about whatever I want, when I want it. Try to beat that." You are right that being a consumer has never been more convenient. But are you enjoying it as much as you used to? That depends on how you use …

12

Your Netflix Time

It is questionable if all the mechanical inventions yet made
have lightened the day's toil of any human being.
—John Stuart Mill

*L*et's now consider the question of whether convenience comes at the price of enjoyment when you go shopping. Let's take the example of renting a movie. Before the Internet, you went to Blockbuster or your local video shop, looked around for a while, argued with a friend, intimate partner, or spouse about which video cassette (or, a decade later, DVD) to rent, and then drove or walked home. Total time: anywhere from half an hour to over an hour.

In the next era of movie rentals, you could order a DVD on Netflix and it arrived in two days. In the current digital age, a movie streams to your TV set instantaneously. Total time: a few minutes, or even just seconds—although the argument with your friend, intimate partner, or spouse may still extend it.

Similarly, compare the time and cost of going to the local bookstore to purchase a book—sometimes including the clerk telling you they don't have it in stock but can order it for you—versus ordering it on Amazon.

Life today is clearly much more efficient than it was twenty or even ten years ago. For me to suggest that you return to dedicating more of your valuable time to logistics or shopping would be the unrealistic idea of a quixotic dreamer relegated to the sidelines as the world speeds hastily on.

A microcosm for how technology has changed our lives is to compare renting a movie on Netflix versus Blockbuster (back when you could find a Blockbuster). In 2000 when Netflix was still sending DVDs by mail to its users, CEO Reed Hastings approached Blockbuster to ask if they would buy the company he founded for $50 million. Blockbuster CEO John Antioco refused, referring to Netflix as a "very small niche business." Notwithstanding our "hindsight bias" rooted in how history subsequently unfolded (in June 2019, Netflix was worth $148 billion), consider this contrast in Appendix B: Netflix Versus Blockbuster.

Something Gained, Something Lost

Let's summarize how shifting from Blockbuster to Netflix is the epitome of the widespread shift in our society from physical brick-and-mortar stores to virtual marketplaces. First of all, let's look at what we have more of now in our dens of electronic commerce such as Netflix and Amazon:

- Selection
- **Convenience**
- Lower prices
- Efficiency
- Higher volume

Now let's look at what we have less of:

- Aesthetic **enjoyment** of each unit
- Physical body movement associated with shopping
- Spontaneity
- Time spent with friends choosing what to listen to or watch

Any rational analysis would lead us to select Netflix or Amazon and all other virtual marketplaces. They are, quite simply, much more efficient, cost effective, and beneficial for the consumer. Yet, on some level, we have lost something: Feeling. Laughing. Enjoying our lives.

Along with yielding more efficiency, technology has also yielded more speed and pressure. Here is the important distinction: the efficiency technology has enabled can in fact increase your sense of meaning in life. You can now get more done in less time, the definition of efficiency. The Internet, then, should really be our friend. It has enabled many business models that provide us with more of our most valuable commodity: time.

Before, you spent twenty minutes to an hour finding your way to and from Blockbuster, selecting a DVD and returning it. Now, you spend a few minutes of your time on Netflix doing the same. In theory, this efficiency should free up a lot of your time to spend with the people you care about, to relax, and to reflect on this wondrous thing called life. Let's see how this works in practice.

How Do You Use Your Netflix Time?

Here's the question that lies at the heart of finding balance in the twenty-first century: *What do you do with the extra fifteen to forty-five minutes provided to you by Netflix?* Let's call these additional fifteen to forty-five minutes contributed to your life by Netflix—and all the similar contributions of Amazon and Hulu and Dropbox and emails and SMSs and smartphones, and so on—"Netflix time."

What you do with your Netflix time is at the heart of finding balance in your life. If you substitute the time you would have spent at Blockbuster with time to go for a relaxing walk or to a mindfulness meditation or to hang out with a good friend, you are using external technological progress to enhance your internal "steadiness of mind," inner peace, and happiness in your daily life. Well done: you have used technology to your benefit.

Such a relationship with technology requires an extremely high level of consciousness and foresight, which very few have. Instead, most of us substitute our Netflix time for more time online engaged in other Internet-mediated activities, such as climbing Email Mountain, nervously checking our smartphone, throwing hours down the craving-for-the-elusive-best-online-deal time sink, or entering the compare-myself-with-others-until-I-get-depressed social media vacuum.

For these people, Netflix and technology in general have not enabled more time for physical exercise, connections with others, or deeper life reflection. Instead, the opposite has occurred: we have permitted technology to take our time for these (usually) wholesome, life-gener-ating activities and replace it with screen time. This shift is tragic. It's why I have written this book.

Technology Camouflages Our Interdependence

"This doesn't work for me," you may be saying to yourself. "There is no 'Netflix time' because I never went to Blockbuster. I wouldn't rent a movie if it weren't so easy to do on Netflix."

That may be true. Yet it's also true that, now that you can do just about anything online, if you don't consciously ask yourself how you will share some of your daily activities with your friends, you may find yourself with no friends. Perhaps for this reason (among others), loneliness has become a global epidemic.

"Okay, I get it, we're lonely," you may be thinking. "But how can we change what's happening? People are choosing to spend so much time on their phones. It seems impossible to stop at this point."

Before we relegate ourselves to a meager social existence character-ized by isolation and loneliness, let's consider how Keith Richards and Mick Jagger developed a lifelong friendship that changed the music landscape forever. This relationship began with Keith meeting Mick as a teenager on a train in London:

> Did we hit it off? You get in a carriage with a guy that's got *Rockin' at the Hops* by Chuck Berry on Chess Records, and *The Best of Muddy Waters* also under his arm, you are gonna hit it off. He's got Henry Morgan's treasure. It's the real shit. I had no idea how to get hold of that.... "Where the hell did you get this?" It was, always, about

records. From when I was eleven or twelve years old, it was who had the records who you hung with. They were precious things.

Today, the next Keith and Mick are more likely to share the same bus, train, or subway car and exchange no more than a sideways glance as they stare down at their phones than to initiate what could become a strong enough connection to launch and sustain a half-century-plus musical career together. With Digital Natives leading the way, we all socialize with each other face-to-face much less often today.

Instead, we opt for convenience: rather than going to great lengths to explore new music with others, the next Keith and Mick are so busy meticulously selecting the music they want and then downloading and listening to it in private isolation that they don't give each other a chance to make history together. Aware of the effects of the rampant individualism accentuated by the Internet on the music industry, seasoned media veteran Lola Ogunnaike of Sky TV recently declared, "Social media has killed the music group."

Do You Choose Convenience or Connection?

Recall a recent situation and ask yourself whether you opted for convenience or connection. If you were having a meal with a friend and they told you about a recent trip with their kids, did you say, "I want to see pictures. Please send me some" or, alternatively, did you say, "I want to see pictures. Can you show me some?" If a friend was going through a difficult issue, did you send a reassuring email or give them a call, or even ask her or him if they would like to meet up in person to talk about it?

If your son or daughter wants a Super Why coloring book, did you order it on Amazon or take them to one of the last remaining bookstores in your town and look over the different coloring books together before purchasing one? I engaged in precisely this activity recently at Barnes & Noble and can vouch for it as a purveyor of connection. Not to mention that we chose much better books because we could touch, feel, and look through them rather than click them unseen (or barely viewed) into an electronic cart.

Clearly Amazon is much more convenient than Barnes & Noble in terms of price and selection, yet there were other intangible benefits of having a Barnes & Noble in our communities: a place to go, an educational family outing on a Saturday, a venue in which to meet other people, to peruse books and become inspired, to listen to an author share their passion, and even a place to write. In many communities across America, the Barnes & Noble acted as a cleaner and more exciting library than the public option, a place where you could also talk with others without the librarian giving you a nasty look or telling you to shut up.

So, once again, the Internet has shifted our society toward convenience and away from enjoyment. Truly consider how much you *enjoy* buying something online versus how much enjoyment you derive from going to a store, touching the merchandise, and soaking up the environment. As the disgraced comedian Louis C. K. put it, "You never feel completely sad or completely happy. You just feel kinda satisfied with your products. And then you die."

Our drive as a society toward convenience—facilitated by the intelligent, often mind-rather-than-heart-driven men who compete with each other for who can create the most efficient apps and websites—is relegating enjoyment to a nostalgic fantasy. Our increasingly mechanical reality represents what only a few decades ago we would have perceived to be a dystopian vision of ourselves immobilized behind our screens, punctuating our otherwise fixed downward gaze to contentedly boast to each other of the great deals we are obtaining online (in the short term) at the price of what we truly value and will bring more fulfillment into our lives (in the long term).

Consider the activities you engage in daily. Make a commitment to spend less time doing them alone and more time doing them outside of the house and in the company of others. As much as possible, try to leave your phone at home or at least in your car or locker during these potential opportunities for social interaction.

Tying the Stake to the Tree

Are you glad you didn't have to traipse around London to listen to someone else's albums? Happy with the convenience of Spotify or iTunes? You may want to think twice: just as the journey toward a goal is often more rewarding than achieving it, social interaction is often more important than the reason for coming together.

Without it, Keith Richards and Mick Jagger never would have become a central part of the underground blues community in London that was an incubator for one of the greatest rock and roll bands in history. In Keith's words:

> Mick and I must have spent a year, while the Stones were coming together and before, record hunting. There were others like us, trawling far and wide, and meeting one another in record shops. If you didn't have money you would just hang and talk.... Blues aficionados in the '60s were a sight to behold. They met in little gatherings like early Christians, but in the front rooms in southeast London. There was nothing else necessarily in common amongst them at all; they were all different ages and occupations. It was funny to walk into a room where nothing else mattered except he's playing the new Slim Harpo and that was enough to bond you all together.... That's what we lived for, basically.

The point for Keith, Mick, and the rest of the Londoners gathered in front rooms across the city was never to just listen to the record; it was having a reason to get together. Having a theme in common provides a context through which genuine friendship can develop.

For the Rolling Stones lead singer and lead guitarist, buying new blues records together was like a stake that you tie to the young tree of their blossoming friendship. Once the tree grows sufficiently, the stake loses its importance—you can even throw it away. The friendship, like the mature tree, remains.

Today, there is a shortage of such stakes. We opt for convenience over the potential for social connection. We dismiss the importance of the stakes—the shared interests explored in person. As a consequence, we end up without the friendships.

It's "Need to Do"

While it is admittedly awkward that we have to make these kinds of choices in our current society, the truth is that, just as socializing with others was "need to do" rather than "nice to do" when I lived in an African village, it is also "need to do" for all of us today—no matter where we live. Making social time a priority will decrease the distressing feelings of social isolation that have become an unfortunate by-product of the digital age and bring untold happiness and well-being back into your life.

Make the life-transforming decision today to look for small ways to choose connection over convenience in your life. I am confident that you can make this seemingly small mental shift and pave a new path that leads to new friends, improved relationships with old friends and family members, and more happiness and social connection.

To get started, take a no-holds-barred look at your relationship with the efficiency afforded you by your laptop, smartphone, or tablet. Question how you are spending your time. Begin by asking yourself, "What am I doing with those extra hours now that I can more efficiently communicate with others and get things done?" Then reflect on what you are doing with your Netflix time.

When you spend two hours in the morning replying to emails, are you using the extra hour or two you saved from visiting others' offices or calling them on the phone to go for a long walk in nature, work on your car, go dancing, or spend a few hours with a good friend? Alternatively, are you using the time you saved by sending pithy, emotionally vacant messages to send more pithy, emotionally vacant messages?

Now that these new technologies have come along to save you time, are you getting even more things done and communicating even more rapidly—using briefer and briefer chunks of typed text instead of looking someone in the eye and speaking from the heart—or are you using this time to enhance your closest relationships, including your relationship with yourself?

In the third millennium, that is the question.

13

So Much Information, So Little Wisdom

We live in a society bloated with data yet starved for wisdom.
We're connected 24/7, yet anxiety, fear, depression and loneliness
are at an all-time high. We must course-correct.
—Elizabeth Kapu'uwailani Lindsey

A few years ago, I was driving to a meeting at California State University San Bernardino. As I passed Rialto, I started to see smoke emanating from a hill I needed to pass to reach the university. The turn I usually take onto highway 215 was closed, so I kept going. The last time there had been a brush fire near the highway, an increasingly common occurrence in this part of southern California, I'd downloaded Waze onto my phone and it took me on a tour of some backstreets of Rancho Cucamonga to reach the university just in time to give a talk.

So I opened Waze again. It guided me to take the next exit and double back onto some San Bernardino side streets. I noticed I was heading right toward the smoke. "It's okay," I thought. "Waze probably knows about the fire and is guiding me toward a way to get to the university while passing near it."

I continued for about a mile; the air was becoming hotter and ashes were flying everywhere. I passed a man on the side of the road shouting at drivers that they would have to turn around anyway so they might as well do it now. A fireman quickly appeared behind him and confirmed the same.

I turned around and drove home. Over the next few days, I thought more and more about what had transpired. What if I had been one of the first to reach the fire, before other cars or even the firefighters? Would I listen to my autopilot, better-reach-this-meeting-or-else voice and follow Waze all the way to my death? It was a lesson to me to prioritize my instincts above any technology-mediated advice and to be more flexible and able to turn off my internal drive that impels me to try to complete a task my mind is set on no matter what.

We really have become dependent on our screens for just about any kind of information. In 2010, Nicaraguan troops were dredging the San Juan River in Costa Rican territory, prompting a clash with Costa Rican police. The Nicaraguan commander claimed he had used Google Maps to plan the work. Google subsequently acknowledged that its map of the border was erroneous.

Too Much Information ...

While most of us are not driving toward a burning inferno or dredging a river along a national border, our daily reality is that we are following digitally mediated social norms in smaller ways rather than trusting our intuition and moving our life toward our own vision of what we know it can become. The collective virtual pressure placed upon us crowds out the space we need in order to live intentionally, rather than as puppets of commercial interests wearing the sheep's clothing of social connection.

How has this happened—that information has become so ubiquitous and accessible from anywhere? The spread of information has become greater in inverse relationship to the size of digital devices, which have not only become smaller but also cheaper and more portable. The first disk drive was manufactured in San Jose, California, in 1953, measured fourteen inches in diameter, had to be used in a protected data center, and was mounted in a standalone box the size of a washing machine.

Three years later, the first commercial disk drive was released, and by 1961 disk drives could store 205 MB of information. Portable wallet-size disk drives that store 4 TB of information (and soon probably much more) are now sold by Western Digital and Seagate for less than $100. To put this into context, a disk drive less than 10 percent the size of the only commercially available drive half a century ago can now store almost 20,000 times as much information.

The information deluge has certain benefits. Think about all the fraying books and documents now preserved for time immemorial on hard drives around the world and in the cloud. Consider the hours spent locating research documents saved by the Internet.

When I was in graduate school, Harvard had a special research computer to locate documents anywhere in the Harvard university system. I remember reserving one hour per week to use this computer to locate scholarly articles for my papers. Now anyone, anywhere who has been granted access can use this system from anywhere in the world.

... Is No Information

A Reuters survey found that two-thirds of managers believe the data deluge has made their jobs less satisfying or harmed their personal relationships. One-third think it has damaged their health.

Jen, the marketing director of a Fortune 500 company, shared in one of our coaching sessions how the proliferation of electronic information is affecting the culture of her company:

> My first job out of college, I didn't have email at all. If we needed to get anything out, we had to write a memo. This sort of what was "memo-worthy" versus what is "email-worthy"... I mean, there's no comparison in just the volume of information to process every day. It's just very different because people will post something on social media or send an email without even thinking about it and we get millions of them every day, like "We have bagels downstairs!" or "Did someone leave a bracelet in the third floor bathroom?" [and] all of these are "Reply All's"!

Protests of managers like Jen notwithstanding, the data deluge unwaveringly marches on. The amount of stored data worldwide, in fact, doubles every eighteen months. A number of phrases have been coined to describe the anxiety produced by too much information, including the first, "information overload," popularized by Alvin Toffler in 1970; "data asphyxiation" (William van Winkle); "data smog" (David Shenk); "information fatigue syndrome" (David Lewis); "cognitive overload" (Eric Schmidt, CEO of Google); and "time famine" (Harvard Business School professor Leslie Perlow).

We've reached an unprecedented level of information creation, categorization, and storage. Is all of this information enabling us to live better, more fulfilling lives?

No Wisdom Superhighway

To answer this question, we must ask ourselves how much of the information posted on the Internet is truly necessary. A woman in Leicester, England, posted 190 Tweets while giving birth, including "Ohh I actually groaned during that contraction—things are looking up!"

I've never heard the term "wisdom superhighway," or for that matter listened to anyone complain of "wisdom overload." It's important to never forget that your screens were designed by programmers living within the constraints of humankind's current level of knowledge.

Einstein once astutely observed that "You can never solve a problem on the level on which it was created." Our screens can replicate some basic human cognitive functions, such as crunching numbers or committing everyday procedures to memory. Yet while knowledge can be outsourced to technology, wisdom can't.

A finance manager I also used to coach, Henry, described the hollowness of most of what we do online. "Email and social media introduced a lot more breadth and a lot less depth," he sighed. "People communicate more but the communications themselves don't necessarily have the same kind of gravitas and depth as they did before."

So what does it mean to maintain our wisdom in the digital age?

Make Discerning Rather Than Distracted Choices

In the digital age, wisdom emerges when, before you crane your neck over your phone, or click on a website, or check Facebook, or reply to a string of emails or text messages, you declare to yourself, "I will use my wisdom to distill which of this plethora of social information helps me live my purpose, and which is an unnecessary distraction."

The other day, my dental hygienist asked me what I had been doing lately and I told her about this book. While I lay back with her dexterous fingers inside my mouth, Diana went on a tirade about the countless hours of her life she had wasted playing Candy Crush Saga and checking Facebook on her phone. At least four times she punctuated her story with the same statement: "If I had used that time to do something tied to a larger purpose, I could have accomplished something great. I'll never have that time again."

Carolyn, a twenty-three-year-old events coordinator in Cape Town, South Africa, also shared her regrets with me for spending so much of her life online:

> When I was in high school, I was more worried about how many friends I had on my Instagram account than actual in-person friends. I felt the more Likes a picture received meant the more popular I was. Looking back at it now, I regret it because it was not until university when I finally started making in-person connections rather than online. Focusing my time on social media made me waste time and energy. Now, I like advising my younger sisters to not make the same mistake as me and have more human interactions and connection.

I think we all—myself included—can relate to Diana and Carolyn. Many of us intend to take a short break by playing Candy Crush Saga or checking social media or doing something else online. We unwittingly make this choice without realizing we've stepped into the fox's den.

Inside our phones, tablets, and laptops reside today's foxes: thousands of brogrammers whose job is to keep you there for as long as humanly possible, engaged in activities most of which hold very little importance to you in the long term. Tristan Harris (the former student of B. J. Fogg referred to earlier) once remarked, "You could say that it's my responsibility to exert self-control when it comes to digital usage, but that's not acknowledging that there's a thousand people on the other side of the screen whose job is to break down whatever responsibility I can maintain."

In many ways, this book is about how to exercise our responsibility in the face of these unprecedented technological distractions and wrest our attention back from the brogrammers.

To Locate Is Not to Retain

It's not going to be easy. Nicholas Carr, author of *The Shallows: What the Internet Is Doing to Our Brains*, describes the digitally mediated cognitive shift affecting our minds:

> Dozens of studies point to the same conclusion: When we go online, we enter an environment that promotes cursory reading, hurried and distracted thinking, and superficial learning.... What we're experiencing is, in a metaphorical sense, a reversal of the early trajectory of civilization: We are evolving from cultivators of personal knowledge into hunters and gatherers in the electronic data forest.

Since the advent of the Internet, the ability to *retain* information has taken a back seat to the ability to *locate* it. Ask many teenagers today to name the capital of Belgium or the first president of India and they won't be able to tell you *now*, but they will in ten seconds.

The upside is that two decades ago most teenagers wouldn't have been able to identify the first president of India either now, in ten seconds, or ever. Perhaps a belated digital assist is better than nothing.

Self-Presentation Versus Self-Development

On the other hand, it may not be: four studies have found that when we are confident we can find information on a particular subject online, we forget the subject itself. According to lead researcher Betsy Sparrow, the Internet has become a primary medium of what psychologists call "transactive memory," or recollections that are external to us yet accessible. What has not yet been revealed are the effects on our personalities of our minds becoming more externally than internally constituted.

To illustrate the effects of our psychological adaptation to the digital age, contrast an individual who spends most of their time thinking about their life and career and family without the aid of external stimuli versus another who spends most of their waking hours on the Internet reading about what others think about their lives and careers and families. Which person do you think will be more genuine and empathetic? Which will be more narcissistic and engaged in social comparison and self-presentation, frequently trying to one-up others to appear superior?

Unfortunately, the first individual is the person many of us were as few as twenty-five years ago before the mass penetration of the Internet. The second is the person many of us have become.

"Now wait a minute," you may be thinking. "Isn't that being overly negative? What about all the benefits of the Internet?" Yes, you are right that we must take into account both the pros and cons of this new communication medium and then determine how to integrate it into our lives.

The challenge is that most of us don't recognize that the need to make this conscious choice *is* the challenge: in fact, some might consider it the paramount challenge of the twenty-first century. Unaware of the urgent nature of this challenge, many of us blindly accept the evolving social mores associated with this new communication medium and gradually become people whom not only others, but *we ourselves*, don't want to be around.

Many Little Brothers Are Watching

Global Positioning Systems (GPS) expand this externally reliant mental orientation. I turn it off sometimes so I have to rely once again on my ability to find my way around. Then, inevitably, I get lost and turn it back on. The more we can locate with digital assistance, the less we retain; we become dependent charges of the digital universe. We have, in effect, outsourced a large part of our brains.

According to Carr, some useful mental capacities, such as focused thinking, atrophy from disuse. Our primal instincts are to rapidly shift our focus from one stimulus to another in order to survive. The Internet capitalizes on this instinct, keeping us in perpetual "survival mode." In this sense, the Internet piques our fear that something is wrong, or someone is angry at us, or we have made a mistake   and we had better check our online accounts to confirm that our sources of approval are still satisfied with us.

Even within Big Tech, remorseful voices are emerging about the effects of new technologies on our brains. These voices include the first president of Facebook, Sean Parker, who recently stated that Facebook is "a social-validation feedback loop" and that "God only knows what it's doing to our children's brains."

The former leader of Facebook's global growth efforts, Chamath Palihapitiya, echoed Parker's sentiments: "The short-term, dopamine-driven feedback loops we've created are destroying how society works."

Instead of Big Brother, we now have thousands of Little Brothers we are incessantly attempting to placate. This scarcity mentality could be at the core of why we feel compelled to check email and Facebook multiple times each hour, even during our so-called leisure or vacation time. We continually attempt to soothe our insecurity that we are okay because everything is okay—all others' expectations of us are currently being met, so we can relax.

Yet here's the Catch-22: since for the first time in history others can reach us within seconds from just about anywhere around the globe, this cat-and-mouse game of satisfying others' expectations has no respite or end or lull—at any time of the day or week, ever. We have become, in effect, prisoners in an electronic maze with no exit. The external quest to please others keeps us plodding forward, dissatisfied yet doggedly driven, further and further, into the maze.

It's not just our surroundings, but also the people we share them with, that impact our happiness. How are we getting on with the other maze runners?

The Beautiful Ones Always Smash the Picture

The Internet helps us create the illusion of omnipotence, omniscience, omnipresence. We believe that it increases our power, our knowledge (through instantaneous access to more information than ever in human history), and our presence in the lives of more people than was ever humanly possible.

This illusion is so powerful that many of us believe we can play the role of God—all-knowing, all-powerful, present everywhere—without even leaving our rooms. We now even have the possibility of meeting the right partner without departing from behind our beloved megapixels simply by swiping left through thousands of one-inch photos, each accompanied by a brief, meticulously assembled self-description intended to induce positive attributions from the viewer—such as carefree, fun-loving, and delightfully intelligent—that will induce the coveted right swipe.

Yet it all comes crashing down, again and again. The real world is not so obsequious or attentive as our screens, which are painstakingly designed to appease so many of our needs. One of the few female programmers in the early years of the Internet, Ellen Ullman, incisively predicted a few decades ago that the on-demand economy would result in antisocial behavior since we would no longer "need to involve anyone else in the satisfaction of our needs."

The ideal person of our fantasies, retrofitted onto an Internet image of a complete stranger versed in self-presentation, rarely delivers in reality. As the writer Andrew Sullivan perceptively observes, "An entire universe of intimate responses is flattened to a single, distant swipe. We hide our vulnerabilities, airbrushing our flaws and quirks; we project our fantasies onto the images before us."

The late musical artist Prince expertly described this phenomenon of etching an image of perfection in one's mind associated with another person. It never works. As Prince croons, "The beautiful ones always smash the picture." It is ironic that these prescient lyrics are from a song, "The Beautiful Ones," that replaced another song originally intended for his album *Purple Rain*, titled "Electric Intercourse."

Back Up and Show Me Your Family

Neither do cameras still purvey the same happiness they once did, when few pictures were snapped and later enthusiastically shared in family albums around the living room sofa or dining room table. Instead, many pictures are now taken and then dispassionately shared online, where people view them individually instead of together, if they view them at all.

Most of the time these days, the only interaction around the sharing of photos is a few words tapped into a social networking site or email, written by each individual while sitting alone behind a screen. Once again, the seeking and sharing of social information do not produce social connection.

When I think back to the years I lived in Kenya, Guatemala, Indonesia, and a number of other developing countries, one common cultural feature they all shared that stands out in my mind is that the first thing you did when visiting a family was to sit down in their living room and look at their photo album. Was it boring at times? Definitely. Yet listening to the stories behind the photos brought you closer and laid the groundwork for discovering common interests.

Now, we no longer listen; we just view.

What has caused us to shift our lives away from developing meaningful social connection and toward sifting through, viewing, analyzing, and evaluating social information? There are many factors, some of which I highlight throughout this book. To better understand this shift, let's consider a disconcertingly deceptive term we associate with a large percentage of the time we while away online: social media.

Most Social Media Is Neither

This is a bold statement. Please allow me to back it up. First of all, social media is often not social. Why? Because it doesn't generate the fulfillment of a social life. As I noted in Chapter 3, social media enables the sharing of social information, but rarely does it produce social connection.

When you go to a party, or go on a hike with a friend, or eat lunch with someone you care about, these activities call upon your social abilities and fulfill a dimension of your life: the part of you that needs and desires to relate to other people. For these reasons, these activities are called "social."

Social media, on the other hand, is a poor substitute. Hunching over a screen typing in information about yourself and broadcasting it to others while reading the information they in turn type into their keypads or keyboards about themselves while hunched over their screens does not adequately fulfill our basic human need to belong. (In Appendix A, Pedro shares what's truly behind the veneer of those attempting to become "social media famous.") Sound miserable? Only a few decades ago, most would have been incredulous if told this would be our current reality today.

Yet our current reality it is. Consider this report from Monica, a wedding planner in the second-to-last week of her Heart of Darkness Challenge:

> I've been reflecting on this experience. It has made me aware of how much we are on our phones, but not really talking. My husband and I went out to dinner with another couple, and it was incredible that most of the time they were on their phones. My friend posted on Facebook, "Having a great time catching up with great friends." But she was on her Instagram most of the night. We really weren't connecting or having a real conversation. I felt like calling them out, like why was I even there? They made me feel unimportant since they couldn't even hold a conversation because they were distracted by their smartphones. But they were not the only ones, as I looked up and around the restaurant, I saw a sea of people with their faces buried in their phones.

Not only is social media questionably "social," but neither are most social media posts "media" in the sense of reporters reporting the news. The viewing of vacation photos, or pictures of a meal soon to be consumed, or a former classmate's diatribe about politics is not exactly the news.

Such sharing of information is not the "news" in pure, distilled form, only weak contacts sharing unfiltered details of their lives, 99-plus percent of which are too trivial for any news outlet designated with the task of sifting through such submissions to print. In other words, Facebook is too much face and not enough book.

Newspapers and magazines serve a purpose: filtering through the thousands of potential news stories to distill those "worthy" of mass consumption. Yes, it's true that a lot of interesting and important news stories are filtered out by subjective editors with personal agendas. Yet it's also true that, without such filtering, reading what anyone deems noteworthy can cause what we ascribe as the "news" to lose its value.

So if social media is neither social nor media, what is it? The director of the Center for Internet and Technology Addiction, David Greenfield, put it well when he told me he's "questioning this idea that social media has anything to do with social contact. I think it's actually completely the opposite. The only reason why social media exists is really to keep your eyes on screens to sell you stuff. That's the model."

Social Riches Aplenty and Available ...

Living a richer life in the third millennium means that the next time there is an opportunity to connect with others in person and an emotion is compelling you to keep on moving in order to tend to the limitless electronic queue of people vying for your attention, you can preempt this socially disconnecting behavior by affirming to yourself, "I will not allow this anxiety associated with my futile quest for an empty inbox to prevent me from connecting in real time with real people. Such connections are the only way to fulfill my social needs. The rest is an illusion."

Making such a bold statement to yourself is the first step toward revitalizing your social life. If you are at a lunch and about to check your phone while a friend goes to the bathroom, resist the temptation and instead think of questions to ask your friend when she or he returns to help them think through some of the pressing life issues they've been sharing with you. Alternatively, just sit and think about your life.

If you are visiting a family and they invite you to stay for dinner, instead of refusing because you want to return home and check your online dating profiles and see who has swiped right on your profile, accept the invitation and hang out with them. The conversation may open up avenues both cognitive (new ways of thinking about what you are looking for in a relationship) and social (their friendship may strengthen you, and they may even have a friend to introduce you to at some point) that will bring you closer to finding the right person.

Amaya, an HR director in Bangalore, India, told me two years ago at one of my leadership conferences there, "The digital age is the wrong period for me, as I'm an empath—I love people."

"Actually, the digital age may be the best possible period for you or anyone else who truly listens," I responded, "as people like you are in such short supply that many others feel a gravitational pull to talk about their lives with you."

If you can do what your smartphone-addled peers are unable to do—stop and truly listen—the social opportunities available to you will be rich and unparalleled. Make the decision to slow down to the speed of real, digitally unmediated life and you will be joyfully surprised to find that you begin to feel stronger and your relationships with the people around you become much more vital and meaningful.

... And the Cost of Ignoring Them

With the volume of information available at our fingertips 24-7 unprecedented in the history of humankind, it should be no surprise that we have trouble focusing on what we most value, or that we are often woefully unable to focus our time and energy on the people and opportunities that are most important to us.

Unfortunately, our inability to make the people we most care about a priority due to our constant digital distractions has resulted in our becoming the loneliest generation to date: as we discovered in Chapter 1, from 1985 to 2004, the number of "confidants" with whom the average American adult can discuss important life issues shrank from three to two. We in effect lost one of our (already few) closest friends.

Moreover, the number of Americans who have *no one whomever* to talk with about what really matters to them more than doubled over the same period, now comprising over one of every four adults. Also alarming, while the modal (most common) response to the survey in 1985 was three close friends, by 2004 it was zero.

We should not be surprised at the surge in shooting sprees and terrorist attacks by lonely individuals: anyone with fewer than two people in their social network with whom to talk about important issues satisfies the widely accepted definition of marginal or inadequate counseling support. This segment of the population that has insufficient people in their lives to act as sounding boards for whatever pops into their minds has grown to almost half of the population.

Without enough trusted friends and family members around them to give them a reality check when they're going off the deep end, more people are going off the deep end. Half our population is now in danger of succumbing to such emotional instability.

Can you recall some moments in your life when the wise counsel of a good friend helped you identify an issue that was bothering you and come up with strategies to resolve it? These conversations have been instrumental in your making wiser choices and becoming the person you are today. How might you have turned out without such a friend? This friendless state is the current reality for most of us.

If we want to develop these trusting relationships with the people around us once again, we have to learn how to manage our use of technology rather than allowing it to manage us. I estimate that this has become one of the most necessary skills for living a content and purpose-driven life in the new millennium.

Part Three of this book is entirely dedicated to refining this ability.

PART THREE

RECONNECTED

14

Direct Your Use of Technology, Not the Other Way Around

We are becoming the servants in thought, as in action,
of the machine(s) we have created to serve us.
—John Kenneth Galbraith

*I*f computers, the Internet, and social media are here to stay—and, like the automobile or any other innovation that has significantly increased efficiency for the masses at an affordable price, they are—then the million-dollar question is "What can we do to recover our friendships and happiness in the digital age?"

I've coached executives and individuals on work-life balance for over twenty-five years, and it's my experience that almost all of the strategies I've seen people successfully implement to reclaim their lives in today's high-technology age have centered around one principle: *Direct your use of technology, not the other way around.*

Your laptop, iPad, or smartphone is merely a tool. A dopamine-inducing, addiction-accelerating, fun little tool, yes. Yet still just a tool. How can we recast the little glowing rectangle in our pockets as merely a tool and not an appendage?

As Tristan Harris once shared, "All of us are jacked into this system. All of our minds can be hijacked. Our choices are not as free as we think they are." How can we heed his words and become more responseable—as Stephen Covey once wrote, able to choose how we respond to any given stimulus—before it's too late?

Align Your Life

The critical challenge in the third millennium is the same as in the first: aligning your values with your behavior. What 90 percent of the Princeton theology students in the Good Samaritan study were unable to achieve. To first develop a vision for how you want to live your life and then live it daily.

To rise to this challenge, ask the best version of yourself—what we could call your higher self—a few questions, such as "How do you desire that I spend my time?", "How do you want me to act toward the people I care about?", and "For what do you want me to be remembered?"

Whatever emanates from this self-dialogue is how you should spend your time. If you can use your clever online tools to achieve some of your most important life goals, all power to you; I'll step out of your way right now. Yet every other moment you spend on your devices is as beneficial to your life as sitting in your car, turning on the ignition, and stepping on the pedal without a destination.

Every moment of every day you are making a decision about how to spend your time. If your goal is to have close friends to share your life with, determine how you will allocate your time to build those friendships. If you wish to spend more time *in reality* and less time sitting behind a screen typing into a keypad *about reality*, take some time this week to design some strategies to limit your virtual time, such as a daily screen-time maximum.

When your laptop or smartphone is adding value to your life, you are more likely to feel at balance and headed toward a destination of which you (meaning your higher self, which you can imagine as you in your much later years, clear about what you value, looking back at you now) can be proud. The moment the use of your devices surpasses this healthy level, it's time to spend some time offline in a place where you feel centered, serene, and inspired and can think about what truly matters to you so you can live your desired life.

This time alone—which, when practiced regularly, will enable you to connect with your heart and deepest values—will guide you to spend less time in front of your screens and more time making a heart connection with others and venturing out into this vast, wonderful world that awaits.

Not a New Question

I'm not asking you to get rid of your social media accounts. What I'm asking you to do is to learn how to direct their use in your life, rather than vice versa. To internalize the words of the ancient Stoic philosopher Epictetus: "Circumstances don't make the man, they only reveal him."

Similarly, just as a gym or a nature trail doesn't make you healthy or unhealthy, technology doesn't make you who you are; it only reveals who you are. If you do not make real, offline time with others your priority, what does that say about you as a person? How does such a choice reflect your values?

When you allow technology to direct you rather than the reverse, your behavior reflects an automaticity not unlike that of a robot. The word "robot," in fact, comes from the Czech word for "compulsory labor." This etymology explains the digitally induced hypnotic state to which many of us have unwittingly succumbed: we act compulsorily, as if controlled by outside forces we do not understand.

This question—whether we will control technology or vice versa—is not new. In 1926, the Knights of Columbus Adult Education Committee posed that its group meetings address the topic "Do modern inventions help or mar character and health?" In addition to concerns about electric lighting keeping people at home, specific questions posed for discussion included "Does the telephone make men more active or more lazy?" and "Does the telephone break up home life and the old practice of visiting friends?"

We only call our present period of human existence the "digital era" because we don't yet understand how to appropriately use technology.

In reality, this isn't the "information society," "computer age," or "digital era" any more than the 1900s were the "telephone society" or the 1950s were the "television era."

The Problem Is Not Technology, It's Us

Those who discovered healthy ways to integrate the television and telephone into their lives are the happiest and most successful now. Similarly, those who now learn how to integrate Internet-ready devices—the modern-day TV, telephone, and so much more—into their lives will be the happiest and most successful in the years ahead.

As is the case with any other new technology, we must learn how to direct our use of it, not the other way around. We must define how we use technology in our lives rather than allow technology to define us and how we experience life.

Another discussion question the Knights of Columbus committee posed to its adult learners was "How can a man be master of an auto instead of it being his master?" Just substitute "the Internet" for "an auto" and you encounter the central question we are still asking ourselves almost a century later.

To successfully answer this question, there is one central premise we must recognize: The problem is not technology. The problem is ourselves, and how we use technology. It is we ourselves, after all, who are the creators of technology: we created technology to fit and enable our desired lifestyle. (Technological innovations that did not fit our desired lifestyle went unutilized and quickly became obsolete.)

We then attributed our unhappiness to technology. We blamed technology for doing too well what we created it to do: increase our efficiency in our obsessive focus on work and the acquisition of social information. This is like blaming a liquor store for your drinking problem, or a condom machine at a local bar for your cheating on your spouse.

Big Tech, like most companies in our capitalistic society, will always pursue the motive to make a quick buck. In their case, maximizing dollars equates to providing us what our baser instincts desire, never mind the consequences to our lives.

To place the blame on their doorstep is like inculpating the producers of slot machines for your gambling problem, or blaming a prostitute for your contracting a sexually transmitted disease. A wiser choice would be to understand the nature of the casino or brothel, to take matters into your own hands, and to become response-able and take responsibility for how you—and, if you have them, your children—use technology.

More Mundane Than You Think

Another myth that needs to be shattered if our relationship with technology is to become more rooted in reality is the idea that technology is an immanent entity, a force with its own interests and purposes. In fact, technology is merely a set of tools we have developed to live our desired life.

The synonyms we have come to associate with the Internet— such as "cyberspace," "information superhighway," "virtual," "cloud computing," and "online"—make the Internet sound ethereal, elusive, and sublime, as if it is a new god or energy force field or parallel universe. This illusion was shattered one day for Andrew Blum, a *Wired* writer, when a squirrel chewed through the wire connecting his house to the Internet.

In truth, the Internet is nothing more than an amalgam of cables and wires originating from sterile, prosaic data centers that transmit bits of information. The images we see on our screens are actually packages of data—millions of 1's and 0's methodically assorted to represent the words, hyperlinks, and still and moving images we associate with the ideas, people, and objects we encounter in our lives.

Technology Marketers Have Killed It

There is tremendous irony in the magical, metaphysical words we have come to associate with machines and the automated exchange of data. If you think about it, the television, telephone, telegraph, or automobile could also have been shrouded with verbal imagery to increase our addiction to them. In this case, perhaps the TV would have been called the "global connection screen"; the telephone "onvoice"; the telegraph "cloud connecting."

Apparently it's not only the brogrammers who have rounded the bases in the digital age, but also the marketers of these new technologies. We have unwittingly imbibed it all like a hungry baby reaching for a bottle of grape soda. The result? The nomenclature surrounding the Internet has become a pandemic form of self-deception taking root across our entire society.

We've collectively drunk the Kool-Aid and are unaware of how technology has changed us; or probably more accurately, we are aware and feel powerless to do anything about it. I hope we figure it out before it's too late.

The author of *The Lord of the Rings*, J. R. R. Tolkien, once stated that the more you immerse yourself in a virtual world—which he calls 'enchantment'—the more "the experience may be similar to Dreaming … but … you are in a dream that some other mind is weaving, and the knowledge of that alarming fact may slip from your grasp."

It's certainly slipped from ours. If we are to emerge from the dreamlike state we have collectively entered, it's imperative that we design and implement strategies to counter those of the brogrammers.

We will explore numerous such strategies in the remaining pages of this book to increase our ability to direct our use of technology. Let's get started with one. This next strategy is a direct and open countermove to subvert the most common technique in the brogrammer arsenal. It is surprisingly simple and directly aimed at the attraction of those candy-colored apps demanding your attention. To understand the need for this strategy, let's first understand the number one technique of the brogrammer brigade to commandeer our attention that it will undermine.

True Colors

A friend at Facebook told Tristan Harris that the social media company's programmers initially developed the notification icon, which alerts users to new activity (such as instant messages, status updates, and "friend requests"), in the color blue. There was a problem, however. "No one pushed it," Harris shares. "Then they switched it to red, and of course everyone used it."

As human beings, we have neurological reactions to specific colors that lead to snap decisions. Sixty percent of consumers, for example, state that color bears a significant influence on their decision to buy a car. This fact has not been lost upon crafty app programmers.

Why did Facebook programmers change the notification icon from blue to red? While product designers know that consumers associate blue with dependability and honesty, red is associated with what is exciting, daring, and modern—psychological associations that stimulate arousal and a tendency toward action.

It is for this reason that, in an innovative suite of experiments, the psychologists Andrew Elliot and Daniela Niesta of the University of Rochester found that if a woman's shirt in a photo is digitally colored red (versus blue), men viewing the photo deem her prettier and more sexually attractive.

In a clever twist, the male voyeurs were asked "Imagine that you are going on a date with this person and have $100 in your wallet. How much money would you be willing to spend on your date?" The women wearing red were more likely to be invited to a pricier outing.

Today, each time you glance at your phone—150 distinct times per day for the average user—you are likely to see red notification icons and dots next to your apps imploring your finger to touch them. Why do we succumb, time and time again? "Red is a trigger color," Harris quips. "That's why it's used as an alarm signal."

Fire trucks, stop signs, blood, fire alarms, and now ... smartphone icons: the color red acts as a cognitive signal that we should immediately drop what we are doing and divert our attention to whatever is encoded with the red color, right here and now. And if that's not enough, we also permit our phones to make buzzing and other abrupt noises to complement the hypervigilance-inducing red icons.

Holding Us over a Barrel: The Brogrammers Prey on and Induce Tense Arousal

When our emotions hijack our thoughts and we are ready to fight or flight, we commonly say that we are "seeing red." The problem you will experience when your stress level is frequently heightened by stimuli that signal danger encoded in the color red—including insects and reptiles through natural selection (a spider with a red carapace is probably one you want to avoid, as its species has survived the millennia for a reason despite its high visibility)—is that you perpetually exist in a state of "tense arousal."

In contrast to energetic arousal—a generally healthy form of activation of the body's subsystem that generates feelings of excitement, enthusiasm, and vitality—tense arousal describes a feeling of anxiety or tension that renders the body similar to a coiled spring perpetually preparing for action.

Mark Williams, the psychologist and director of the Oxford Mindfulness Centre, incisively explains how our busy lives keep us in a perpetual state of tense arousal: "What we know ... from looking at the brain scans of people that are always rushing around, who never taste their food ... is that the emotional part of the brain that drives people is on sort of high alert all the time ... biologically, they're rushing around just as if they were escaping from a predator."

Tense arousal is an adaptive response to negative, unanticipated events or situations that can lead us to over-focus on these events and even to engage in fight, flight, or freeze behaviors. Our body tightens and our stress level rises so we can preempt other negative events from transpiring.

Energetic arousal, which is related to feelings of joy and satisfaction, does not similarly tend to cause us to focus on the specific event or situation that has stimulated our positively aroused emotions. Instead, as I've discovered in a research study with Yih-teen Lee of IESE Business School, we feel a "diffuse contentment": all is good, just enjoying being alive if you don't mind, no need to focus on anything at all.

Hence, you don't have to be a rocket scientist to understand why app developers prefer us to be in a hypervigilant, self-damaging state of tense arousal rather than a joyful state of energetic arousal: our tense arousal causes us to focus on the stimuli of that arousal—the apps and websites with the colors, notifications, and abrasive noises they've developed to acquire our attention.

Running on Empty

Try living in an area where fire trucks pass with whirling red lights and abrupt noises numerous times daily and see what it does to your level of stress and well-being. As a color, red has always been used sparingly to signal emergency or crisis, as it shifts us from energetic arousal (again, an emotional state in which we tend to relax and enjoy life) to tense arousal (a state in which we are hypervigilant and releasing cortisol, which increases our stress).

You can think of energetic arousal as clean, high-quality fuel that will help propel you toward your long-term goals. Tense arousal, on the other hand, is like junk fuel that will only help you achieve short-term objectives at the price of burning you out before you reach your longer-term life goals.

Since the release of the first iPhone just over a decade ago (at the time of publication), we have unwittingly permitted app developers to insert the color red into our lives—often accompanied by the halting noises they also designed—on average, 150 times daily. With mobile technology's unprecedented ability to dazzle, notify, and remind us, it's no wonder our experience of life has headed south.

If you are still in doubt, consider this remorseful apology of an inventor: "It is very common for humans to develop things with the best of intentions that have unintended, negative consequences." Do these words hail from Robert Oppenheimer, the University of California at Berkeley physicist who developed the atomic bomb?

Not even close—they are from Justin Rosenstein, the former Facebook and Google engineer who helped develop the "Like" button. According to Rosenstein, "Everyone is distracted. All the time" because of the "bright dings of pseudo-pleasure" from his now-ubiquitous design feature.

Roger McNamee, a former adviser to Mark Zuckerberg who introduced the Facebook founder to the head of advertising at Google, Sheryl Sandberg (she subsequently became the COO of Facebook and spearheaded the social networking company's advertising efforts), echoes Rosenstein's sentiments: "The people who run Facebook and Google are good people, whose well-intentioned strategies have led to horrific unintended consequences."

Make Your Smartphone Duller

A couple of years ago, I figured out how to reduce these horrific consequences in my life by discovering a way to remind myself regularly throughout each and every day that my phone is just a machine and not a candy-colored magic glowing rectangle to turn to in every moment in which I feel a tinge of boredom or anxiety and desire a distraction. (Ironically, a recent 2017 study led by psychologist Ryan Dwyer of the University of British Columbia found that smartphone use increases rather than decreases boredom.) How? I stripped my phone of its bright, candy-colored, radiant allure. How did I pull off this countercultural, seditious feat?

I set my smartphone display to "grayscale": shades of black and white.

Through this simple yet treasonous act, I downgraded my phone into a much less inviting machine that I use less to placate inner existential angst and more to get things done, which, as I understand it, is why I bought it in the first place.

Seeing its boring, mundane gray screen is also a continual reminder that my phone is just a tool: that's why it's in black and white, after all. In perpetual contrast, the iridescent, breathtakingly beautiful real world in front of me is in color.

Viewing my phone in grayscale helps me make this distinction. It also helps me not mistake my (prosaic gray) phone for the activities in the (stunningly colorful) real world—such as spending time with my wife, kids, and friends and going on walks in nature—that bring so much color-imbued joy into my life. It helps me discern between viewing and seeing.

Do you think these technology companies make it easy to circumvent their addictive algorithms and fade to grayscale?

Not at all. To accomplish such a countercultural feat requires about six steps: they bury this act of treason as far down into the dark basement of your phone as possible, in visibility or accessibility options. You actually have to pretend you're blind to pull it off. You can use their algorithms to beat them at their own game, however, by doing a web search for "Change my Android (or iPhone) display to grayscale."

Boring ...

It turns out I'm not alone. The CEO of Neurons, a Danish company that uses eye-tracking and brain-scanning technology to analyze apps, Thomas Ramsøy, admonishes, "Color and shape, these are the icebreakers when it comes to grabbing people's attention, and attention is the new currency."

After learning about how Big Tech uses color to hijack our attention, Ramsøy also went renegade—to grayscale. According to Ramsøy, this maverick decision reintroduces choice, or "controlled attention."

Bevil Conway is another color defector who went grayscale. A researcher on color and emotion at the National Eye Institute, Conway concurs: "Silicon Valley is in a battle for our attention, and often I feel like the last person in charge of my own eyes. After going to grayscale, I'm not a different person all of a sudden, but I feel more in control of my phone, which now looks like a tool rather than a toy … If I'm waiting in line for coffee, this gray slab is not as delightful a distraction as it once was."

Going grayscale has helped me relegate my phone to its proper role—a tool designed to increase our efficiency so we have *more* time for real-time presence in this radiant, technicolor life, not less. It's only worked because I also receive no notifications—so no audio or visual cues impelling me to abandon what I'm doing and tend to someone who has condescended to spend less than ten seconds sending me an electronic request of my time. The only way anyone can reach me in real time through my phone is to—imagine the horror of it—call me.

The Fun Is Over

I've since taught hundreds of people how to go grayscale. They consistently, and sometimes comically, extol how this simple strategy diminishes their interest in their phone. Pilar, an interior designer from Pereira, Colombia, shares: "I am actually not caring for the grayscale too much anymore. It makes everything dull. When I check my emails or messages the grayscale is making my phone unattractive. I can now understand how brightness and color can be eye catching. My phone is literally less attractive."

Kiran, a mechanical engineer from Melbourne, Australia, concurs: "Most notably, the B/W screen is far less engaging than with color. That is helping to keep my phone interactions short. I definitely like keeping my phone in grayscale. The times that I do switch it off, I am annoyed by the color and find it distracting to whatever I need to do."

And my favorite, from Paula, a librarian from Albuquerque, New Mexico:

> [First week of the Heart of Darkness Challenge Journal] The grayscale is proving to be an effective detractor … it's making my phone seem boring … [Fourth week] Now for the big cheat: I turned off the grayscale so my husband could use the camera last Friday, and didn't turn it back on until today. I really saw how color is like candy to me … [And in her seventh week] Part of me has felt like I'm overcoming the mass appeal of the smartphone phenomena; it's been like the digital age version of flipping society the bird.

These experiences fit squarely with the sage advice the University of Connecticut psychiatrist David Greenfield shared with me in a recent interview:

> We can do small things like gray out your phone, which is actually a remarkably useful strategy. If you gray your phone out, you're not going to want to look at it as much and your interest will drop by about thirty to forty percent. So, if you want to just cut down the intensity of your desire to look at your phone very quickly, just gray it out. Pictures don't look so good. You'll still get your texts and your emails. You'll still be able to handle the business that you need to handle on it, but you will not necessarily want to spend a whole lot of extra time scrolling around because it won't look very good.

Perhaps the greatest benefit of picking up a silent, prosaic gray sliver of plastic, glass, and metal instead of a colorful, random noise–emitting device is that it is a constant reminder not to confuse real life with the illusory, tense arousal–filled dream the brogrammers would have us exist in for most of our waking hours.

Stripped of color and sound, my phone is, quite simply, boring.

No Color, More Relax

My own life is much calmer now that I'm not experiencing frequent dopamine releases throughout the day as a result of hearing stop-what-you're-doing-right-now-and-pay-attention-to-me-yes-you   sounds from my phone. As Greenfield shares about smartphone sounds, "That ping is telling us there is some type of reward there, waiting for us."

I asked him to explain in detail how this process works. "The thing about a notification is that it's letting you know through anticipatory dopamine release that there might be something there," Greenfield replied. "[The] anticipation of pleasure actually elevates dopamine at an even higher level than the actual pleasure itself ... that blip of dopamine is letting you know that you want to check the phone ... that's part of what compels us to do it, over and over and over again with no end in sight because you never get enough of it ... Notifications are one of the most dangerous aspects of the smartphone because you're chasing the high. Most addiction is really chasing that original hit that you got that [you] might have liked at one point and now you're just chasing it forever."

It's not only the noises your smartphones makes, but turning off notifications entirely that is critical to reclaiming any semblance of peace in your life. (Remember, seeing that a message is waiting for you and not checking it induces stress and anxiety.)

Declawing it of sound, color, and notifications notwithstanding, my phone would still accelerate my addictive qualities were it not for one other strategy I've employed to stifle its previous long-running reign over me, which I'll share in the last two chapters.

From Automatic to Conscious

"Okay, I get it," you may be thinking. "I should direct my use of technology rather than have it direct me. Yet I still don't know what to do about it and am in the same predicament as when I picked up this book." Yes, you have a point. It's time for some more concrete strategies to direct your use of your smartphone and other screens.

As a first step toward this goal, bring to your mind the image of a small tree surrounded by a little fence. The purpose of the fence is to help the tree grow straight up toward the sky. Once the tree has proven it is capable of advancing toward this goal, there is no more need for the fence, and it can be discarded; it no longer helps the more mature and developed tree continue to flourish and grow toward the light.

In the remaining chapters of this book, I will share some strategies designed to help you create guidelines to limit digital access. You can consider these guidelines as the equivalent of placing a fence around your impulses that digital media capitalize on: the desire for social approval and the ephemeral increase to self-esteem that comes from favorably comparing yourself with similar others (Facebook), the desire to accumulate (Amazon), the desire for task completion (email), the desire for intimacy and companionship (Bumble, Tinder), and the desire for instant information (Twitter, Google search).

These strategies will enable you to grow not toward the myriad distractions customized and tailored by Silicon Valley's finest to extract every last dollar from your wallet, but toward becoming a free, self-actualizing human being once again. To rediscover the more holistic, authentic life you once had and, with a bit of effort, can reclaim. The strategies that follow will help you replace *automatic* behavior with *conscious* behavior in all areas of your life, including how you spend time online.

15

Downgrade Social Media, Upgrade Your Relationships

Social media is the new gold, and will remain a high-supply, high-demand commodity until we reduce its perceived value in our minds. Until then, we will continue to eke out our existence and live low-vitality, unfulfilling lives. To reduce the value you place on social media, ask yourself how much of your day you are spending in real-time, genuine, face-to-face conversations with the people you care about.

If you find yourself depressed by the scarcity of genuine interactions in your life, take a few steps now to revitalize these connections. When you receive a text or email from a good friend, you can make the decision to respond by picking up the phone and calling them.

If you call family members or friends and they don't answer or return your call (they may resist your efforts to wrest them away from their parallel digital universe), what can you do? Make a list of people who actually do respond in real time—who value you enough to dedicate more than the slight nerve twitch required to type a few words into their phone and send them in your direction—and start calling them.

Here's the stark reality of life in the third millennium: *The only way to downgrade the value of social media in your life is to upgrade the value of authentic, real-time connections with the people you care about—or could care about if you took the time to get to know them better.*

Once you take this inward leap into the depths of your true nature, which centers on and finds comfort only in your own and others' humanness, you will find that love is still there, surrounding you in many forms. Most likely, you will discover that the forms in which love exists in your life are different from what you perceived them to be for years.

Before you embark on this challenging yet ultimately rewarding journey, a spoiler alert: some of the people whom you identify as your close friends or family members simply will not want to allocate more time from their lives for you than a brief textual exchange allows. Their reality is that they only apportion such premium time to a select few—perhaps only their spouse, children, parents, and one or two close friends—and you just don't make the cut.

Before the advent of the Internet, these people may have maintained a broader network of confidants of which you were an important part; you now may no longer be a member of this much more limited group.

The Specter of Loneliness

Where does this heightened exclusivity leave you? Starving for affection from increasingly unavailable people who only toss you the electronic crumbs from their social diet? I don't think so. If love isn't being served at the table, it's time to stand up and seek nourishment elsewhere.

If you are unwilling to break out of your comfort zone and meet new people, don't expect to transform your social life. How can you improve your relationships if you cannot let go of those people whose reaction to the available new technologies has left them with abridged social capabilities and you without the social support you once received?

I know it's not easy to desist in your attempts to be close with family members and friends who once made a genuine effort and recipro- cated your social overtures. Yet we are living in a new era in which our phones and other devices have created a false sense of social overload when in fact we are lonelier than ever before.

Most people are unaware of how they have been baited-and- switched by their devices: they unwittingly consider themselves more in demand than ever when in fact they are discarded daily by the people they consider their friends, who choose gulping from the digital spout over sustaining a high-quality connection with them.

As countless studies have shown, it is precisely these close connections that provide a buffer against physical and mental malaise and keep us healthy. Lonely people do not sleep as well, are more depressed and anxious, and possess less self-control and lower self-esteem than non-lonely individuals.

In addition to these psychological detriments of loneliness, the physical effects are no less alarming: lonely people experience reduced functioning of the immune, endocrine, and cardiovascular systems, the latter leading to reduced blood pressure regulation, increased heart rate and cardiac contractility (tension of heart contractions), and increased risk for heart attacks. As a result, they die sooner than their non-lonely counterparts. The physical wounds of lonely people even heal more slowly than the wounds of those who are not lonely.

Given the Cigna study released in 2020 that found that over 60 percent of Americans are lonely and the well-established link between high technology use and loneliness—a recent meta-analysis, for instance, found that lonely people spend more time on Facebook than non-lonely people—it is likely that most of the people who return your calls with a text or email are actually lonely. They have likely dug themselves into a digitally circumscribed hole, one small finger-tapping chunk of digital text at a time, from which they do not know how to exit.

Stop Digging

Either tone deaf to the increasingly ubiquitous specter of digitally mediated loneliness or intent on selling his products in spite of it, Google's former chairman Eric Schmidt once said, "Now you're never lonely, because your friends are always reachable. You're never bored, because there's infinite streams of information and entertainment." It is this type of messaging from Big Tech that has created the widespread illusion that the social information accessible on the Internet will result in social connection.

To understand how misguided Schmidt's proclamation is, consider one study that found women with breast cancer who used the Internet to research their disease felt more socially supported than those who did not. These same women, however, found that the more time they spent on the Internet, the lonelier they became.

Social information in the form of posts from doctors and other women with breast cancer helped these women better understand what they were going through. This social information, however, actually distanced them further from the social connection with and socioemotional support of others they so desperately needed in the most vulnerable time of their lives.

One of the first rules of holes is that if you find yourself in one, stop digging. You do not have to continue excavating yourself into this new nadir of social connection we have collectively created. Neither do you have to feel any less about yourself because some of the people you care about are no longer reciprocating your social efforts. Instead, you can develop more compassion for them.

Keep in mind that in addition to the debilitating physical and psychological effects of loneliness they are likely experiencing, lonely people also experience an increased evaluation of everyday activities as stress provoking, which is likely influencing their other relationships. Neither is work immune from the toxic tentacles of loneliness: lonely people experience more stress and burnout and do not perform as well in their jobs.

Hence, your compassion is merited: unless you also choose to spend your day touching your smartphone over twenty-five hundred times (which, considering that it's the average, may include you), it's not you—it's them. The by-product of the brogrammers having hit the ball out of the park is that "them" has become most people.

"If that's the case, it will require tremendous self-control not to cave in to the new digital norms," you may be thinking. Yes, what you say is true. So let's dive deeper into how you can regain your self-control—starting with how you manage your emotions.

Enhance Your Emotion Regulation Abilities

Taking stock of the dangerous and highly detrimental effects of loneliness, you can transform your perception of the people who were once in your close social circle but have edged out and become less communicative. While "It's me, not you" is a commonly contrived line during a breakup, in this case it's probably true: in their search for digital gold, the people who no longer have time for you have likely stopped making an effort in most of their relationships and have been left with worthless fool's gold with no redeemable value.

This mental transformation in how you view less-available family members and friends is called "cognitive reappraisal": a psychological reassessment of how you view a person, event, or situation in your life that can effectively change the emotion you experience when you think of this person, event, or situation. Numerous studies have found cognitive reappraisal to be the most effective form of emotion regulation.

Loneliness is one of these emotions. It is associated with the psychological belief that your social relationships are not as abundant and meaningful as you would like them to be. Feeling socially excluded can precipitate the onset of this emotion—loneliness—very quickly.

The good news is that you can use cognitive reappraisal to understand how phones and other devices have led many of the people who used to occupy a more central role in your life down a lonely road. This understanding can help you transform the negative emotions you associate with their flight (e.g., your own resentment and loneliness) into positive emotions such as compassion and concern.

This transformation of your inner emotions related to the people you care about will help you find the strength to be compassionate about their reduced social abilities. It will also help you seek out and bring into your core group of confidants new people who have better resisted the digital onslaught.

Fake It and You Won't Make It

Transforming the thoughts that induce a negative emotion such as loneliness through cognitive reappraisal becomes that much more important when we contrast this strategy with the other most common form of emotion regulation: suppression. Numerous studies on emotion regulation—including a field experiment I conducted in Madras, India, in collaboration with Brett Peters and other psychologists at the University of Ohio in which conference participants either suppressed or cognitively reappraised their nervousness and fear before giving a speech in public—support the finding that cognitive reappraisal is a much more effective strategy than suppression.

The reason is that suppression tends to lead to stress, burnout, and feelings of self-alienation (you're faking your emotions, after all), not to mention alienation from others. In short, it's hard to connect with others when you feel like an imposter.

Do you remember the "marshmallow test" experiments at Stanford we reviewed in Chapter 6? One of the most practical findings of these experiments is that the most effective way to delay gratification is to use cognitive reappraisal to mentally reframe the situation.

Instead of focusing on how sweet and delicious the marshmallow would be to eat, preschoolers who could alter their mental representation of the marshmallow—for example, envisioning it as a little cotton ball or a cloud—were able to avoid eating it for much longer. The other form of emotion regulation, suppressing the emotion of desire or hunger to pop the tantalizing, fluffy little treat into one's eagerly awaiting mouth, was much less effective.

In other words, spending your days denying the loneliness you feel (e.g., suppression) when the people you used to count on no longer return your calls or stop by because they have become tethered to their phones is a recipe that will only create the conditions for your loneliness to compound and become less manageable. Instead, you can reengineer your thinking (i.e., cognitive reappraisal) about their social distancing and call it by a new name: their digitally induced atrophying of social abilities that's exacerbating not only your loneliness, but their own.

The existing evidence admittedly paints a desolate picture of the social effects of the Internet. Does this mean that all of the social effects of the Internet are negative? No, it turns out. There has been an unanticipated finding of our digitally mediated lives no one expected.

Yes, a Relationship-Oriented Benefit of the Internet

While many prior friends have been expelled from the inner circles of most people, there has been a surprising benefit to another social group: direct family members. Many people now only make phone calls to their closest family members—especially their Digital Settler parents. Why? Because *they are the only ones who will actually answer the phone!*

When you call anyone else, your desire to converse in real time is often met by their voice mail greeting. It then takes a while for them to return your call—if they return your call, that is.

So when people are looking for socioemotional support, who do they go to? Someone they can count on. Someone who will answer the phone or at least call them back soon. The gap between the responsiveness of close family and everyone else has widened to the point where oftentimes people will elect to call family repeated times per day and certainly per week because they're the only people they can reach. Thank God for Mom and Dad.

Many people rely on family even more now for socioemotional support because they don't feel fulfilled communicating solely through digital means with friends. Hence, one consequence of the Internet is that we're becoming more clan-like.

Friendship networks are shrinking and family relationships are deepening—at least in terms of speaking more regularly by phone with those few family members who are reachable (relationships with less-available family members, like many friends, are becoming shallower). Feasibly, more phone time with those select family members will also lead to more in-person time.

In my own case, my mother and father will usually answer the phone. My brother and sisters are more hit or miss. I'm fortunate to have a few friends who will usually pick up or call me back the same or next day. My parents and these few friends—like a rare, almost impossible-to-find, coveted commodity—have appreciated in value immensely in my life.

To satisfy our need for social connection, each of us has a choice to make. When you desire to connect with another human being and you're alone and want to talk with someone, who will you call? For most, it will be the people who will answer the phone, which is likely to be a few family members and only the closest of friends.

I once came up with a saying: "Your closest friends are like brothers or sisters. Your closest brothers or sisters are like friends." The select group of people I'm referring to are the ones who will answer the phone or call you right back: for most of us, they are also the only people who still bear much influence in our lives.

Before you construct too rosy a mental image of a new society of family-oriented people cozying up to the fireplace with their parents or children, consider what scientists have to say about this phenomenon.

... Actually, Not So Fast

There is a downside to narrowing the people we still speak with to those who share our genes. Evolutionary psychologists claim that "kin selection," or favoritism toward family members who share your genetic makeup, is at the root of ethnic conflict. According to the biologist E. O. Wilson, kin selection is "the enemy of civilization. If human beings are to a large extent guided ... to favor their own relatives and tribe, only a limited amount of global harmony is possible."

The uptick in kin selection is the only phenomenon I can point to in order to understand the increased fear of child abduction that impels many parents today to hover over their children and keep them off the streets. There hasn't been a significant increase in child kidnappings—about 100 to 150 children are the victims of successful abductions in the US per year—so it's difficult to understand the motives of the current helicopter parent generation unless we consider the insularity that digital devices–induced kin selection fosters.

The less parents are able to develop friendships outside of their families (feel my Daddy pain here: social overture by phone with potential new friend semi-rejected with the return of a short text either because they are single and I've lost my game and am not a good wingman or because they are married with kids and too busy raising them for much of a social life), the more they rely on their children for social connection.

This desperate attempt to mold their children into friends often actually prevents these parents from being parents. Later, the same helicopter parents often blame their involuntarily insulated kids for not having sufficient friends of their own.

These underlying reasons notwithstanding, the insular nature of relationship development in the current smartphone era seems to run counter to the proclamations of enthusiasts (which we discovered in Chapter 1) extolling their anticipation that our screens (first the television and now our phones, laptops, and tablets) will usher in an era of global interconnectedness and understanding.

The Communication Reciprocation Downgrade

"Okay, I get it," you may be thinking. "Mostly talking in real time with my family members unfortunately does describe my life on some level. But what can I do about it? Don't leave me hanging, oh distant author."

While some of your friendships may have become social casualties of the digital age, it's better to accept this situation than to waste even one more day striving for pole position in a relationship you will never again experience as it once was.

Instead, you can acknowledge that you are going through a commonly experienced feeling of deflation in the digital age that emerges from the Communication Reciprocation Downgrade. This event occurs when you make a media-rich overture to someone (e.g., a phone call) and they offer a media-poor reply (e.g., a text or email). We have all fallen prey to the Communication Reciprocation Downgrade. (A few of my friends from college who don't answer my calls, but instead reply with a text or email a few weeks later, come to mind.)

Make a pact with yourself to start taking note of the family members and friends who do consistently pick up the phone or call you back when you reach out to them: they are your best social investment and, from here on out, your buffer from the ever-expanding tentacles of digitally induced loneliness.

Perhaps before, you did not afford them the value they deserved. Maybe you took them for granted while pining over others who, truth be told, have not reciprocated your efforts for years—unless you have been willing to join the ranks of their multitudinous social contacts to whom they condescend to send the occasional brief email, IM, or text message.

Compassion Fades Resentment

I'm not suggesting you end these relationships. A weak contact who is dealt a wake-up call in the form of the loss of health, intimate partner, or job may become a strong connection in the future. The compassion you generate for people who have exited your social stage by cognitively reappraising negative emotions such as anger, resentment, and anxiety associated with their digitally induced departure will help you to welcome them with an open, nonjudgmental heart if or when they return.

This compassion is not just for them, but for yourself. Why? Because any person you once liked who re-enters your social stage may become a good friend again if you welcome them with empathy and caring.

Given the scarcity of people who both recognize the futility of seeking social connection (and instead receiving social information) online and are attempting to rekindle face-to-face relationships, you cannot afford to spurn them based on a festering resentment for past inattentiveness or other negative emotions you have been unable to cognitively reappraise.

Even if a once-close friend or family member only wishes to be in your life on a limited basis, it may grow into a more meaningful relationship in the future, especially if they also begin to recognize the value you provide to them as a human being willing to connect in real time. Even if it doesn't, one of the most well-known findings of social network research is that weak ties are often the ones who forward your email, post a listing on Facebook for your dream job, or introduce you to the right person to help you access a new career opportunity.

While I'm not proposing that you unnecessarily end relationships out of spite or resentment, I am suggesting that you reply to an email or text from someone with whom you were once close with a phone call. If your call is not returned, leave the ball in their court and shift your social effort and attention toward those who place more value on you and your friendship. Today. Now. In the only moment in which your happiness resides.

Placing less value on social media, then, is really placing more value on yourself. It's placing more value on those with whom you wish to develop a meaningful connection and who similarly value that connection.

A Rock and a Hard Place

I know what I'm proposing will not be easy. You may fear that you will disrupt the current momentum of your relationships and cause others to resent you—even to perceive you as intrusive for calling and interrupting their digitally curated social lives.

It is true that they may initially feel threatened by your attempts to derail the meticulously titrated social distance they aspire to in their relationships. They may even resent you for your attempt to impede their efforts to keep countless relationships slowly advancing simultaneously and to keep themselves impervious to the messiness and potential hurt of real human connection.

To pick up the phone and call requires self-confidence and a willingness to cede the detached control of texting. As the writer Andrew Sullivan put it, "Think of how rarely you now use the phone to speak with someone. A text is far easier, quicker, less burdensome. A phone call could take longer; it could force you to encounter that person's idiosyncrasies or digressions or unexpected emotional needs."

"Now hold on a minute," you may be thinking. "If no one is using the phone to make calls anymore, won't what you're suggesting be threatening to others? Doesn't seem like very socially sound advice to me." It's a valid point that this suggestion can lead to rejection, as others may no longer be accustomed to receiving phone calls. They may feel awkward or inconvenienced and consequently balk at your challenging what has become the status quo for social overtures.

Yet at the same time, sending and receiving small bits of information rather than talking by phone is leading people down a desolate path of loneliness, anxiety, and depression. Picking up the phone and calling increasingly unavailable people may be the lesser of two dauntingly unattractive options.

If You Build It, They Will Come

If you wish to reinvigorate your relationships, the question you have to answer is how you can circumvent the increasingly digitally mediated habits of others. Design some strategies to develop more meaningful connections with others—such as calling an old friend, or going on a group hike, or going sailing or fencing or to a local park and being friendly with the people you meet there—and then give them a try. In the process, remind yourself that new friends do not come along every day and you will have to try and try again to bring the kinds of people you desire into your life.

When you participate in social activities you enjoy—such as hiking, dancing, sports, ferret racing, or playing cards or board games—you'll have fun independent of whom you meet. While you're engaging in such a personally fulfilling approach to your social life, new friends will magically appear, as per the old saying "When you least expect it, expect it."

Just as another old proverb reminds us that a watched pot never boils, new friends enter our lives not when we insist they appear, but when they are ready—which tends to be at roughly the time when we are happy with ourselves and radiating that joy out to others.

To understand the link between reduced screen time and real-life social activities that fortify your sense of self, remember the displacement effect from Chapter 1. Not only does more screen time equate to less time to develop your relationships with family and friends, but it also translates into less time to cultivate your relationship with yourself. Flowers that do not receive water do not grow; you are no different.

Short-Circuit the Displacement Effect

If you doubt how the displacement effect of technology applies to growing your sense of self, consider a recent interview with Francine, a high school history teacher in Riverside, California:

> My reliance on social media has separated me from the real world. I have focused my attention on perfecting my image on social media and have lost touch with my real-life experiences. Social events or memorable moments are spent capturing every minute so that people sitting at home can also somehow be a part of my personal experiences. While I am uploading the events of my life, I am forgetting to enjoy the moment. I am losing touch with the people who are standing right in front of me and creating a lonely environment for myself.

Consider how you can learn from people like Francine and short-circuit this displacement effect by spending less time online and more time engaged in real-life activities that strengthen you. Then derail the displacement effect even further by making bold attempts to connect with the people you care about—or could care about if you got to know them better—in person and by phone. Give this strategy a try and you will soon find that digital substitutes for real connection cease to hold much significance or attraction to you.

Rather than continuing to show up as Exhibit A for the social media–loneliness link—a recent study found that the top 25 percent of social media users among Americans ages nineteen to thirty-two are twice as likely to report they are lonely as those using social media the least—you will begin to experience a new freedom from email, text, and social media. Why? Because you will no longer recognize these platforms as viable substitutes for spending real-world time with family and friends.

As you extend your new approach to your career by converting emails into phone calls or face-to-face meetings (sometimes by just picking up the phone and calling, often by emailing back to schedule a phone call or meeting, sometimes even by walking down the hall and knocking on a door or popping your head into a cubicle) you will be pleasantly surprised to find that you are able to get work done more effectively and develop more trust and loyalty with your coworkers now that you take the time to listen and talk with them and better understand their motivations.

Make a pact with yourself to upgrade how you communicate with others. Your humanity and enjoyment of a life that feels vital and worth living again will become the ultimate benefits.

"Okay, I understand that private victory comes first, and that I need to regulate my use of my phone and laptop," you may be thinking. "But I still need some more concrete strategies I can really use. There are many books decrying what is happening to our society since the brogrammers, as you call them, took over, but still so few answers."

Yes, you are absolutely right on all counts. We need more practical and practice-able strategies that enable us to live with our devices. Our phones and other screens are certainly not going anywhere soon. They are too deeply integrated into our lives for us to sanguinely throw them off a bridge or under a bus, so we need some specific strategies to help us live with them without losing our deepest humanity in the process. In the next chapter, I will continue sharing concrete strategies that enable us to retain our freedom while living with our phones and other devices.

16

Digital Limiting Strategies

*M*y greatest struggle with email in any relationship in my life has been with my mother. I asked her for years to call rather than email me, but she instead insisted on constantly sending me emails. Many of these emails were sent to a group of twelve or more family members and friends and included such intimate messages as "Just had a wonderful dinner with Maria and Charles. Will be back in Washington tomorrow."

Whereas before she had called me a few times per week, once she became hooked on her iPad—which, little knowing the outcome, I bought for her—I would sometimes go for months without hearing her voice unless I called her. Even then, sometimes I would call and receive a Communication Reciprocation Downgrade in the form of an email response a few days later.

I asked my mother politely and then insistently for years not to send so many messages, but to instead save up what she wants to tell me and then to call me, all to no avail. It all came to a head when she was preparing to visit us in Barcelona and we spoke by phone from the hospital a few hours after our first child was born.

As a newly minted dad, to say I was feeling anxious would be an egregious understatement. Not sleeping for a few days wasn't helping. Making the difficult choice between being able to sleep at night or listening to the desperate wailing of a newborn, my mother opted to stay in a hotel for a week. I suggested she consider renting an apartment on Airbnb, which could be both more comfortable and cheaper than a hotel. She said she would and we hung up the phone.

An hour later, I was asleep for the first time in about twenty-four hours with our baby nestled in the crook of my arm. My phone vibrated and abruptly woke me up. My mother had texted me the message "Check out this room" with a link to an option she favored on Airbnb. Sound innocuous? Yet another brief, instrumental text not unlike the hundreds you probably send and receive each month?

I was infuriated. My accrued angst surrounding the birth found its opportunity for release, directed toward my mother. I felt a sense of self-righteous anger: our baby had just been born and my mother was sending me the first of most likely a litany of messages about possible Airbnb rooms.

I replied with the following message, verbatim: "No texts please Mom thanks just make notes for what u want to talk about next time we talk no more electronic communication I really mean it."

Not Wanted: Maternal Downgrade

Feeling the delicate breath of our son—who didn't even have a day to his name, or for that matter a name yet—as he nestled so innocently on my chest, I experienced an overpowering surge of a visceral, unusual feeling within me. This feeling told me, with unequivocal clarity and intensity, that I didn't want him to grow up in this kind of world.

After sending the text, I fumed for a few more minutes and then called my mother. Here's what I said to this poor woman who had digitally stumbled onto the wrong phone at the wrong time: "I can't believe that you are asking me to go look online at rooms for you two hours after our child has been born. I love you Mom and you can call me ten times a day if you like and I'll always be happy to talk with you. But no more electronic communication. For at least the next three months."

That was six years ago, and I have sent no more than about thirty emails or text messages to my mother since. We now have agreed upon a rule: no more than one email per week.

About once every three months, I remind her of the rule. She still routinely breaks it; I don't make a big deal about it, but at the same time I don't reply to her emails. Instead, I pick up the phone and call her.

Now I know I am coming across as an analog dinosaur: The Unabomber 2.0, Not in HD. It was an extreme solution, I realize. Yet it was the only way. Alex had to come into this world for me to finally be able to create the kind of relationship I wanted with one of the most important persons in my life: my mother. We now speak by phone a few times per week and have more of a heart connection once again.

It's not perfect: sometimes we don't talk for a couple of weeks and I wonder how she is doing, and think perhaps it would be better to receive one or two emails than nothing at all. But it was never possible to only receive a few emails and also receive phone calls, and I will never return to the type of relationship we had for almost ten years: speaking infrequently and instead exchanging brief chunks of text across cyberspace.

She's the human being who brought me into this world, after all. I can acquiesce to the phone-to-brief-electronic-missive Communication Reciprocation Downgrade in many other relationships, but not with my own mother.

Building Fences

Alan works in San Francisco's Marina District and lives in the Mission District. A biotech engineer who came to see me in search of work-life balance, Alan explained to me that he can either take the bus or bicycle to work. He prefers to bicycle, as it provides him with twenty-five minutes during which he cannot use his phone. Whereas if he takes the bus, he will spend most of the ride on his phone.

After Alan's session I couldn't shake the thought of what a shame it is that we need to rely on an external catalyst or condition—such as having to be on a bicycle where it's impossible to (safely) text—to be able to carve out a break from our phones. There is also a whole host of technologies designed to save you from technology, such as apps that warn you when you've passed a threshold of a certain amount of hours on your smartphone, or a specific app, on a particular day.

These solutions seem a bit ironic: we have to admit some kind of defeat when we purchase one technology to protect us from another—or even from itself (the new iPhone comes replete with such limiting apps). We should be able to do that ourselves. It brings to mind the antismoking messages that tobacco companies released. As the writer Evgeny Morozov wittily notes, "Technology companies produce apps to fight noise, overload, and distraction—having first produced noise, overload, and distraction."

Nonetheless, clever technologies abound to save us from ourselves, including an admittedly clever "smartphone safe" that can be programmed to not allow you to retrieve your phone for a pre-specified period, such as a few hours or days. It does not allow overrides.

An impetus for me to write this book has been to help you create internal mechanisms for taking regular breaks from your phone so you can actually experience your life rather than letting it slip away in a digitally induced trance you only become aware of once it's too late.

Hence, the Digital Limiting Strategies I propose in this book do not rely on any external app or technology. They are internally designed and enforced—by you.

It's Alive

The solution to too much CO_2 in the atmosphere that was agreed upon by 169 nations in the Kyoto protocol, with the striking exceptions of the US and Australia, has been called "cap and trade." This international covenant requires a cap, or limit, on emissions—nation by nation, company by company, household by household—until acceptable levels are reached.

The solution to too much CO_{mputer} in your life? Also cap and trade. Limit its usage. Like the traditional horror movie character who barricades himself in the basement so he won't be able to harm others once he transforms into a bloodthirsty monster, give the current you permission to regulate the Digital Drift–prone future you. (And don't be disheartened by the fact that the horror movie protagonist always breaks free.)

Digital Limiting Strategies have been tested in organizations. Recent attempts by some large companies, such as Atos in France and Volkswagen in Germany, to limit interoffice email reflect a growing recognition that constant connectivity—to give you an idea of the velocity of professional communication today, 70 percent of office emails are opened within six seconds—can become unproductive and impede healthy organizational functioning. Some companies, such as Canon, Deloitte & Touche, U.S. Cellular, and, ironically, Intel, have introduced "no-email days."

According to Stacey Villarrubia, payroll and benefits coordinator at PBD Worldwide Fulfillment Services, a three-hundred-employee company in Alpharetta, Georgia, when PBD instituted no-email Fridays, she thought, "Email has become our right arm, and now you've cut it off." Stacey continued to write emails on Friday, but instead of sending them, she stockpiled them in her outbox and set them to be automatically sent on Monday.

As a result, each Monday all of the employees' inboxes overflowed. Soon Stacey's boss started running down the hall and calling her out, along with other strategic offenders, for this digital sleight of hand. Then, rather than drafting emails on Fridays, she began to step out of her office and walk over to the warehouse to talk with employees face-to-face. According to Stacey, more people now stop by her office "to say hi" and "pass on family plans."

Have you set any limits to the amount of time you spend checking emails, texting, or surfing the web?

Help the Tree Grow

Here are a few Digital Limiting Strategies some of my clients and friends have successfully practiced:

- A parent enforces "blackout periods" for their kids during which they are not allowed to access any digital technology.
- Meals are off limits (e.g., no smartphones). One client and his wife purposefully leave their phones in their bedroom when they have breakfast and dinner. This practice began when, on a few occasions, he asked her during dinner, "Did you see that email I sent you?" and she replied, "No, because my phone is upstairs. I'm not looking at it."
- Bedrooms are also off limits. The problem with having a phone in your bedroom is that you begin and end your day with your device, resulting in an increased heart rate at both of these otherwise (and, for some people, only) relaxed moments of the day. Better to start and finish your day not thinking about what others want from you (in the queue of electronic messages your phone contains) but about what you want from yourself and your life.
- One family has a basket next to the door to their dining room where phones are turned off and deposited before meals. Whether you leave your phone in your bedroom, the foyer, a basket, or a closet, the point is to leave it far enough away so you will not see or hear alerts or notifications and will hopefully be too lazy to retrieve it to punctuate (and, if done enough times, derail) a conversation about a fact check on Saturday's weather or the birthplace of Genghis Khan.
- Create and plan in advance distinct phone-free events with your family and friends. Obtain their buy-in early so they're psychologically ready for it when it happens.
- My favorite, which merits much more practice: when a group of friends goes out for a meal, the first person to check their phone pays the bill.

It's Not What You Say That Counts

Parents can play a vital role in helping their children construct a fence around the tree until the tree can grow healthily on its own. Yet as parents we tend to succumb to Digital Drift ourselves, losing our time and self-direction online; these tendencies are also our "children"—the more innocent, naïve parts of ourselves that need our vigilance and protection.

Our physical children observe how we regulate our own cravings vis-à-vis any new technology, and they tread in our footsteps. They learn more deeply not from what we say, but what we do.

What we call "play" is, at least on some level, children preparing for their future lives. Children create games with cars, action figures, dolls, food preparation, or cowboys as a way to assimilate what they perceive they are likely to encounter later in life. Most importantly, children observe their parents and take cues for what they need to learn to survive and thrive in life. Reinforcing this dynamic, the University of Washington pediatrician and epidemiologist Dimitri Christakis shared with me in a recent interview:

> Parents should be aware that they are children's first and most important teachers and that their actions are providing a very potent example for their children. So, even as infants, they're looking to you and seeing how you spend your time, what you value. In fact, it's not coincidental that one of the most popular toys, even for babies, is essentially these fake phones.... the reason is because children recognize these as valued devices in the family. They see everybody holding on to them and they want one of their own.

So we really need to be mindful of what we say and do around our kids, especially in relation to how we use our phones and other devices. Yet most of us are not saying or doing much of anything. According to a 2013 report from the American Academy of Pediatrics, two-thirds of children and teenagers report being held to "no rules" whatsoever regarding their screen usage. The majority also report that they continue to use their devices after the lights are turned off at night.

How could this be happening—that so many of us are so naïve when it comes to regulating our children's screen use? There are two primary reasons. The first is what psychologists call the fundamental attribution error: when things go wrong in our lives (such as returning home to a brood of glazed-eyed zombies who rage when we suggest they put away their devices), we attribute it to external circumstances (those #*/!#-* phones!).

However, when things go wrong in other people's lives, we attribute it to their intrinsic characteristics. So when you run a traffic light, it's the damn light. When someone else does, it's because they're an idiot. (The corollary is that when good things happen to us, it's our internal characteristics—"I worked really hard for that award." However, when fortune strikes others it's their external circumstances—"She was lucky.")

The second reason is what's called the Dunning-Kruger effect: the least competent among us (e.g., at regulating our children's screen use) are the most susceptible to overconfidence (e.g., Johnny will do well in life despite his inability to comfortably interact with anyone without a screen mediating the conversation). Even imprisoned criminals believe they are more trustworthy, honest, and kinder than the average person.

The Natives Are Restless

Your home can be different. You can set Digital Limiting Strategies for yourself and/or your children depending on who most needs the fence constructed around their tree so they can grow toward the light. Which light? The one illuminated by the values you hold dear and are attempting to instill in your children.

Others can also design creative Digital Limiting Strategies. Fed up with worshippers texting during Mass, Father Michele Madonna of

Naples, Italy, installed a cell phone jamming device. "It has solved the problem," the priest shared.

The oldest son of Tony Fadell, the co-inventor of the iPod, was born weeks before the introduction of the iPhone. Fadell noticed that when he took a phone or tablet away from his kids, similar to adults "they would get really anxious and upset." Fadell banned smartphones in the morning and started "screen-free Sundays" in his home.

Expect resistance. After shutting down the Internet in his home in 2014 and only allowing his children one hour of access per day, university professor Martin Kutnowski reports "piercing screams" from "inside the fortress of [his ten-year-old daughter's] bedroom.... She is angry with me because she has discovered that her iPod cannot get online."

Seeing many of his students out of shape, lethargic, and lacking the focus to write a coherent essay or even read a book, Kutnowski wanted something different for his kids. Months after his seditious act, his kids are once again "avid talkers" stimulated by going outside, playing games, reading books, and generally acting "like fish returning to a river that had been polluted for decades."

Let's consider some more Digital Limiting Strategies you can practice in any relationship, beginning with your relationship with yourself.

Create Discrete Online Periods

In the well-known legend, Ulysses asks his crewmates to tie him to the mast of his ship and put wax in their ears in order to avoid temptation by the Sirens, whose beautiful songs would otherwise likely lure them to run aground onto jagged rocks.

To withstand one of our greatest modern-day temptations, some of the rope and wax we can use to cordon ourselves off for most of the day is to minimize online entry. What does this mean? To keep even going online in the first place (including checking your smartphone) to a bare minimum. To achieve this goal, you can collapse the time during which you do anything whatsoever online—attending to work and nonwork tasks that require the Internet, for example—into discrete time blocks in your work schedule.

To make this strategy practicable, I've created the term "Online Entry Points" (OEPs) to represent specific times of the day during which we go online for any reason. At the beginning of each week, I measure (in a spreadsheet) my evening and weekend OEPs from the previous week. My goal is to have at most one weekday evening OEP (with a maximum of one hour online, but in practice it tends to be just a few minutes) and one weekend OEP (also maximum one hour).

Yes, I realize the OEP strategy and the idea of structured online time sounds indescribably anal. It is. But it works! Because I know it will count as one of my OEPs, I stay offline almost all weekday evenings and one weekend day, enabling me to spend much more quantity and quality time with my wife, children, and friends.

It's absolutely absurd that anyone would avoid going online during their personal time because they then have to mark an OEP in a spreadsheet that only they, and no one else, will look at on Monday morning. Yet this is precisely what happens for me and for many of the people I coach.

Why? Two primary reasons: First, it's like having to admit the breach of an important value, something most of us would prefer to avoid. Second, it finally puts dopamine to work *for* you rather than *against* you—quite an accomplishment in the digital age. By writing down the limited number of OEPs you have permitted for the week, you feel like you are achieving an important goal, which induces the release of the reward-oriented neurotransmitter.

Staying on Track Without Losing Your Enjoyment of Life

For the OEP strategy to work, try as much as you can to not go online at all during your personal time. One way to achieve this objective is to make a list called "Evenings/weekends screen list" and put on the list anything you need to do online during nonwork hours.

For example, suppose it is 8:30 p.m. and you are finishing dinner and not sure if someone is going to meet you for lunch the next day. You're beginning to feel anxious about it. Going online to check is likely to lead to Digital Drift, where you then engage in other activities online and soon you've drop-punted your evening (unless you practice the Side Door strategy described in the next chapter).

Instead, write down in your planner to check the following morning whether the email has come in and the lunch is confirmed. (Alternatively, use the Side Door strategy.) Writing down a task you would like to complete tomorrow is an excellent way to relieve your stress and preoccupation with the task, as one of the healthy functions of stress and worry is to ensure you pay attention to something that would be damaging to you to forget.

Waiting to check a lunch confirmation is one example, but there are many other tasks we think are urgent in the moment that, through slowing down, we realize are really not that urgent at all. You can table them to discrete time blocks in your schedule—online periods—where you tend to all such issues. Keeping online and offline periods distinct is likely to result in much more offline time, which will reduce your stress level and yield more strategic thinking and time to reflect on what's most important in your life.

"That creates anxiety just thinking about it," you may say to yourself. "I want to know what I will be doing the next day." The truth is that, even when you check the next message, you are likely to continue cruising down the road you've been traveling on, called Feel Anxiety About What's Next Avenue. Actually, it's more like a cul-de-sac from which you can't escape. Whatever it is, that's too long a name for a street.

Make an effort to slow down and schedule times at which you will go online and you will find that what seemed so urgent really wasn't. You will also find that a slower pace of receiving messages from others, if managed well, achieves the dueling objectives of keeping your life on track and enjoying it along the way.

Make It Happen:

1) Acknowledge how you spend your time online. Identify the specific online "projects" you embark on that seem to never have an end in sight and continually pique your acquisitive instinct, such as downloading music or movies, or researching potential partners to date, or emptying your inbox.

2) Give yourself a weekly maximum of time to dedicate to each of these activities. Select the amount of time depending on how this activity aligns with your deeper values and life vision.

3) Share these weekly maximums with a good friend (who ideally also does this exercise and shares their weekly maximums with you), perhaps in a spreadsheet. By transforming this exercise into a social commitment, you increase your chances of adhering to it as you and your friend hold each other accountable.

4) At the end of each week, compare your hours spent on each of these activities with the weekly maximum. You and your friend can share your respective progress over lunch, while going on a walk together, or at a café.

5) If you surpass the limit, together with your friend, design strategies to reduce your hours. Alternatively, make adjustments to the weekly maximum if you deem it necessary.

The Cognitive Miser Meets the Internet

As with any addiction, the addict must limit their use of the object that captivates their attention in order to transform their behavior from compulsive to intentional. While the long-term goal is to no longer crave the object as much (e.g., cigarettes, sex, drugs, TV, chocolate), in the short term the cravings rage. For this reason, the focus of the OEP strategy, like other behavior-limiting strategies, is on not allowing the cravings to dictate your actions.

While the early-stage beat-the-addiction strategies center around regulating *behavior*, or how you *act*, the later-stage strategies emphasize regulating *cognition*, or how you *think*. We follow this order because it's easier to change how you *act* (e.g., "I won't check email tonight after 9 p.m.") than how you *think* (e.g., "I understand the reasons why checking email is harmful and therefore do not want to check email after 9 p.m.").

What if one of the primary reasons that breaking an addiction to an activity mediated by your phone or laptop is so challenging is that it requires you to reengineer the way you think, which goes against a natural human tendency to think as little as possible? As it turns out, this is precisely the case.

Psychological research has found that we tend to act as "cognitive misers" and process social information automatically and unintentionally. In fact, this is one of the most agreed-upon, central findings of social psychology.

People are convinced by a ten-to-one margin, for example, that the candidate they support has won a presidential debate. Why? To think otherwise would require a greater expenditure of cognitive resources, including thoughts such as "What did the opponent say to which my candidate could have better responded?" and "What mistakes did my candidate make?"

How does the cognitive miser phenomenon relate to digitally mediated addictions? Let's take a look.

Cold Turkey Not an Option

Addiction to any activity (e.g., gaming, porn, gambling, shopping ... name your poison) now easily accessed on the Internet is different from other addictions, where the only way to break them is to go cold turkey. Breaking other substance-involved addictions often involves making a dichotomous choice, a difficult decision involving only two options: smoke or don't smoke; drink or don't drink. This all-or-nothing choice is both cognitively simpler and much easier to uphold.

For this reason, more people quit smoking by going cold turkey than by reducing their intake to two cigarettes per day. Yes, it's hard as hell and involves intense suffering—that's why they're called "addictions": the person has subscribed to a conscious or subconscious belief that they rely on the object of their addiction.

Yet for many smokers, it's easier to drop their intake to zero rather than two cigarettes per day. The same is true with drinking: cold turkey is excruciatingly difficult at first, but easier in the long run than years of futilely attempting to tote back only one glass each day.

With an addiction to something accessed on the Internet, it's different: we've swiftly reached a state of mass penetration—called "the network effect"—where there are so many users that we feel like we have to engage in some measure of online activities to effectively function in our work and personal lives.

At this point in our collective history, to try to live without going online is impractical. As Andrew Martin, a librarian in Washington, D.C., once exclaimed, "We can't just go cold turkey. We rely on [our phones] too much for legitimate, logistical stuff like navigating."

Online for Legitimate Reasons, Addiction Sets In

The pediatric neuro-endocrinologist Rob Lustig poignantly shared with me how legitimate social media use becomes an entry point for addiction:

> My wife is an endocrine nurse practitioner. We knew about this danger. We kept my oldest daughter off Facebook until the ninth grade, when she went to high school and joined the debate team for

her local high school. And the debate team did all of its practices, all of its logistics, all of its carpooling, etc., on Facebook. So if you wanted to be on the debate team, you had to be on Facebook. No choice. So reluctantly, we relinquished the blockade of that Facebook site. Two years later, she was an addict. We would catch her under the covers at four in the morning doing "likes" and "dislikes" and all sorts of things that we were, shall we say, not too happy about. And to this day, she still has a very bastardized relationship with her phone. And that's with good parents....What do you think happens with the parents who don't really know what's going on?

If you have children of your own, hearing this experience from two dedicated and highly educated parents may make you want to kick your phone to the curb. Yet whether it's staying in touch with people; buying airline, train, or bus tickets; checking up on a work project; finding a restaurant; or inviting friends to a party, the Internet, if properly used, indisputably makes our lives more efficient. To deny these efficiency gains would be quixotic.

In this sense, the OEP strategy enables a life in which you combine the efficiency of the Internet with the effectiveness of pursuing self-initiated goals. Just as going from being an alcoholic to two drinks per day is very challenging if you're having a sip of vodka every twenty minutes, we will never beat our technology-accelerated addictions if we briefly check our phone or laptop every twenty minutes or even more frequently "just to see one quick thing."

Yet, again, not to check our devices at all is also impractical. The Stanford University psychiatrist Anna Lembke likens phone use to "a spectrum disorder" with "mild, moderate, and extreme forms." She also makes the comparison to alcohol, with moderate consumption benefiting some people. "Let's be very thoughtful about how we're using these devices," Lembke cautions, "because we can use them in pathological ways."

So set up your daily OEPs and you're all set, right? If only.

Starting Strong and Finishing Weak

Despite their *initial* practicality and usefulness, many OEPs *subsequently* lead to Digital Drift. They begin strong (in terms of their alignment with our deeper values) and finish weak, ultimately debilitating us as we lose our self-efficacy multiple times daily under the thrall of Digital Drift. Before we know it, our lives have become digitally mediated. What we could have wisely utilized as an efficient tool becomes a life support we can no longer live without.

So why does our natural propensity to be cognitive misers propel us toward a fully digitally mediated existence? Because there are no quick-and-dirty strategies to end addictions to technology-mediated activities. Unlike drinking, gambling, casual sex, or porn, we can't go cold turkey and just stop the activity; living an Internet-free life is simply not a viable option for the vast majority of us in the third millennium.

To strengthen our resistance to the allure of our glistening devices and become less Screened In, we have to develop new, as yet untested competencies; we have to become pioneers in work-life balance in the digital age; we have to read books like this one and others that suggest how to develop such strategies. All of this requires a tremendous amount of psychological effort and expenditure of the limited cognitive resources we strive so hard to conserve.

Doesn't sound like much fun, does it? This is precisely the challenge that confronts us in the digital age, like it or not. It's psychologically draining. Certainly those pioneering families who moved their televisions back into the living room faced a similar challenge. As did the drivers who decided they didn't need to sit in their car anymore while watching a movie.

An Unprecedented, but Not Insurmountable, Psychological Challenge

Yet these earlier cognitive challenges pale in comparison to the one you face right here and now. When you attempt to think through how to divert your time and attention from devices constructed to appear to meet innumerable human needs, keep in mind a daunting fact: these needs include all those met by history's previous technological marvels put together.

To meet such a challenge, the purpose of this book, is no easy task. Consider that if you were to take a small drink every twenty minutes, you'd be slightly drunk all the time. That's more or less our state of mind—tinged with the adrenaline rush of constant connection, continually tipsy with the online buzz—when we take just a slight sip from the digital goblet.

I have developed the final strategy in this book (which you will learn about in the next chapter), the Heart of Darkness, with a singular goal: *to address our need to check our phones from time to time without looking at them all the time*. In other words, the goal of the Heart of Darkness is to help you achieve the equivalent of temperate alcohol consumption: to moderate the attention you give to your phone.

Why is moderate phone consumption such a critical make-or-break for our well-being in the digital age? Because otherwise we walk around perpetually intoxicated in our dopamine-high stupor.

All it takes at any given moment—to be precise, each moment occurs on average every six minutes—is a quick craning of the head to glance at the phone in your hand, and once again you are a bit woozy, slightly high from the adrenaline rush of feeling important, of feeling that others want you or want to get in touch with you or are interested in what you have to say.

The alternative is to emphasize the part of your self-development that does not come from digitally mediated interaction but from time spent connecting in real time with yourself and others—time in which the emotions that accompany such connection teach you important lessons about who you are.

Be the Prism

Herein lies an important reminder about addiction: *All addictions are to something external to you.* If you want to kick any addiction— including one (or many) mediated by your phone or laptop, such as porn, gambling, or seeking Mr. or Ms. Right—the first step is to acknowledge that the object you crave is separate from you. Most importantly, it is not you. You are much larger than it.

A useful metaphor is to think of yourself as a prism. If you set a prism next to a rose, it takes the color of the rose. If you place it next to a puddle of mud, it assumes the color of the mud. Yet the prism is neither the rose nor the mud; it is a prism.

To break an addiction means to face the fear of confronting yourself that led you to overattach to something external to yourself (the metaphorical rose or mud) in the first place. That means constructing a fence around the fledgling sense of self you are trying to revitalize. The fence, the Digital Limiting Strategy, is the defining of your daily OEPs: how many, how long, how often.

Make a commitment to only go online during premeditated OEPs and you will be taking a stand for developing a meaningful relationship with yourself. Your limited OEPs (the fence) will protect you from the brogrammer brigade competing for your attention *away from yourself* and onto the profitable, candy-colored, addiction-generating distractions on which they build their livelihoods.

The Ideal Is Above the Real

If you are going to embark with me on this journey, it's important to go easy on yourself when you don't meet your OEP goals. Recall that this level of psychological effort to adapt to a new technology is unprecedented in the history of humankind, and to expend this effort goes against our natural human inclination to conserve our limited attentional resources (i.e., to think as little as possible).

"Today I didn't do so well, as I gave in and checked my phone and email more often than I should have," Doug, a disabled veteran from Sarasota, Florida, shared in his Heart of Darkness Challenge Journal. "It is strange, but I actually feel guilty since I have grown accustomed to this new norm of resisting technological influences that are not necessarily healthy. Even though I fell off the wagon, I plan to grab myself by my bootstraps and get back up again."

If you are to join me on this mission to limit your Online Entry Points, it's critical that, like Doug, you learn not to beat yourself up not *if*, but *when* you lapse. Instead, return to your center. Recall that your OEP goals are the ideal, and *the ideal is always above the real.* Nonetheless, it's important to have an ideal. Otherwise, you never know which direction to move in.

"I like this idea, but it seems impractical," you may be thinking. "There is a whole host of apps, notifications, and buzzing sounds that emanate from my phone and conspire against any attempt I make to limit online access, as you suggest."

You have a point. If you are to be able to resist the best efforts of the brogrammer brigade to divert your attention to your phone and other screens on average 150 times daily, you must have a secret weapon beyond limiting your online entry. Without a more potent arsenal at your disposal, they will eat you for breakfast.

Please allow me to provide you with such a weapon: the ultimate fence-building strategy that will enable you to take back control of your life.

17

The Heart of Darkness

Around the end of each year, I often think about what I want to do differently in my life. I take a couple of weeks off for the holidays and it's always in the back of my mind. At the end of 2017, I was experiencing an existential uneasiness.

I had made quite a bit of progress in regulating email about five years earlier, and was only checking my email account about five times per week, usually on weekday afternoons. That had worked well. Yet without realizing it, I had developed an automatic habit of checking texts and WhatsApp, sometimes over thirty or forty times per day— basically, all the time.

For me, text messages had become a substitute for email. Like emailing, texting consists of a brief electronic textual exchange. As we saw in Chapter 4, communicating solely through the written word comprises about 7 percent of the full experience of communication. I realized I had whittled the richness of my connections with others down to this 7 percent, and was engaged in it addictively.

I realized the duplicity of what I had been doing every day for years. I had tried to kick the habit without success. About a year earlier, I had taken notifications off my phone, so text messages no longer popped up on my phone or buzzed or vibrated. This strategy wasn't working, however, because since I knew I wasn't receiving notifications, I was checking my phone for texts all the time. Go figure.

My family, good friends, and some coworkers knew I didn't check email often and that texting me was the best way to get a rapid response. So now, in addition to climbing Email Mountain every time I logged in to my email account, I was trekking up SMS Mountain every time I picked up my phone—which was often.

I had tried many times to stop checking my text and WhatsApp messages so often, but nothing seemed to work. Then, on New Year's Eve in 2017, in a small town in Mexico, I realized why.

Mission Possible: Check Your Phone Infrequently

Every time I picked up my phone, the home screen showed me the text messaging and WhatsApp icons, each with a badge indicating how many messages were waiting for me to open. Seeing a message and not checking it or hearing your phone ringing and not answering it causes your heart rate, blood pressure, and feelings of anxiety to increase.

Impossible: *not* checking or answering is simply not going to happen. You open your inbox and the social pressure-cooker thoughts heat up—"Oh, Fred needs this," "Maria wants to reschedule a meeting," "These friends are trying to get together"—and not attending to these messages doesn't feel like a viable option.

Hilary, a woman in her early forties who works at the Environmental Protection Agency in Washington, DC, shared how she managed her anxiety vis-à-vis her email inbox by the fourth week of the Heart of Darkness Challenge: "I used to constantly check my text and Facebook messages because I did not like the notification icon on the top of my phone. It may sound silly but that is why I would check my phone constantly. I am slowly getting used to this experiment."

Rather than being stressed, I preferred the dopamine rush of checking my messages and both crossing "check messages" off my invisible mental list and placating the deeply ingrained craving for social information and recognition (e.g., "It looks like someone wants to reach me. I guess I'm important to them. I wonder what they have to say.").

I had tried to go cold turkey, to not check my phone at all, but this strategy had not worked in any way whatsoever. As I mentioned earlier, in our current digital society with our phones mediating numerous transactional daily activities such as navigating, listening to music, and monitoring logistical and social information, it's just too impractical to not look at our phones at all. I needed a solution that would allow me to use my phone sporadically as a tool without it becoming an inseparable bodily appendage.

It became clear to me that the only way to check texts and other apps without becoming addicted to glancing at my phone every five or ten minutes would be if I only opened the inbox (the badge showing me how many messages each app contains for me) once or twice per day.

After years of being plagued by this issue and using my phone way too much—including when I was purportedly watching my kids at the playground and other shameful, life-contracting moments such as at a restaurant when family or friends were ordering their meals or had gone to the bathroom (after which my mind became preoccupied with some other issue galvanized by my phone and fell out of sync with the conversation)—it finally hit me. I knew what I could do if I only wanted to see my text messages and other addiction-facilitating apps once or twice per day so my life would no longer be controlled by social media companies.

It was very simple, it turned out, although it took me years to discover.

How Often a Visit from the Postman?

Imagine that you can have your (postal service) mail delivered as often as you like. You can choose precisely how often the postman will show up and bring you your (snail) mail.

Will you choose once per day, once every few days, or once per week? Alternatively, will you select a frequency of two or three times per day, ten times per day, fifty times per day? Before reading any further, make a mental note of how often you would like to receive your postal mail in an ideal world.

I've asked thousands of people this question in my conferences, and the most common responses are once per day or once every few days. Almost no one has ever chosen to have their mail delivered more than once per day in this imaginary world where the postal service is willing to deliver your mail as often as you like.

Why doesn't anyone choose more than once per day? Reasons commonly stated are that such a rate of mail delivery would be intrusive, distracting, or just downright annoying. "How could I get anything else done if I were constantly checking my mail" is a commonly shared sentiment.

Can you guess where this is going? If you would only select to have paper mail delivered at most once per day, why is it that you allow the new form of mail that has all but replaced paper mail—electronic mail—to be delivered to you over seventy-five, and for some, over two hundred times daily? (Recall that 70 percent of office emails are read within six seconds.) Whether in the form of text messages, email, or IMs from apps such as Facebook, WhatsApp, Bumble, or Twitter, all such brief textual missives are the new form of (electronic) mail.

Regulating the Use of Our New Toys

The Heart of Darkness model has a very simple objective: to enable you to bring the frequency with which you check your (now electronic rather than paper) mail down to a reasonable number. Why? So that, quite simply, you can focus on your larger life goals rather than spending your inheritance (called "life") checking your mail over, and over, and over again.

Additionally, research has found that the more often you check email, the more stressed you become and the less you check the less stress you experience. So any strategy that reduces the number of times you check incoming messages each day is likely to contribute significantly to your overall well-being.

This model will enable you to once again gain control of how often others reach you. In implementing it, you will be able to shift your attention from the goals others have for you to the goals you set for yourself.

Rather than reacting to the vicissitudes of the good opinions of others by craning your neck down an average of 150 times per day to read their latest thoughts about how you should live your life, you can elect to make this shift and receive the new (electronic) type of mail from others in its various textual forms five, three, or even one time per day. Yes, really.

I'll share with you how I managed, after years of failed experiments, to pull off this feat. But first, why did all of my previous experimenting not work?

Because, as I mentioned earlier, going cold turkey on our phones or laptops is not really a practical option anymore: we use them for too many vital purposes, ranging from finding our way to a party to listening to our favorite songs to letting someone know we're running late.

The reason the Heart of Darkness model works is because it doesn't require you to throw your phone into the sewer, or shut down your social media accounts, or trade in your smartphone for a retro flip phone that can only make calls. Far from it. It allows you to continue to enjoy what almost all of us have come to enjoy too much this past decade, often to the exclusion of the rest of our lives.

With this model of measured phone use, we can continue to take advantage of the historically unparalleled opportunities our new toys avail without losing our values, our larger vision of what we want to accomplish, and ourselves along the way.

How does the Heart of Darkness pull this off? By enabling us to finally check our phones for incoming (electronic) mail with the same frequency we would desire to receive regular (paper) mail.

'Nuf said. Let's get to it.

The Heart of Darkness

In the book *Heart of Darkness* by Joseph Conrad, the protagonist, Charles Marlow, searches for a megalomaniacal ivory trader, Kurtz, in the Congolese jungle. Marlow travels along the Congo River from the outer station to the middle station to, finally, the inner station—the heart of darkness. There, in the middle of the dense forest, he encounters the eccentric ivory trader's personal fiefdom.

In smartphone parlance, you can consider the inner station to be the apps you find the most addictive—whether they are apps that enable you to find a date, see what your friends are doing, check the news, find the latest bargain, view the latest stock prices, or communicate with others via email or text.

Your phone probably has about nine screens (and it's possible to create more). You can move the most addictive apps (in my case, the text messaging, WhatsApp, Skype, BBC News, and Amazon apps; consider which apps are most addictive for you) to the final screens. You can place the less addictive apps, on the other hand, in the outer station or middle station (your home and middle screens, respectively, in progressive order of their addictiveness). Because you will have to swipe numerous times to reach your last screens, you will permit your higher-order values an opportunity to reassert themselves and stop you before you arrive.

Provided you first turn off all notifications on your phone, your final screen—which you will have to swipe seven or eight times to reach—becomes your inner station, the Heart of Darkness, the not-so-accessible den of your most alluring addictions, your go-to vices. The outer station is your home screen: what you see when you open your phone. It should not contain any apps that enable digital interaction with friends because, as has been well researched, it's the social functionality of smartphones that makes them so addictive.

I personally have been using the Heart of Darkness model for over two years. Most of the time, I check my text and WhatsApp messages at most once or twice per day when I venture to the final screen on my phone—the Heart of Darkness.

Every day, I actually say to myself, "At what time will I check all my texts and WhatsApp messages?" At some point in the afternoon or evening, I check them for five minutes and, especially at first, there aren't as many as I anticipated … that's the irony—you'll think, "Well, I'm checking forty times a day, must be that I'm receiving all these messages because I'm so in demand."

Spoiler alert: it's not true. I no longer receive that many text messages because I'm not replying to them quickly. As I learned the hard way, replying rapidly often snowballs into a texting avalanche of brief, barely decipherable replies that communicate next to nothing, like copulating bunnies who self-generate until all you can see in any direction is fur.

Enabling Presence

This new system has led to my being much more present with my children. Sometimes it hits me, a feeling of "Wow, here I am with my kids. I'm not distracted. We're spending the whole day together."

Why? Because there's nothing to do on my phone. First of all, it's in grayscale and is boring (see Chapter 14). Second, hardly anyone is calling me because no one calls anymore. Third, thanks to this strategy, I can't check text or any other (e.g., WhatsApp, Skype) messages until midday and then again at five or six.

This strategy works almost all the time. It just did this morning. I walked Alex to preschool and felt like checking my phone on the way home, no doubt due to some existential angst associated with being alone and just walking and thinking (remember from Chapter 2: addictions stem not from the need to seek pleasure, but from the need to soothe psychological distress). Happens sometimes. Couldn't check my phone, since I don't check messages until late afternoon.

Sure, I could have checked some other apps or the news, but

somewhere in my subconscious and sometimes conscious mind, the Heart of Darkness has etched the intended message, inescapable and clear as day: you don't check text messages until late in the afternoon because you have a deeper vision of not being distracted by your phone. So just walk. Enjoy the morning.

From Toy to Tool

On some afternoons around five, I'm with my children and want to check and I think, "Well, it's sunset now. It's beautiful and I'm with my kids. Why don't I wait until it's dark?" I don't want to be sitting there on my phone for a while checking messages during the sunset; neither do I want to cash in my chips just yet, considering that once I do check, that's it for the day.

In general, we subconsciously accept the idea that "Okay, well, I'll just check my text messages or email or whatever and it will just take a couple of minutes." However, when you become aware that you've been waiting all day to check your phone, you start to think, "Well, maybe it's going to take longer. So let me wait until the right time when I can really focus on it."

As a result, I'm no longer shamefully ignoring my kids with my head craned down (looking not at them, but at my phone) at the playground. Instead, after we return home and it's dark, I pick up my phone. The moment that was at first deflating has now become normal and emotionally vacant: there aren't that many messages. I send out a few replies; it takes a few minutes; I put down my phone. Done and done.

Being more relaxed, present, and upright rather than stressed, distracted, and hunched over my phone has also yielded untold benefits for my creativity. Exhibit A: this book.

You can also reap the creative benefits of heeding a warning from Stanford psychiatrist Anna Lembke: "What people don't realize with their smartphone usage [is] it can really deprive you of a kind of seamless flow of creative thought that generates from your own brain." With this new approach to moderating your phone use, you can strip your phone of the role it has usurped in your life—an irresistible toy— and relegate it to the role you (hopefully) intended for it in the first place: a useful tool.

The Reemergence of Our Humanity

Participants in the Heart of Darkness Challenge consistently report that once they limit the checking of their text messages and other addictive apps to a few times per day, they start making more phone calls and spending more time in person with the people they care about. Almost always, this shift in the medium of communication they use for connecting with others leads to a few closer and more meaningful relationships.

Given that, as we saw in Chapter 1, the average number of people we feel close to and can confide in has shrunk from three to two since the advent of social media sites such as Facebook, this is a huge increase that can have a tremendous impact on one's life.

According to Linda, a pharmacist from Bristol, England:

> This is the third week since I started this experiment. I am noticing that I am making more phone calls. It made me reflect on when the last time was that I called someone besides my immediate family (hubby and kids). I started thinking about my sister who lives in London. I really don't get to see her much because of work. So, I took a chance and called her this week. She usually doesn't pick up her phone, but this time she did. It was nice to have a quick chat, but most importantly I told her how much I love her and was very happy to hear her voice. It really made me feel so good inside. I made that connection. And I think she was also impacted by that simple phone call.

Paola, a surveyor from Milan, Italy, shares: "A relationship with one friend, Sofia, has been strengthened by swapping texts for phone calls. We try and get together once a week and rather than coordinating our meetups through text, we pick up the phone. Sometimes our conversations are brief, but sometimes we get the chance to catch up and be more open and honest about how we are feeling and how our weeks have been. I have been noticing this with my coworker, Giovanni, as well."

I'm also making more phone calls. Why? Because I still have that desire for connection. Why do you think I was checking my text messages forty times per day in the first place?! I wanted social connection. But what was I receiving? Social information. I wasn't finding what I was seeking. Looking for something you need (social connection) repeatedly—an average of 150 times per day, in fact—and not obtaining it is the sad and poignant state of most people in our society today, and the reason depression and anxiety are at all-time highs.

A Guideline, Not a Rule

"I appreciate what you're trying to do with this Heart of Darkness model," you may be thinking, "but checking my text messages once or twice per day would be impossible. That's the way my coworkers and friends communicate, and to reduce my responsiveness to such a low level would be personal and career suicide."

Your need to be responsive to others is no small matter. Reconciling this need with the ideal that I lay out in this book (which, again, will always be above the real) requires a return to the famous line from the (original 1984) movie *Ghostbusters*.

"I make it a rule never to get involved with possessed people," Bill Murray says to Sigourney Weaver.

Weaver closes the door and reopens it, this time wearing lingerie. She grabs him and writhes against him.

Murray continues, "Actually, it's more of a guideline than a rule."

The same is true for the Heart of Darkness model. It's important to not become a poster child for this model or any of the other reclaim-your-freedom strategies in this book. Like not sleeping with ghosts (which I don't recommend—it certainly didn't work out well for Murray's character in *Ghostbusters*), each strategy is a guideline, not a rule.

Making It Your Own

In your case, while perhaps you can try to check your phone an average of a few times per day, there may be some days when you check more often. Alternatively, maybe the average number of times you check your text messages and other apps is five times per day rather than fifty.

Whatever your unique situation, you can acknowledge your current state of text messaging and app checking and then set a goal—a finite threshold you will set out not to cross—and continually move toward that goal, which hopefully will be a lot less online time than your current text/app-checking habits yield.

The Heart of Darkness model—like all the other strategies in this book—needs to be personalized and customized by you. Don't become that poster child and then get down on yourself when you set your goal for four times per day and there are a few days when you check eight times. The important takeaway from this model is to move toward much less text/app messaging than before, enabling much richer and more meaningful (face-to-face and phone) interactions with the people you care about.

I promised to share a concrete tool with you to help you set in place a workable Digital Limiting Strategy and reduce your time on your phone and other devices. As it turns out, however, there is a chink in the armor. To be effective, this tool, the Heart of Darkness, requires an attachment, a patch if you will, to help it work its magic.

The Side Door

There are times when you may need to check for a text message from a specific person—to see if they are trying to reach you or cancel an appointment, for instance—and if you do, you'll surpass the goal you've set of checking only once or twice per day. Why? Because you'll see all the other text messages waiting for you and end up also checking them—not opening them, as research has found, would produce too much anxiety.

In such situations, you can create a "side door" into a text message—a way in to read it without seeing the others that may also be languishing in your inbox.

How can you pull this off? You can open the contact profile of the person you are expecting a message from: for example, if you have a meeting with someone and wish to see if they've sent you a message to let you know they're running late. In their contact profile, tap on the text message icon and it will take you to the texting history between you and them. If they've just sent a message, it will appear there, and you can then text them back if necessary.

Importantly, this doesn't count as one of your trips into the Heart of Darkness. It serves, therefore, as a way to check periodically for an important message from someone for logistical, social, or professional purposes.

Then—and this part is very important—tap "Clear All" or the bottom button that returns you to the home screen rather than returning to the text messaging app, which would take you to a screen showing you all of your other text messages and send you traipsing once again up Email or Text Mountain for the next half hour.

How can you do the same with email? You can set up your email account such that all incoming messages skip the inbox and go to "All Mail" (or the equivalent term your email provider uses). This way, every time you open your email (from anywhere—your laptop, phone, watch, or tablet), you will see only an empty inbox. You can check all of your messages once or twice (or the number of times you set) per day (in "All Mail") and put important messages into various files that you can label. This practice will give you more control over your email account. It only works because you have created a Side Door to search for a specific message at any time without seeing all of the other messages waiting to propel you back up the mountain.

Freedom Is Not Free

Parents desiring to keep frequent tabs on their children have found the Side Door model their only way to avoid being glued to their phones all day, anxiously awaiting news from their kids. "The Side Door helped me when it came to reading simple messages from my daughter, since she is a teenager and plays sports and I need to know when she gets home," Samantha, a bank manager from the Philippines, told me.

In my case, I have Gmail on my phone, and I don't receive notifications or check it because, as I mentioned earlier, I only do that once per day on weekdays (usually late morning) on my laptop. Yet I will open Gmail on my phone to send a message or just to check for a message from a specific person, again by using the Side Door model: I search for their last name rather than clicking on "All Mail," and, as a result, I don't see any other messages.

In effect, I'm recognizing that email, texting, WhatsApp, and instant messaging on Skype, Facebook, or any other app are all the same: forms of electronic communication that circumvent richer means of communication, either in person or by phone.

This admittedly anal process—the Side Door—is important for self-regulation. It enables you to feel in control and experience balance in your life. Whether in your email or texting account, the Side Door is like a shopping incursion—go in, get what you need, get the hell out. Stroll past the impulse buys (the awaiting messages) without even a glance.

Give this strategy a try and you will be amusingly astonished to find yourself feeling light, spacious, and ultimately free as you experience what it's like to be in control of your little portable digital tool rather than vice versa.

"I just can't be too restrictive in how I use my phone," you might be thinking. "These strategies go against the grain of the freedom with which I wish to live my life." Your freedom is paramount—I agree. Why adopt a strategy that would limit it? The Heart of Darkness and Side Door models will certainly take away a lot of the short-term fun of using your phone. Doesn't sound like a very good idea, does it?

Unless you ask yourself this question: "Am I truly free if I am unable to walk outside or eat a meal or hang out with a good friend without looking down at an electronic slab that has been found to induce stress, envy, and a lonely existence?"

Can you see the irony in wishing to feel free to use your phone whenever you want, yet when you do, no longer being free to develop meaningful relationships with yourself or others? Why? Because you have ceded your freedom to a few technology companies that have you firmly under their control, mired in an ineffective, media-poor mode of social interaction while they profit from your pain.

Consider the benefits to your life your phone could provide if you were to gain control of how you use it instead of permitting it to continue its reign over you. What would be possible if you were truly free again? How would you experience this thing called life?

Let's consider how you might answer this question in the next and final chapter.

18

Contain Your Phone, Expand Your Life

*T*hese arguments aside, does the Heart of Darkness model described in the last chapter seem way too limiting? Consider the alternative to the admittedly self-constraining model of the last chapter: if you check your phone often, or hear or see buzzes, rings, or messages popping up on it all the time through push notifications, you end up so distracted that you can't focus on anything substantial for any extended period of time.

The cognitive psychologist Daniel Willingham notes, "One of the most stubborn, persistent [aspects] of the mind is that when you do two things at once, you don't do either one as well as when you do them one at a time." It is for this reason that multitasking has been found to be a poor use of time.

In fact, research has uncovered that attempting to do two tasks at once takes longer than performing them one at a time, burns more cognitive energy, and hence wears down the brain more—which causes more stress and produces more mistakes.

Perhaps for this reason, a study conducted by the late Stanford communication professor Clifford Nass and his colleagues found that adult media multitaskers exposed to multiple streams of electronic information simultaneously do not remember facts or solve problems very well. Why? They become unable to prevent irrelevant information from surfacing in their minds.

In other words, they become so highly distracted that they cannot concentrate effectively on what's most important, leading "to the surprising result that heavy media multitaskers performed worse on a test of task-switching ability."

Let Freedom Reign

Participants in the Heart of Darkness Challenge consistently shared their newfound feelings of freedom as they became less tethered to their phones. "Not having to look at my phone the moment I am alone is a really liberating feeling," wrote Earl, a museum director from Cincinnati. "I really like the way I feel being less attached to my screen. I find that it is making me more engaged in conversations with friends. It prevents me from wasting hours on mindless content, only to feel guilty for wasted time."

The Heart of Darkness and Side Door strategies are self-regulatory tools we can use to prevent ourselves from perpetually—in my case, it used to be about forty to fifty times per day, every day—seeking social connection but only obtaining social information. These strategies can help us prioritize face-to-face and phone over digital interactions and then walk our talk. Why? Because we have a shield to fight off the brogrammers' rapid fire.

For myself and so many of my conference participants who have used the Heart of Darkness strategy to reduce phone use, the reason it works is because within days, you begin to experience the amazing, liberating feeling of being less dependent on your phone. Changing your attitude or values in relation to your phone—which the rest of *Screened In* encourages you to do—is an important first step. Yet as the Princeton theology students demonstrated, attitude change is not enough to prevent you from acting in ways you'll later regret (i.e., engaging in an addiction).

The way to kick any addiction is not just to change your values or attitude about the external object capturing your attention (in this case, your phone)—so many smokers, for example, *know* it's not good for them but just can't stop—but to actually *experience the benefits* of new behaviors aligned with those values.

Why? Because as the Canadian neuropsychologist and associative learning expert Donald Hebb once remarked, neurons that fire together wire together. New behaviors create new synaptic linkages between nerve cells: in this case, positive feelings associated with highly regulated phone use. Without these new feelings of freedom from your digital devices, you may find it difficult to reduce their use.

"These strategies sound great," you may be saying to yourself, "but I'm not ready to take the popularity plunge of removing myself from the most utilized means of communication among my friends and peers." Yes, disconnection from others would not be a good idea. These social pressures are very real, and there is definitely risk involved. Let's consider how this bold act may affect your social life.

Not as Popular as You Think

A civil engineer from Colombo, Sri Lanka, who tried out the Heart of Darkness model after coming to one of my conferences, Chamath was surprised that the pace of communication slowed down once he started checking his phone only twice per day. "I'm not as in demand as I thought I was," Chamath shared. "I realize how little people care if I take ten to twelve hours to get back to them."

The Heart of Darkness model is humbling. Before you use it, you think you're so sought after, with so many people texting and emailing you. Once you try this model, however, you quickly realize that so few people actually call you.

We're not as important as we think we are. It's really sobering—a wake-up call to our true popularity.

A study of Facebook found that although the average person has about 150 "friends," they only actually communicate in a given month with a few; many Facebook users only communicate with one or two.

Henry, a software engineer who attended one of my leadership conferences in Washington, DC, shares: "Since I started checking text messages only twice per day, I've discovered that most of those messages were from my wife. She would send me these quick messages such as 'Hey, can we meet you at three at the park with the kids?', 'Can you pick up the kids at eleven?', or 'I was thinking of buying this coffee table on Amazon. What do you think?' When I told her about my new twice-daily text regimen, she said, 'Okay. Well, I guess I'll just call you instead of sending you text messages.' That's already reduced my text traffic by about sixty percent."

Since most of us communicate regularly with only a few people, we can just tell them about our new Digital Limiting Strategy. If you are having lunch with a friend or colleague, you can say, "Oh by the way, I don't receive notifications on my phone and only check text messages about once per day, so if you need to reach me urgently, please just call me." The more you tell others about your limited text-checking protocol, the less you will need to check for text messages before a meeting or social engagement because they'll know you've relinquished the electronic leash.

In the end, our phones, laptops, and tablets are only tools. If we use them in the right ways, they can add a lot of value to our lives. If we do the opposite, they remove value from how we experience life. Our digital devices are like fire, a hammer, or a car—tools that can produce either positive or negative consequences for us depending on how we use them.

Make It Happen:

1) Turn off all notifications on your phone and, if you are willing to take a bold, courageous step to severely reduce the allure of your phone, set it to grayscale (see Chapter 14 for why and how to perform this sacrilegious, countercultural transgression against Big Tech).

2) Rate your apps in terms of how addictive they are. Which are the few apps you are always checking? Write down their names.

3) Acknowledge how many times per day you are checking your text messages and other addictive apps (which may include email, WhatsApp, Snapchat, Bumble, Amazon, CNN or BBC, Zillow, or Facebook).

4) Envision what your life would be like if you were to check these apps much less often. Write a few sentences describing how your life would be different and how it would feel, including how often you would like to check each app if you were controlling your use of technology rather than technology (meaning the brogrammers who design it) controlling its use of you.

5) Write down the maximum number of times you will check these apps daily.

6) Move your text messaging and other addictive apps to the inner station, the final screen on your smartphone, the furthest screen from your home screen that you have to swipe to the highest number of times, the Heart of Darkness—the heart of your addiction.

7) Check in with yourself daily about how you are doing in terms of only treading into the Heart of Darkness and checking those apps with the frequency you specified in Step 5. (Please feel free to check for individual text or email messages once in a while using the Side Door, but don't abuse this option.) Make a concerted effort to travel into and check the apps within the Heart of Darkness for messages quickly—usually for no more than a few minutes. Note the times of the day when you will use your limited access to your texting and other addictive final-screen apps.

8) Note how you feel, and how your experience of life is changing (as I and a number of my conference participants have done in the preceding pages) now that you travel into the Heart of Darkness much less frequently. Don't get down on yourself if you exceed your desired frequency on any particular day. That would reduce your self-esteem and be counterproductive. Instead, be honest with yourself about the basic human needs that induce you to open any particular app more than you would like. Then recommit to your goal of only checking that app the next day up to the maximum you

identified in Step 5. (Alternatively, if you feel that your goal was too draconian, be more realistic and allow yourself to enter the Heart of Darkness one or a few more times daily. Create a goal that is "ambitious yet attainable.")

9) Periodically recalibrate. Every week or two, return to Step 1 and make updates if necessary.

Facing Our Inner Demons

It was New Year's Day, 2018. Out of habit, each day when I'm not working I spend some time after waking up with our daughter, Chloe, who was one year old at the time and was playing house, so I taught her how to put together a little table for her dollhouse and then take it apart. Once my wife woke up, I returned to our bedroom and picked up my phone.

Subconsciously, I wanted it to entertain me somehow. I wanted to know there was more to the coming year than watching my kids play with toys. I wanted some kind of stimulus. But there was none because my text messages, WhatsApp, and Skype instant messages were all seven or eight screens away, as per the Heart of Darkness model, and I knew I wouldn't look at them until late afternoon.

Consequently, there was nothing to do on my phone, which was causing me some serious existential angst. I put it down. It had taken me a few years to reach the point where I could actually do that.

The poignant stories from conference participants who rose to the Heart of Darkness Challenge and wrestled with the anxiety produced by their phones helped me realize I'm not alone and increased my motivation to write this book. Florin, a media entrepreneur who attended one of my conferences in Bucharest, Romania, wrote in his first week:

I am not doing too good. I feel bored while on break at work. I started trying to remember what I used to do before I even owned a phone and did not have anything at all. I honestly could not remember and then it dawned on me. I used to smoke before, that is what I looked forward to on my breaks at work or simply just killing time throughout the day. I am feeling uncomfortable with myself. As what I hate to admit the most is now coming to light: I have major addictive behaviors.

Struggling with a tough week, Chris, a mechanical engineer in San Jose, California, wrote in his fifth week: "Yesterday was a huge day-long cheat-fest. I lost control … I was bored, but kept scrolling through Facebook looking for something interesting. It was almost like it felt as if I couldn't put the phone and social media down until I came across something worthwhile. Well that never happened."

Like Florin, Chris, and many others who have been courageous enough to share their challenging experiences with moderating their phone use to a few times per day, the feeling I sometimes have since using the Heart of Darkness model is also similar to withdrawal. Quite simply, it's a craving to check my phone.

With this new system, however, there's nothing to check. You would have to embark on the shameful voyage to your last screen, which requires enough conscious decisions (each swipe) that you are likely to catch yourself in time, and before you take one of these actions, your deeper values are likely to assert themselves and impel you to do what the Princeton theology students couldn't—stop.

You are more likely to wait because you only intend to go into the Heart of Darkness twice daily. At just about any given moment, you are likely to prefer to leave time for more messages to come in than to play your hand early. If you can pull this off, your phone will become dull. Mundane. Deadweight in your pocket.

Less Becomes More

Could you make such a commitment? What would your life be like if you were to only check your phone for any kind of textual message or entertaining video once or twice per day? Would you feel bored at first? What would you do with all of the resulting free time? This level of liberation from your phone may intimidate and scare you, as it did me. "I'll lose my productivity and connection with others," you may be thinking.

Yes, it is true that this adjustment may result in a short-term loss of productivity and a less than enthusiastic reaction from the people in your life who keep you in their text-but-don't-call/Communication Reciprocation Downgrade social roster. Yet it's also likely to be true that all of the time that becomes available once you are no longer spending so many of your limited moments on this earth checking your phone will enable you to develop more meaningful connections with yourself and the people around you. Such a sea change in your daily phone etiquette will likely generate a tremendous shift in both your long-term productivity and your well-being.

Make a pact with yourself to only stop in once or twice per day at the Heart of Darkness—the place where you send and receive social information rather than experience social connection. In so doing, you will reduce the darkness in your life that comes from subscribing to our current societal norms: loneliness, low self-esteem, and vitriolic anger at distorted virtual apparitions of the people around you.

Instead, you will begin to fill your life with the light that only shines from within human beings connecting with themselves and others in real time. You will also experience a freedom unparalleled in today's digitally influenced society: a freedom mediated by the genuine, real-life connection you continually build and rebuild with yourself and the people you most care about.

The Reemergence of the Phone

Charlotte, a veterinarian in Nelson, New Zealand, documented how she began her transition from primarily communicating with others through her phone to more in-person interactions. In week two of her Heart of Darkness Journal, she shared: "I am realizing how often I wake up with the immediate urge to look at my phone. I started plugging in my phone across my bedroom to limit my late-night/early-morning browsing. I wake up feeling like I am missing a limb!"

Then in week four: "I have reduced my texting down to two times per week (down from three). This change was surprisingly easy. I have tried to make it a rule to not even look at my phone until 10 a.m. This made me realize that there is literally nothing that happens between when I go to bed and when I wake up that requires immediate attention."

And then in week six: "I have decided to try and open up my social circle ... This feeling of need for more healthy relationships is directly related to my decrease in screen time. When I am not doing work, I realize how much empty time I used to fill with browsing my phone ... I have to start thinking of ways I can connect with other people without the reliance on technology."

My own situation was similar. It wasn't until I started using the Heart of Darkness model—where, once again, I check electronic messages from texts, emails, or any source whatsoever only once or twice per day—that I realized that in many previous instances, a friend or family member would call me and I wouldn't answer the phone because I was so caught up in texting.

One thought would pop into my mind after seeing their name flash on my screen as the phone rang: "I don't have time to have an extended conversation with this person right now. I'll call them back later." I often felt like I didn't have the bandwidth to receive their call right in that moment because I was attending to a queue of electronic messages and experiencing the dopamine rush of the slow, steady climb up Email and SMS Mountain in search of the impossible: the empty inbox.

While at times I just didn't feel like talking right then, texting stimulated the feeling of wanting to order and control the uncertainty associated with speaking with people. It was also just easier to hide my emotions behind texting.

Even worse, when I eventually called people back, many of them didn't answer; they were also calibrating their phone communication to make time to reply to all their texts and electronic messages and continue their dopamine-addled e-mountain ascent.

Since I started checking text messages and so forth only once or twice a day, I've noticed that I'm answering the phone and talking to people more. The reason? Simple. Once you start using the Heart of Darkness model, there really is not much else to anticipate from your phone than a phone call. If you are like me, since you only allow yourself five to ten minutes per day to check texting and communication apps, you will become more enthusiastic about answering the phone when it rings.

I'm sure my friends and family members are sensing my renewed enthusiasm in our phone conversations. I've also noticed that because I don't check text messages more than once or twice per day, some people call me anyway when they don't receive a reply to a text they've sent. So my phone is just naturally turning into more of a … phone. It really has come full circle.

It's been over two years now, and my foray into the Heart of Darkness is instilling a deep appreciation for the rare, infrequently sighted members of the phone-answering tribe, who are becoming my close friends. Perhaps nothing has changed: I value potential friends not only for how much I like them, but also for whether they reciprocate my social overtures. Without a Communication Reciprocation Downgrade, that is.

Valuing Your Social Gold

Returning a text takes a few seconds and is a meager reciprocal social act; returning a call is a more significant investment in the relationship. Over time, the people who return and initiate calls, and collaborate to parlay those calls into in-person meetings, become the friends we need in the digital age.

These people become our most coveted social resource, our social gold. The only ones who enables us to revitalize our social life. The only people standing between us and the formidable, ever-encircling tentacles of loneliness.

Practice this strategy of isolating your most addictive apps on your phone and committing to checking them at most a few times daily and you will find yourself feeling relaxed rather than stressed, and focused rather than distracted as you enjoy the many hours that are freed up once you are no longer nervously checking your phone throughout the day.

When you relegate the apps you check frequently to Smartphone Siberia—the most distant screen from your home screen, the Heart of Darkness—you make a bold statement about your life priorities and your determination to start living them again.

The other day, I was walking outside and experienced a moment in which I felt so appreciative of my phone and laptop and the convenience they offer me. Thanks to the Heart of Darkness and Side Door strategies, I now embrace my devices as useful tools. Why? Their net effect is now positive: they add value to my life. It took years of figuring out how to manage their use to arrive at this point.

I am proud to say that I no longer feel at the whim of any candy-colored app or website. I choose how and when to use the Internet and access the vast treasures it contains. That treasure hunt now rarely obstructs my experience of life.

Why? Because I've recognized it's a treasure hunt with no finish line, and the only way to join the feeding frenzy of treasure hunters without losing your soul is to limit your engagement: to design and then adhere to hard and fast principles guiding your participation. In this new era of unprecedented access and choices, it's imperative that these principles—whatever they may be for you—immobilize the distractions that will cause you to lose your way if you are unable to contain them.

Give this strategy a try. With this shield against the best efforts of

Silicon Valley's finest in place, you can expect to see an increase in the meaningfulness and connectedness of your relationship with yourself and others and a decrease in your feelings of loneliness. You will be pleasantly surprised by how this simple shift in how you choreograph your smartphone apps—along with your steadfast commitment to only make that treacherous journey by swipe into the Heart of Darkness a few times per day—will enable you to regain control of your life.

Make It Happen: The Heart of Darkness Challenge

Create a Heart of Darkness Journal: Write at least twice per week for the next seven weeks in your journal about how you are experiencing this change in how you use your phone. Use these questions as a (loose) guide to help you write about your experience (e.g., creatively free-flow write rather than answering these questions one after the other; like sleeping with ghosts, let the questions be a guideline, not a rule):

1) How does this practice feel for me?

2) Am I experiencing any changes in my life as a consequence of this practice?

3) Am I experiencing any changes (from when I first started) in terms of how I feel about this practice?

4) How (if at all) are my relationships changing as a result of this practice?

5) What (if anything) is this experience changing about how I view my phone and its role in my life?

6) After you complete the Heart of Darkness Challenge, go to Appendix A and read a few sample Heart of Darkness Challenge Journals. Compare your own Heart of Darkness Challenge Journal to those in Appendix A and ask yourself what you have learned from this self-imposed social experiment. What will you do differently going forward based on what you've learned?

COMMENCEMENT

One of the major themes of this book is that our smartphones and other devices impair our self-regulation, which in turn impairs our relationships. While I emphasize the effects on children and youth, the connection between devices and self-regulation creates a vicious spiral based on a four-step process that affects not just young people, but all of us.

How does this process work? First, as we have seen from various angles throughout this book, each supported by numerous studies, our digital devices promise social connection, yet only yield social information. Second, the displacement effect (more time online equates to less in-person time with others) impairs our self-regulation, which in turn (third) diminishes our future connections with ourselves and others. So then what do we do? Recall that addictions stem primarily not from the search for pleasure but from the search for relief from psychological distress. So finally, we turn even more frequently to our devices to ease the pain, and they only end up compounding it.

While the rest of the book will hopefully help you change your values or attitudes about your phone and other devices, the final strategy in *Screened In,* the Heart of Darkness, is critical for sustaining long-term change in the habits you actually adopt. Why? Because when it comes to preventing behaviors that are inconsistent with your values (i.e., addictions), attitude change alone has been found to be insufficient.

The Heart of Darkness and other strategies I've laid out in this book, especially in Part Three, will enable you to actually *experience the benefits* of new behaviors—new neuronic associations—aligned with those values. Without these new feelings of liberation from your devices, you may find it difficult to reduce their use.

In the end, this book has been about how to reduce Internet-accelerated addictions. There is hope: thanks to social activism, many addictions have been reduced over time. The percentage of

Americans who smoke, for example, had dropped to 21 percent, half of what it was forty years ago. A similar decline has been reported in Canada.

A similar pattern has emerged with alcohol. According to UCLA's Higher Education Research Institute, the number of college freshman who claim abstinence from beer has also changed dramatically—from 25 percent in 1981 to 41 percent in 2007.

This book follows in the footsteps of the hard work of so many featured in these pages to reduce our dependence on a digitally mediated external object to fill a gap inside of ourselves—in other words, addictions. These people have been working day in and day out to help us understand the bait-and-switch of the Internet: that we go online seeking social connection and leave with only social information.

I have had the privilege of working with and/or interviewing some of the people in the preceding pages who have joined this burgeoning global movement to help us understand how our phones and devices have accelerated the natural human tendency to overattach to something outside of ourselves (such as approval, porn, drugs, nicotine, or shopping). I am encouraged by their dedication and progress in stemming the influence of the brogrammers before it's too late.

I hope you too will join this movement, beginning by developing new habits that enable you to reclaim your essential humanness. Collectively, our humanity lies in the balance.

I leave you to apply what you have learned in this book in your own life with the deep, heartfelt wish that you will discover the key to the digitally-3D-printed shackles that have ossified around your ankles, and, ultimately, your own path to achieve freedom from the technology that has ensnared us all. I would like to end with the powerful call to action by the rabbinic sage Hillel the Elder that has been adopted by many social activists:

If not you, who? If not now, when?

Appendix A

Contents

William, Forty-Three, Software Engineer, Houston, Texas

Week One

I must admit the Heart of Darkness Challenge has me a little nervous and I am hoping that I can follow through until the end. The reason why I am nervous is because I rely on my phone quite a bit throughout each day. I would say that I use my phone about 75 percent for work-related activity, 20 percent for social media, and 5 percent to speak via phone. Not checking my phone every five minutes for work is what has me most worried. However, I do recognize the value in this challenge because it seems like I have a habit of checking my phone every few minutes. I am hoping that these seven weeks will help me reflect and gain greater insight into my patterns of communication and, more importantly, help me reconnect with others in my circle on a more intimate level.

My first week was a little rough at first. It took me a second to get used to the gray screen. My initial reaction was that the phone was bland and boring. Because I am partially color blind, it was also kind of hard on my eyes. Regardless of this, I noticed that I was still checking my phone frequently with a bit of fear that I would miss an important email or text. While I don't check the phone quite as much as the first two to three days of the assignment, I must admit that I am still checking it at least once an hour. I am hoping I can do better next week.

I told my wife about this challenge and that I was not going to participate due to all the other items currently on my plate. However, after thinking about it a bit more I decided to give it a try. I am hoping that this exercise will also help in my personal life, as most of my family members spend a considerable amount of time on our phones. If I can make a change in my life, maybe it will spread to other members of my family ... fingers crossed.

Week Two

This week I noticed that it was a little easier to not check my phone so often. I am down to maybe every three or four hours before I pick it up. This is a big step, as I would normally check the phone minimally once per hour. This exercise has already helped me understand the hold that my phone had over me. Being inundated with a large number of email responses was a big fear of mine going into this study. However, I have noticed that many of the emails that I receive are not urgent and I am still able to go through my inbox quite quickly. This has freed up a lot of my time.

I have grown used to the screen being grayed out now. The screen is bland and boring, which is not very appealing. This is a huge factor, I feel, in not wanting to check my phone. I have also noticed that I am using the phone more for video conferencing with my daughter, who just had a baby. Seeing her and the baby via video has been awesome, as normally I would just text and/or wait weeks before I would see them in person. I feel this has been helpful to my overall energy and feelings of being connected. Looking forward to next week!

Week Three

At this stage of this exercise I find myself not even wanting to look at my phone. The gray screen is extremely frustrating to look at and is unappealing. I have also noticed that over the past week my urge to check the phone has decreased. Although I do have to admit that I am still checking the phone more than the maximum two times per day. I will continue to work on this next week. Having to use the back route to respond to text messages has definitely helped reduce my desire to use the phone. On a positive note, I had lunch with three different people this week. Up until now, I had not noticed that I normally eat lunch alone in my office. I think folks were a bit surprised when I accepted the invites, and one person even more surprised when I reached out to invite. Getting out of my shell was good and it felt nice to get to know my coworkers on a more personal level. I also found that the in-person interaction was much more engaging than social media and texting. I found myself laughing more, which felt good. Looking forward to another week!

Week Four

I have good news to report this week. I can say that I have officially experienced a noticeable decrease in my phone usage. I still say the graying out of the phone has been one of the primary drivers. I tried to show my wife a picture the other day, and even she said she no longer wanted to see my phone because the phone screen was gray and "ugly." This week I also spent a lot more time reflecting and trying to understand why I have invested so much time and energy in my phone over the years. I realized that I cannot pinpoint a specific event or date that I became hooked on the phone. However, I believe the change occurred when phones switched from flip mode to smartphones with apps and games. Social media apps like Facebook (FB) also acted as a sort of quicksand where before I knew it, I was already in up to my neck. At first, I saw FB as an amazing tool to reconnect with old friends and to make new ones. As part of this week's journal entry I went onto my FB account and just realized I have 338 "friends." I was blown away, as I had not realized the number of contacts had reached so high. What is even more fascinating is that, aside from liking posts, I probably only really communicate with four to five on a regular (daily/weekly) basis. The Heart of Darkness Challenge has definitely opened my eyes and made me realize how few friends I really have. It's a little depressing when I think about it in that light.

Week Five

This week flew by with a flash. Not much to report on, as I don't feel I stuck to the challenge guidelines of only checking my phone two times a day. Following the Heart of Darkness framework was challenging because this past week was extremely busy with celebrations for work, as well as school award ceremonies for my own family. As a result, I spent a considerable amount of time on FB going through the threads to view and acknowledge the achievements of those in my circle. While I did make several visits and phone calls to wish folks well, most of the communication was through posts on FB. One interesting observation was I found myself repeatedly checking for comments and "likes" for posts that I placed on social media regarding my two sons' academic achievements. This got me thinking and asking myself why? I struggled with this question, as I have often told my kids not to worry about what others think as they make their way through life … yet here I was in the shadows of social media looking to see who took the time to acknowledge their accomplishments.

Week Six

I found that I had an easier time this week in checking my phone. While I would like to say that the decrease in phone usage was due to the impact of participating in the Heart of Darkness Challenge, I believe that workload played a larger role. This equated to a greater amount of my time being spent on reading and writing, resulting in less opportunities for me to check my phone. On a positive note, when I did have an opportunity for free time, I found myself unplugging and hanging out with my family at home. The time away from digital devices was welcomed and much needed, as my human battery is on low.

Week Seven

This was the last week of the Heart of Darkness Challenge. I am happy that this exercise helped me to reflect and acknowledge just how much time I was wasting on social media. I can also attest that while I thought I was using social media to "connect" with folks, in reality it was often unidirectional forms of communication, with an occasional "thumbs up" to show either I or someone else had enjoyed what had been posted. The Heart of Darkness Challenge also helped me to increase other forms of communication. For example, I used the actual phone feature on my mobile device at a much higher rate. I also found myself having many more face-to-face interactions. I was never able to reduce the number of times I checked my phone down to two times per day; however, I did notice that my usage and desire to check every few minutes went way down. I still believe that the graying out of the phone had a large part in this change, as my screen literally became so unappealing that I didn't want to use the device any longer. Overall, it was a cool experiment … it will be interesting to see if there is sustained change … or if I will fall back into my old patterns of behavior.

Seven Months Later . . .

Two months ago I was asked to write a few thoughts about how my relationship with my phone has evolved after the conclusion of my participation in the Heart of Darkness Challenge. At first, I was excited about the opportunity. My ego jumped into high gear with the thought of Dr. Silard wanting to know how the experience might have impacted my life.

Once I sat down to write, the initial energy quickly diminished as I realize that I had nothing positive to report. In fact, I had reverted back to my old ways. I stared at my phone with Facebook and other social media apps centrally repositioned on my home screen. I began to realize that I was once again checking my phone every few minutes to see what's happening. Had anyone in my circle taken the time to "like" any of my recent or past posts? That yearning of feeling recognized and acknowledged was like a drug calling to me.

That night I decided to disable my Facebook and other social media accounts. I also completely deleted the associated apps from my phone. I only told my wife and two adult daughters what I had done and my rationale. I recall my daughter and wife placing wagers on how long I would last … one week, maybe a month at the most. Hearing that conversation hurt, yet it also inspired me to go all in.

The first few hours after I deleted the apps I contemplated re-downloading them, afraid that I would miss something. The next few days were tough, but I soon realized that I was in a much better mood, more productive and inquisitive about what was going on around me "in real life." I began to engage more purposefully with my family and friends and saw that we were talking in more depth during our interactions. I was back to feeling free.

Call it human nature or a moment of weakness, but I was curious to see if I had missed anything after being away from Facebook after two months. Surely someone in my circle had reached out to me during that time. I reinstalled Facebook to satisfy my curiosity. I quickly realized the only posts to my page during my absence were from advertising agencies. Crushed, yet resolved, I realized that I really don't need social media to stay connected to those I care about.

Later that week, as if the universe was listening, I received an instant message from my niece. She reached out just to reminisce about a time I drove out to San Diego to take her and my nephew out to lunch. She thanked me for being a part of her life and for the little acts of purposeful interactions throughout the years. It was at that moment that I recognized that we are all seeking the same feeling of acceptance and connection. I also realized that these connections don't occur through digital engagement, but through our willingness to sacrifice our time to be with one another "in real life."

Krystle, Thirty, Systems Analyst, Menlo Park, California

This is my new home screen on the left. On the right is the screen that I must swipe twice to get to all the other apps that are "off limits."

Week One

Check-in 1, Tuesday

This week I have already failed in my attempt at only checking my phone four times a day. I am trying not to check my emails in meetings, be present for them. I think this is how I can get closer to my goal of four checks per day. Little improvements. Being present for my meetings is critical because I am typically the one who is driving action items from different constituents. This means my teams will only deliver on action items if I am organized in assigning the items to them.

Check-in 2, Saturday

It is Saturday afternoon and I spent the day working. We had our payroll manager unexpectedly retire at the beginning of January and I have taken on a majority of her leadership role with the team. I am exhausted. My eyes hurt from overexposure to my laptop and my mobile device. It feels like there is not enough time in the day. I will attempt to give Sunday fully to this challenge. I was also on my phone periodically throughout the day to talk to someone I am dating. We haven't had an in-person date/meeting yet so most of our relationship is over text. I met him through mutual friends, so we are trying to move things slowly and get to know each other. "Getting to know each other slowly" today means texting for hours on end. About every ten minutes I was texting back and forth with him. Between my personal life and work life I exceeded my three checks for a weekend and possibly even exceeded my normal of twenty checks before I took on this challenge!

Week Two

Check-in 1, Wednesday

Going back to Sunday earlier this week, I was able to commit to the three times per day check. Quick check in the a.m. and a short check in the afternoon. I was busy most of the day running errands that I was not able to do because I was so busy during the week, which I think helped keep me off my phone and distracted with activities. I am a runner who is always preparing for my next marathon, so part of my training plan includes about two to three short runs of about three to five miles during the week and one long-distance run on the weekends. I like to run outside because it makes it a little more difficult for me to check my phone. Being outside lends a sense of stress relief as well since running just a mile away from my house allows for the remaining eight miles of my run to be on mountain trails. This part of my weekend is critical and seems to be in line with the Heart of Darkness Challenge. I did however spend hours talking to the guy I am dating from 6 p.m. to about midnight as I did housework, laundry, cleaning, etc. But this was part of my challenge that I could do this. Maybe I need to put a limit on the end of night talking. Six hours in hindsight seems a little excessive 0_0.

This week is also fairly heavy with work. I am finding that my new rule of just not checking my phone during meetings is helping me feel more focused and get more work done. Since I am paying closer attention in meetings, I am able to better plan out my action items for the team that is in the room with me. Usually I am distracted with the needs of other team members who are attempting to reach me through my phone. I think I am now showing a new level of respect for the people I am meeting with in person that I was not giving them before. I think this is helping the relationship with my immediate team members. This idea of not checking my phone is stressful for me. I keep thinking what am I missing by not checking. However, I am finding that once I check my phone after the meeting the only messages I missed were not urgent.

This check-in reminds me of a quote I once heard: You teach people how to treat you. By me checking my phone all the time and responding quickly, I am teaching people in my life what they can expect of me and I need to basically reteach people in my life that I am not as reactive as they have been led to believe.

I was also asked to apply to a new position. It would be a promotion for me but a big change in work responsibilities. I would no longer work in Human Resources. I would be a project manager in the Information Technology Services division working on company-wide system implementations. I spent some time applying to the position and am a little nervous to interview with people I work with daily. I have changed jobs every single year since college so I would be happy to remain in my current position if possible but can't pass on an opportunity that is being offered to me ... This is making me feel like I have to be perfect over the next two months because I am being watched to take on a higher-level leadership role so my sense of needing to be perfect is extremely high at work. I feel this is making me anxious and making it so I want to calm my mind by sorting through my Facebook or NPR news feed, but I know I can't. I am realizing how much I rely on random app surfing to alleviate feelings of anxiety this week.

Check-in 2, Saturday

Throughout the week, I have been talking to the person I have been dating every night for about four hours after 6 p.m. until I fall asleep around midnight. For me this challenge has shifted the primary use of my mobile device to personal. Before my mobile device was all about work, even my text messages were work related. Having this distinction of personal messages and work messages is helpful for my mind to separate the two. We are planning on meeting in person for a date tomorrow (Sunday) so depending on how this goes it may impact my last check of the night utilization, maybe?

I still find myself checking my phone about fifteen times a day at work during the week. This is less than my forty times per week before so there is progress, but nowhere near my goal of only four checks.

Week Three

Check-in 1, Thursday

I am feeling extremely anxious at work for two reasons: (1) I am being considered for the new job so I need to be perfect, and (2) I have my system that implemented in January still needing further configurations, and two new systems going live in about two months that still require a lot of attention. This anxiety I usually deal with by sitting down at the end of my day and scrolling through news feeds and social media to calm my thoughts and mind. It helps my mind dwell on other things. However, I am finding that the scrolling through social media just makes me feel less confident in myself. Seeing my friends' success on social media makes me feel like I will never be as good as them, why am I even thinking I can do this new job? I think it is called imposter syndrome. The scrolling that I thought was helping my anxiety seems to be making it worse, creating a lot of self-doubt in me when I need to be feeling my most confident. Social media preys on your insecurities, only amplifying them.

Check-in 2, Saturday

I am planning on a third date tomorrow, Sunday, with the person I have been dating. If anything, the two previous dates we had last week went so well that I think we are texting more throughout the day than we were before. He is also a serious professional with a high-stress job like mine, so we weren't texting during the day, but now we send a few back and forth. I have responded a few times to his personal messages during one of my afternoon work-only checks I had told myself I would do. I feel like the fact that I only have these designated times to talk to him actually makes the conversations have more substance. He knows about my challenge and that it is almost like we have scheduled time to talk. Usually when dating, anytime is fair game for texting. It is like we have a texting date. I actually think we both like this idea.

Week Four

Check-in 1, Wednesday

This weekend is Valentine's Day. I am attempting to take Friday off from work since I haven't had a day off in four months. I would like to be out of town for this holiday. Long story short I broke up with my boyfriend of nine years, one year ago. While it was my choice, it is still something that I struggle with. My ex-boyfriend has made it a point to "visit" me at work last month to go to lunch unexpectedly. He also sent me flowers to my place of work. He has been making himself present back in my life and I'm worried he will show up over the weekend, so I don't want to be in town. I feel that I followed the rules of Heart of Darkness a little closer this week because I didn't want to see text messages from my ex-boyfriend and I didn't want to be stressed out while I was at work. If I really wanted to see my outlook/emails, I travel from meeting to meeting with my laptop and that need can be met. I was able to only check my phone five times on Tuesday so yay!

Check-in 2, Saturday

I was unable to take off Friday, so instead of traveling somewhere I have just made plans for the whole weekend that will keep me out of my house and busy. If anything, I was under my daily checks today but we will see how tomorrow goes.

Week Five

Check-in 1, Monday

This week I have been unexpectedly asked to attend a conference for three days to present on one of my system implementations. I have been on the phone rescheduling meetings, making travel plans, preparing my presentation, all while supporting payroll and just my regular job. I am feeling extremely stressed and unprepared for my week and it is not a good feeling. I have my interview next week for my new job and I haven't even started preparing. I find my phone to be more of a stressful thing than an anxiety relief nowadays. If anything, I don't want to check it because my work life is so stressful, I don't want to see who needs what from me. The relationship with the person I am dating is progressing and he is moving the relationship forward emotionally and that makes me scared. I'm not sure I am ready for that type of commitment again this soon. I don't really want to check my phone that much because I want to place some distance between him and me. Which sounds horrible because things are going really well, but it is stressing me out to check my messages to see what is sent to me personally.

Check-in 2, Friday

I am in the airport in Oakland waiting for a delayed flight, so figured I could do my check-in. My conference went well. I know I have been feeling like an "imposter" in my own life lately, but today is probably the worst. I spent the last hour scrolling through news feeds to pass the time since my flight is delayed and again, it has made me feel even lower about myself. To top it off, the guy I am dating hasn't seen me in a few days because I've been traveling and busy, and he wants to see me when I get home tonight. I want to see him too, but I think I need time to myself. Saying no over text message is hard because I don't know how he will take it. Instead of texting at night I will suggest today that we talk on the phone—maybe that can be the solution to solving my screen time issue and still talking to him. Talking on the phone is more valuable in my opinion than texting so we would still be working on the relationship.

I have a friend in the Peace Corps in Mongolia and we talk through WhatsApp. She has been feeling really depressed lately. They are right on the tail end of a long, really, really cold winter and she is really struggling. I want to check my phone more to chat with her and keep her company, but I don't want to check my phone because of all the other things going on in my life. I feel guilty that I am not always on my phone talking to her. I told her about this challenge and trying to be better with my phone, but she isn't convinced. It is making me feel guilty not checking my phone and giving her that interaction. She will be back in four months, so it isn't that much longer that she has to go.

Week Six

Check-in 1, Monday

I am feeling extremely anxious with my interview for my new position at the end of the week and all these conflicting needs in my work life that have really started to become my personal life too with the traveling and long hours. Checking my phone used to be a way to relieve stress for me but now with the scheduled check-ins, I almost dread them. I am feeling better when I am communicating in person, almost clearer somehow, since there is no longer that temptation to check my phone while someone is talking in a meeting, even if they aren't talking to me. I feel I am more present to see all the nonverbals of communication when I am physically with someone.

Check-in 2, Saturday

I had my interview for my new position yesterday and am glad it is over, but I don't think that I did as well as I could have. I feel apprehensive about my career and projects at work. I typically work six days a week and it is feeling like I am still struggling to get the work done. If anything, I think I may try not to check my phone at all tomorrow. I am taking the guy I am dating to my winery in St. Helena for the day, so I really shouldn't have a reason to check my phone the whole day. I am excited to have a day without my phone really being needed. I think there is a change in my thought process now about my phone. Do I really need it?

Week Seven

Check-in 1, Wednesday
I heard back that they would like to offer me the new position in Information Technology Services. This is a huge change for what I do at work. I have a very intense job as it is, so transitioning my current position to another will be difficult and is bringing a lot of stress. While my current job is intense, I know that I have job security. This new position is more of a leadership role, less in the weeds, so I am a little nervous about this change. I have a few nosy nellies who have been texting me to see how everything is going. These folks only got my cell phone number when we were traveling for work a year ago and we needed to communicate with each other for work purposes. These people are now texting me on the weekend to get dirt on the recruitment process and gossip about me. I do not appreciate this—it feels like a violation of my personal space. It is interesting that a text message can make me feel this way. I guess everyone sees different forms of electronic communication differently. I see text messages as more personal, and only a few work folks are permitted to text me. This text from a coworker that I am not very fond of is very unsettling to me.

Week 8–9-ish

As a final entry, I will answer these questions.

i. How does this practice feel for me?
This practice has made me feel more anxious about checking my phone, because I now know the power it has over my emotions. It has made me feel like I do not want to check my phone and I am much more willing to put it away. It makes me feel more empowered to teach people how to treat me. I don't need to answer a text message within a few minutes—that is an arbitrary expectation that I set for myself. Not something that others set for me. I have to set that boundary.

ii. Am I experiencing any changes in my life as a consequence of this practice?

Yes, I feel I am more present in my conversations in person. Or that my mind is less distracted with electronic communication that I "have to send" as soon as I am done with this or that. Instead of texting my director a few doors down from my office, I will get up and physically check in with her, even if it is a small thing. I feel those few personal interactions over the past weeks have been valuable for us because we both have busy schedules.

I find when I am leading my team members at work I can be more present and focused in meetings. I don't feel as anxious during meetings because I am focusing on one topic at hand.

iii. Am I experiencing any changes (from when I first started) in terms of how I feel about this practice?

I thought this practice was "new age BS." I thought Dr. Silard just needed to get with the times and that technology is our new reality, so get to it. But after this experience and seeing how fragile my emotions were to the effects of simply scrolling through news feeds of friends or news across the world, I see it can be dangerous. It is something that needs to be monitored and used with careful discretion.

iv. How (if at all) are my relationships changing as a result of this practice?

I think this has helped in my personal relationship with the person that I have now been dating for about two months. Both of us being working professionals, it was a nice change of pace to almost have a scheduled time to talk. I think with my generation and texting, it is almost as if you are on a mini-date throughout the day if you are texting them. I don't think that helps build a meaningful relationship or substantive dialogue. Texting can be a good way of communicating for short messages, but if you are truly trying to date someone as an adult, I think it is actually counterproductive. It may even create an unhealthy dependence on the other person for frequent text messages. Maybe an idea for research: dating nowadays and texting impacts on long-term relationship development or something.☺

I feel that I am more present and calmer to be with. Most of the time people in my life say my blood is coffee and stress. I am typically lean because I run so much training for marathons, so when people ask me how I stay skinny, I joke and say, "Thanks, it's all the stress," and we all laugh because we know it is true. But since I have been trying to have a break from my phone this has actually led to a work-life balance improvement for me. The technology doesn't allow me to break from work, and I think I was on the brink of burnout. I wasn't sleeping due to work-related stress. I saw my mom two weeks ago and she mentioned that I seem more at peace. I really do think it is because of this challenge.

v. What (if anything) is this experience changing about how I view my smartphone and its role in my life?

Like I mentioned above it has led me to have a better work-life balance and understand how much my smartphone impacts my moods. It is a powerful thing.

Nancy, Forty-Eight, Program Manager, Tucson, Arizona

Week One

I updated my phone settings and notifications and the grayscale wallpaper is ugly and drab as intended. This reminds me of the puce refrigerator lightbulbs once sold as "diet aids." After five days, I'm finding that around 11 a.m. and 7 p.m. seem to be good times to split the day.

I fruitlessly tried to convince my immediate family members to do this with me, but at least they admitted they won't die if they must call me for urgent needs. I was surprised how upset everyone was since I am already quite remiss in responding in a timely manner to texts or noticing Facebook posts.

I believe I will weather this well. I can resist Facebook and am not cool (translated: young) enough to have gotten hooked on Instagram or Twitter, so I'm safe there. I think the toughest part of this will be missing sweet nothings from my honey throughout the day. He was the biggest, loudest, and most vehement objector. After five days, we are both adjusting to my midday check-in, so he has simmered down.

Week Two

Last week started out a little rough, but this week has been terrible. I've had two people who KNOW about this exercise break confirmed appointments with me at the last minute. I'm left waiting and wondering what happened until enough time has lapsed for me to call and they seem shocked that I didn't get their text. My patience is really thin since I've been so sick and haven't been getting much sleep, and I really wanted to bail out.

Instead, I decided to stick it out and start confirming all appointments that fall in the "dead zone" by phone call. This is going to be awkward. Many people now find phone calls to be rude. I was always taught that just because other people are being rude to you does not mean you can be rude to them. I want to be mindful that not everyone wants to help me in this social experiment.

One positive note has been my chats with my good friend who moved to West Virginia earlier this year. It has been great to reconnect as we have been missing each other since she moved.

Week Three

I expected this to get easier, but it seems to be getting harder and harder each week. Being in another time zone than my family this week made communicating even more complicated. This is primarily because my kids were the targets of my calls of "Did you remember to feed the cat today?" and "Don't forget my plane lands on Friday at 1 p.m." and "Linda, you do remember you're picking me up, right?"

Calling my kids is a little like wildlife photography, but instead of hiding in the bushes with the camera poised, hoping for a doe to step into the frame, I just keep aiming my phone [calls] at them and hoping one of them will accidentally answer. I text them too, but my "check-in" times and their conscious hours are wildly out of sync, so by the time they see my text, I'm back into "darkness" and we keep missing each other. Finally, as the return flight approached, I cheated and had my honey send them a flurry of texts from his time zone until all was settled. Finally, I can breathe a sigh of relief.

Week Four

Things are settling down into a comfortable routine now that I'm back at home. Funny, I have read that it takes three weeks to establish new habits and this has proven true in this, as well. I'm sensing a shift now in how I view the exercise. No longer am I seeing this like an experiment with controlled parameters. I'm beginning to consider that, instead of a seven-week, deprivation-style diet from unhealthy phone habits, this is a new lifestyle I'd like to keep.

This change in perspective surprised me. After all, my boyfriend still chafes a little at the limitations on instant text contact during the day when phone calls wouldn't be feasible. I don't think that is going to change. Perhaps, in time, he will be my one "cheater snack" that gets me through an otherwise healthy diet. I have manipulated the rules a bit for sanity purposes. If my kids have a yes-or-no question that is not time sensitive, they just text me and know they will get their answer at my next sanctioned "peek." If they have something cool to tell me or a complicated question, they text me to call them. That's working out well. I didn't expect them to adjust this nicely. I do love surprises!

Week Five

I have another convert to the Heart of Darkness! My best friend—the one who moved to West Virginia—is going to do this with her social media and texting, but not change her screen saver. Plus, we have switched to using video calls to get as close to face-to-face as we can to make sure our relationship stays healthy across the country. We laughed so hard the first few times when we were worrying about double chins, wrinkles, and age spots and accidentally NOT hanging up and leaving it going all night once. Since no one else in my family wanted to do this with me, it's nice to have a "diet partner" out there on my side.

It has been weird, though. At first, I was anxiously watching the clock and aching to pull out my phone. It made me get cranky and overly sensitive to criticism of the exercise. Now I'm seeing positive changes and can more confidently defend this to others and even ask them to join me.

Week Six

This was my first holiday weekend in a long time not spent with family and friends around a barbeque grill or pool. This left me feeling a little wistful at first. My daughters both work in retail, so they were dealing with the influx of shoppers seeking out summer deals or simply supplying the cookouts and parties they were hosting. I chose to relish the time without the interruptions and external distractions that normally provide background noise to my days. My phone sat, forgotten, on the charger in the bedroom for most of the weekend and then it was back to the normal grind of alarm clocks and meetings.

As another week comes to a close, I am chagrined to consider how long it had been since the last time I spent any significant time alone and in silence. My Tuesday morning alarm did not hurt as bad as normal Mondays do. I'm not sure why, but some of the people who consistently rub me the wrong way just couldn't bother me this week. I have read over and over that adding silence and meditation to your life and to each and every day brings about a variety of positive changes. I never felt I had TIME to add this into my crazy schedule. Last weekend combined with the increased silence from my phone is showing me that 1) I DO have time for silence; and 2) I NEED it.

One caveat to this new revelation for myself is that I also need the craziness, the unpredictability, and the loudness that social events and groups of friends bring. I just spent my entire lunch hour talking with my West Virginia friend about how frustrated she is that her daughter's Social Security hearing for benefits was denied. We ALWAYS laugh, cry, and hug each other no matter how far away she is. Thank you, Heart of Darkness Challenge, for giving her back to me!

Week Seven

It feels surreal coming to the end of this exercise. I don't even think about this challenge anymore until my weekly "Heart of Darkness Journal" alarm goes off.

Enjoying the brief respite of Friday evening, I was sitting on my back patio sipping with my sweetheart as we chatted about our latest challenges and successes. As I apologized for the need to largely ignore him the rest of the night and most of the weekend to finish up some work, the phone burst into its jarring alarm. After giggling over my little shriek, he commented that I don't seem to care about my phone anymore.

Is that true? I still value my phone as a tool, but not as an extension of myself. When did that happen? I think that began around Week Four and has become truer as each week passes. I still use my phone to contact people but only text those holdouts who really WON'T talk on the phone (my kids) and am using video calls more and more. I consciously strive to use the closest method to face-to-face as I can and often only briefly use the phone to set up in-person contact later. I don't put undue value on the phone anymore, though.

I blushed as we reminisced about the time my phone was pickpocketed at a hockey game and I spent over $800 to buy a replacement unit instead of waiting four extra days for insurance eligibility to bring the cost to only $150. At the time, I was crying and panicked at having to wait that long without my phone. If I forgot my phone and had to last a morning without it, I felt naked and distracted until I could go home and get it.

This exercise has allowed me to reclaim my right to respond to people in a reasonable amount of time rather than immediately. Ever so slowly, it has helped my partner stop checking his phone during meals, which had previously been a thorn in our relationship. It has given me back several friends who had become buried behind a wall of Facebook and Instagram posts and stopped getting together.

The Heart of Darkness Challenge has been life changing for me. I feel lighter. I am smiling more often as I think of something a friend told me or something I want to tell someone else. Each relationship that rekindles over the phone has me dancing and jumping around the house. I'm not exaggerating! I'm like a little kid on Christmas morning. Our summer calendar is looking like the old days with parties here at our place and others to attend.

All I needed to do was take a chance for seven weeks. This exercise has paid off in more ways than I can share. I am so glad I decided to participate!

Two Months Later . . .

I'm surprised upon consideration that the changes since I began the Heart of Darkness Challenge have been very small. First, I changed my home-screen photo of myself and my husband back to color. Now that there are no apps and icons across our faces, this is a treasured photo of beaming smiles when my phone lights up with a call. Nothing else needs to change back. Second, very few people text or email me with time-sensitive information anymore. Those who still prefer texting over calls will text me and know they will wait for my response. (Four hours? One day? It depends on when I look.) I realize that no one complains about it anymore. It has become normal for THEM too.

This feels like the kind of lifestyle change that diets are supposed to be. The first couple of weeks of the challenge were like the detox phase of a diet when your body breaks its addiction to sugar. I'm no longer addicted to my phone. I only check my phone just a few times a day. I turn up my ringer volume for calls, but leave all other notifications silent. Unlimited minutes actually matters again.

I'm so glad that I participated in this challenge, but I'm grateful that the lessons have stuck. Truly, Dr. Silard, I thank you for this opportunity. I stuck with it because I saw positive change despite some early conflict. It was a true challenge, but, wow, what a difference it continues to make in my relationships near and far.

Pedro, Thirty-Seven, Chief Financial Officer, Mendoza, Argentina

Week One

It is day one of using the Heart of Darkness and Side Door models. I want to first begin by saying that turning your phone to grayscale does make your phone less appealing to look at. However, I still ended up checking my phone more than a handful of times today. I noticed the battle that I had with scrolling through social media. What was I looking for? Absolutely nothing. I noticed how much time I was wasting away browsing through my phone. I noticed how my phone was disrupting my sleeping time. I would lie down to sleep and be on my phone, and next thing I knew two hours had passed by and I was not giving my body the rest that it needs. I realized that I needed to take control by first acknowledging the impact that the smartphone was having on me and my life and then changing my habits and practices by enforcing a couple of rules. Such as not being able to use my phone more than three times a day, and each time I checked my phone I could not exceed ten minutes.

As a few days passed I did notice that I was not checking my text messages or emails. I did notice, though, that I was less tempted to check my social media (Snapchat, Facebook, Instagram, and YouTube) because my phone was on grayscale. Everything seemed less appealing to look at. It was crazy to realize that everything in black and white seemed alike. I never noticed how much color appeals to your eyes and attracts your attention. I feel that I just have a bad habit of wasting my time browsing on my phone. I feel annoyed about how much I relied on my phone to keep me entertained and also about how much time was being wasted away.

Week Two

So far, I have been great with checking my emails and text messages and calls only three times a day. I have cut down browsing through social media when I have down time. I do get tempted to browse and see what new videos have been uploaded to YouTube. Limiting my phone use, I realized how much more time I had. It really sickens me when I think back to how much time I wasted. I began to make a list of to-dos, chores, errands, and things that I have been wanting to do or places that I have been wanting to visit.

Checking my phone has become easier. It is no longer something that runs through my mind. I feel like it is there for emergencies or for personal use when needed. Other than using my phone for my bank account and camera apps, I really do not need to depend on my phone. I have been able to accomplish more tasks, such as going to the gym, keeping up with daily chores, and playing with my dog, Ventura. Spending time away from my smartphone I began to realize the loss of relationships that I had with friends and with myself. It is definitely time to make a change!

Week Three

Limiting phone time has given me more time to live. I am starting to really appreciate this practice. I am learning about things that I used to like and then lost interest in. I am able to be more creative. I feel like I am able to see what it is that I like and what I want without having any outside influence. I never noticed how much I made myself feel lonely and relied on my phone to fill that void. I know that I still need to continue to pursue better friendships and relationships with others and with myself. Phones are literally so great for their resources, but can be very dangerous socially and psychologically.

I feel the freedom of having so much time on my hands. Checking my phone two to three times for text messages, phone calls, and emails has not been a problem. I have never really been a person to call or text much, and I cannot stand emails, so this practice allowed me to just go into my phone, reply to and delete messages, and get out. One thing that I did notice over the past two weeks is that when I was using my smartphone prior to this practice I was not fully engaged in communicating with others. It is hard to express how at times I used to choose being in my room on my phone over spending quality family time. I question myself—Why would I choose my phone over my family? What has it done for me? It wasn't like it was my job, but just a sad habit. This practice then opened my eyes to see how much influence phones had on others around me. I noticed how many kids were glued to watching cartoons and how parents easily hand them their phones to sit them still. They are kids—they are supposed to be playing and learning. Yes, a phone can teach you things but does not teach you communication skills.

Week Four

So far so good. I have kept my time of checking my phone to now two times a day. I make life a priority. When I have down time I go to the gym, or hang out with my family or friends. It makes me remember how things were prior to relying on electronic devices. We have to communicate and talk to each other and not text each other. In most cases I do not think that texting is a good way to communicate with one another. Only for a quick question or short reply, such as "I am here" or "I'm on my way home," should a text be made. I try to share with others that they should make a change with using technological devices. The impact of technology is eroding people's creativity, intimacy, empathy, conversations, etc.

Week Five

I began to make a few changes with family members and friends, such as not being able to use electronic devices while we are eating together or while we are spending time together. It is funny to see that many people have a bad habit of checking their phones to find nothing. The majority of the time, there is nothing that is needed to be attended to. People can just scroll on their phones for hours. Eventually, the phone gets boring and all you are doing is comparing, judging, questioning, and dreaming about things that are not even real. Social media especially has such a huge impact on our generation. Everyone wants to be social media famous, and for what? The majority of the people who are social media influencers are the least influential people out there. Many have anxiety issues, depression, lack communication skills, etc. What you see is not reality.

Week Six

I wish more people would try to cut their technology device time in half. Maybe people will be much happier and build more relationships. I think people think that phones make them happier, but it is a device that blocks the void of reality. Technology is only a stimulator that has a rise and end point. It is a short-term feeling. It attracts people like a drug. People think they need it and become anxious when they don't have it. How many times do people freak out when they realize they left the house without their phone?

Cell phones have benefits, and this is something I really agree with, but only to an extent. I think it is amazing to have a small device that has Internet access, mobile banking, GPS, a personal calendar, a built-in camera, etc. These applications I believe are necessities for our daily living and should remain a necessity. Social skills are very much needed and are really important in a job. How do people expect to work together if they cannot adapt to change? A lot of the issue, I believe, falls on Millennials. I have a younger brother and I see the impact of needing these devices to keep them happy. At times I had to confront him that he was being a hermit and staying cooped up in his bedroom playing videogames and on social media. Life passes by so fast, and was it that important to miss spending time with family?

Week Seven

This practice opened up my eyes. I do not have to limit myself to checking my phone two times a day. I am able to check it as many times as needed. This allows me to not feel confined to reach out for my messages to friends or missing phone calls and using certain time gaps to reply. I like to simply reply and go on about my day. I feel that when I do it instantly I do not have any urge to wait till a certain time to check my phone. I have noticed that I spend my time on myself more than I ever have before. I allow myself to watch a show or two but at the same time I am being productive, such as doing house chores, or going on a walk. I feel happier within myself. I just know that I need to learn how to reach out to others more. I need to learn how to communicate with others better in person and not have this awkwardness that I believe my phone allowed me to have.

This practice has taught me the importance of communication. The reality is no one is really going to give up their phone time, but we change our behaviors. It has been great finding more time for myself and others. What I used to be interested in is not the same. I feel like social media had a major influence on me and I didn't even know it. It is so easy to get caught up in what people like and not what you like. I did delete a few games and applications that I felt were not necessary. I always carry a book with me in my car or in my briefcase in case I have down time. I have come to the agreement that I will eventually cut out social media completely. It is going to be a challenge but there are much better things to do with my time.

Four Months Later . . .

I enjoyed the Heart of Darkness Challenge as it allowed me to see the common distractions that were affecting my life and sometimes happiness. It is very easy to get caught in virtual existence, impacting our creativity and appreciation of life. After the challenge my relationship with my phone has gone back and forth. Phones today have become such a necessity. I feel the need to have my phone with me at all times. However, I do not depend on my phone for distraction or to make me happy. I am continuing to appreciate living in the moment. It is very easy to get your mind caught up based on what you see. Therefore, it is very important to understand that what you see and hear is not entirely true. This challenge helped me come to the realization of how easily phones cause distraction and decrease productivity.

Carol, Twenty-Four, Sales Representative, Missoula, Montana

Journal #1

Week one of having my phone on grayscale. It's different, I'm not 100 percent sure how I feel about this. I feel like this experience is going to be good for me by disconnecting from my phone. I gave my family members the heads-up this week that I will start this experience. So far I am having a difficult time letting go of my phone. I want to look at my screen and at the same time I don't. When I'm at work I put my phone away in my bag. When I'm at home that's when I want to use it the most.

So far, it has been hard for me to not use my phone throughout the day. I normally use my phone the most to check social media. When I have down time I check my social media. Since I haven't used my phone, I can't wait to go to bed at night because that's when I use it really fast to check my social media and to respond to text messages. This experience is going to change my life since I can't use my phone throughout the day. I didn't realize before how bad I want to be on my phone. I keep wondering if I have any text messages. It's almost like a natural habit that I didn't notice I was doing before. Using my phone before was just something I got used to.

Journal #2

Week two has been difficult, I am getting a little better without depending on my phone. I really don't like the screen gray. It bugs me. I like that I can still listen to music on my phone. At least that helps me think that I am still using my phone but I really am not. I am calling people now when before I would not do that. I also like that I put all my apps on the last page on my phone and turned off the notification. I decided to check my phone in the morning before I get up and before bed. I gave myself a time and I have been doing pretty good so far. Before going to bed I respond to my notifications.

I am so used to my phone, especially during the weekends. So far for this experience the weekends have been harder than during the week. During the week I am busy with work and I'm okay leaving my phone in my bag, but on the weekend I am at home and want to check social media during the day. It's really hard to wait for the evenings. I felt really disconnected from social media and everyone I know. Instead of having my phone in my back pocket, I decided to leave it in my purse so I can try not to think about it. I found this helped me. I didn't realize how hard it would be for me. I didn't realize how much I depend on my phone. It was so hard for me to not check my screen throughout the day.

Journal #3

Week three: this week I found myself wanting to check my phone less. I think it's because the gray screen frustrates me. I only use my phone to listen to music and I had to use the GPS. I only used it when I went somewhere that I'm not familiar with and plus because I am really bad at directions and get lost very easily. Other than that I am starting to learn how to separate from my phone more and more every day. I like that I can use the Side Door model. I had to use it because my daughter was sick this week and I had to leave her with my mom. My mom would send me text messages letting me know how she was doing. I'm glad I was able to use the Side Door model just because my daughter was really sick and I had to take her to urgent care this week.

I am actually enjoying not being on my phone as much. I started to notice when I use my phone for a little bit before bed I am not as interested in using it anymore, especially with the screen being gray. Having the screen gray has helped me disconnect from my phone so much easier. My family members now call me rather than text me. Since I don't text them back right away they are calling me when it's important. I would say this week has been a lot different compared to the first week. I am not as anxious about wanting to check my phone anymore.

Journal #4

I can't believe it's week four already. I'm not active on social media anymore and when I check social media at night I'm starting to realize its actually nice disconnecting from the social media world. I am less interested in knowing what is going on. The gray screen makes it boring for me and I'd rather not use it. I actually like that I have disconnected myself. I like that people do not know what I have been up to. I don't get a lot of notifications anymore because I am not on social media like I used to be. My emails are adding up on my phone but I am not worried about reading them right away like I used to be, and I also realize if I check my emails that will take too long and I'd rather not spend time checking emails before bed.

Even though I told my family members and friends the reason why I am not responding to them right away and I have gotten used to not responding if I feel like it's not important, I can tell my friends are starting to get annoyed with me. They'd rather not call me and when I see them that's when they talk to me in person. I actually like the communication in person rather than on the phone. Yes, the phone is a big part of our lives now but I have realized it's not important. Another thing I noticed with my friends, they will ask me, "Where is your phone? I messaged you asking you a question." And half the time I tell them I don't know, somewhere in my bag. Then I tell them call me if you have a question and they look at me with a crazy face expression.

Journal #5

Week five. I used to take my phone with me everywhere even when I took my daughter to school. I had to make sure I had it before walking out of the house. Now when I take my daughter my phone doesn't even cross my mind and I'm leaving it at the house. When I take my daughter to school, I feel like it's not a big deal if I take my phone or not. It's actually really nice not worrying about the phone. I didn't realize before when my daughter would talk to me I would just say okay or that's good because I was so busy using my phone. Now when she is talking to me I'm listening to what she is saying and I am not distracted.

Journal #6

I am starting to notice others around me are using their phones all the time. I can see how people are so addicted to their phones now. This weekend my boyfriend and I went to dinner and it was nice having the phones put away and just talking. He didn't bring his phone out because I wasn't using mine. We were able to catch up on life and talk about the upcoming weeks and everything that needs to get done. Not using the phone can change your life, and I even realize how much time your phone takes up when I was always using it before this.

Journal #7

Week seven, yay!!! This is the last week and I can officially say I no longer feel like I need to use my phone. This experience has helped me disconnect from my phone and connect with my family instead. I have noticed during the weekend I am spending more time with my family, keeping busy, and I don't think twice about my phone. I don't feel like I need to have my phone with me all the time and I still get to read my messages when I wake up or before bed and surprisingly that's enough time for me. I have noticed a big difference in how I used to be with my phone compared to now. Before this experiment my phone took over my life, but now I am enjoying my life.

I would say this experience was interesting and life changing. The way I view my smartphone and its role in my life, I would say a smartphone comes in handy for emergency use only. Social media is not important enough to continue using my phone the way I used to use it. Now I see my phone for emergency usage only. The apps I have on my phone I decided to leave them where they are at on the last screen and I haven't changed my notifications back—I got used to them off. And if I need to get on Amazon for example, I can always use my computer. I don't need my phone anymore for every little thing.

Appendix B

	Netflix	Blockbuster
Decision making	Argument with your spouse, roommate, or friend only once, when you establish the queue of movies you will watch over the next few months.	Potential argument with your spouse, roommate, or friend every time you rent a movie.
Physical effort	You do not move your body from its entrenched position in front of your screen.	You walk or at least drive to Blockbuster and walk around the store. In so doing, you move your body in a different way than you do when you drag your mouse or move your finger across your touch screen. You engage in real activity and get at least a little exercise.
Professional reviews	You can check lots of movie reviews on Rotten Tomatoes or IMDB, which amalgamate (a skill the Internet fcilitates) the opinion of hundreds of movie critics and give you a composite score—helping you weed out the bombs and select movies that have been well received.	There are fewer movie reviews on the DVD box, which may be misrepresentative of the film; after all, they are the reviews the film company has selected to put on the box for you to see. As a result, you're more likely to rent a low-quality movie.

Personal reviews	You can link your own reviews to those of your friends and search for films your friends on Netflix have rated highly. Without even making this effort, Netflix's AI algorithms attempt to predict your film proclivities and tee up films for you that suit your taste. Any way you cut it, the Internet has democratized movie reviews, giving you a much more informed means of selecting a film to watch.	You have to call your friends and ask their opinions, which takes more time (with your friends; but wait—isn't that *why* you have friends, to spend time with them and ask their opinions?). Opposing argument: You can spend your time with your friends talking about more important things than their opinions of movies, which you can now read on the Netflix website. First argument again: Yes, but relationships are not efficient. Conversations about mundane issues such as which movie to see lead to deeper conversations about life, family, and relationships. Without the more mundane conversations to give us an excuse to meet, we often choose not to meet. Interdependence is greater when we recognize our need to be physically present with each other (as I learned while living in a rural African town). With our material needs and access to plentiful movie reviews taken care of, time with friends starts to feel like "nice to do" instead of "need to do." All our time becomes focused on what we "need to do"—all of which must be done on our screens.
Social connection	No spontaneity; no challenges; "life" at home as usual.	You may bump into someone you know in your neighborhood on the way to Blockbuster or while in the store. If you do, you may be forced to navigate a spontaneous conversation, developing your social skills. You may meet a new friend, or even someone to date. You may come up with a new idea with the down time you access when you get out of the house and walk or drive.

Late fees	No late charges.	I don't know about you (if you are also a Digital Settler), but I rarely returned a Blockbuster VHS (remember those, or the Beta videocassettes, or Laser Discs?) or DVD on time. It annoyed the hell out of me. The Internet wins this round hands down.
Availability	The movie you want is (just about always) in. Between Netflix, Amazon Prime, Hulu, and other Internet video offerings, you can get just about any movie you want, at any time. "The tyranny of convenience" is that you can obtain movies so easily you stop appreciating them. You can also return them with so little cost or effort that if you are not sufficiently entertained within ten minutes, you can cancel one and watch another movie. You lose the art of patience, "sticking through" something. On the other hand, you have an easier exit from a bad movie (more convenience). For those who have stuck through *really* bad movies, this is well appreciated.	The movie you want may be in or out; roll the dice, similar to trying to find a book at a bookstore. Yet you get to touch and "feel" the DVD you rent. You appreciate it more for the time you put into selecting it, and are likely to enjoy it more. This feeling is similar to enjoying a record album more when you pick it out at the record store and then sit on your floor and pore over the lyrics and the cover art to connect with the artist's creation, versus tapping a song to listen to on Spotify before quickly moving on to the next song.
Selection	Much more selection, including esoteric indie and foreign films.	Limited selection.
Price	It's cheaper, as Netflix has much less overhead (no storefronts).	It's more expensive. Okay, that's four straight rounds for the Internet.

Acknowledgments

To my wife, Karla: thank you for your patience and support throughout these past ten years as I researched and wrote this book. Thank you also for inspiring me with an example of a mother dedicated to raising her children with steadfast connection in the digital age.

To my editors, Sheridan McCarthy and Stanton Nelson of Meadowlark Publishing Services: thank you for your integrity, patience, authenticity, and uncanny ability to catch even the minutest of errors. I am so grateful to have had the opportunity to learn from you.

To my reviewers—Jeffrey Brudney, Annie Costa, Tim Gray, Laszlo Gregor, Peter Harms, Jeremy Murray, Kris Olsen, Bradley Owens, Kate Perry, Ronald Riggio, Karla Silard, and Ken Thomas: thank you for providing such thoughtful and detailed feedback on the manuscript. Your painstaking efforts have significantly improved *Screened In*.

To my cover designer, Mark Eimer, and layout designer, Diana Wade: you each were a joy to work with. Thank you.

To you, the reader: thank you for purchasing *Screened In* and enabling me to live my purpose of helping people experience and facilitate connection and create personal and social change.

Notes

Chapter 1: A History of Praising and Criticizing a New Technology

6 | stop working by then, like it or not: I had spent years unconsciously rebelling against starting my guitar lesson at six o'clock as I wrestled with an internal voice telling me I had inadequately tackled the day's tasks—translation: "You're inadequate." Yet, without fail, after an hour of playing guitar, my mind had completely let go of work and was solely focused on strumming the right chords.

7 | more depressed and lonely than they were only a few decades ago: Konrath, S. Bushman, B., and Grove, T. (2009). Seeing my world in a million little pieces: Narcissism, self-construal, and cognitive-perceptual style. *Journal of Personality*, 77(4), 1197–1228; Konrath, S. H., O'Brien, E., and Hsing, C. (2011). Changes in dispositional empathy in American college students over time: A meta-analysis. *Personality and Social Psychology Review*, 15(2), 180–98; Twenge, J., Konrath, S., Foster, J., Campbell, W., and Bushman, B. (2008). Further evidence of an increase in narcissism among college students. *Journal of Personality*, 76(4); Twenge, J. M. (2017). *IGen: Why Today's Super-Connected Kids are Growing Up Less Rebellious, More Tolerant, Less Happy—and Completely Unprepared for Adulthood—and What That Means for the Rest of Us*. New York: Simon and Schuster; Twenge, J. M., Catanese, K. R., and Baumeister, R. F. (2002). Social exclusion causes self-defeating behavior. *Journal of Personality and Social Psychology*, 83(3), 606–15.

7 | less emotional connection with others: Tromholt, M. (2016). The Facebook experiment: Quitting Facebook leads to higher level of well-being. *Cyberpsychology, Behavior, and Social Networking*, 19, 661–66. Twenge, *IGen*.

7 | less time face-to-face with family and friends: Nie, N. H., and Erbring, L. (2000). *Internet and Society: A Preliminary Report*. Palo Alto, CA: Stanford Institute for the Quantitative Study of Society, 3, 14–19.

8 | social isolation, depression, and loneliness: Kraut, R., Patterson, M., Lundmark, V., Kiesler. S., Mukopadhyay, T, and Scherlis, W. (1998). Internet paradox. A social technology that reduces social involvement and psychological well-being? *American Psychologist*, 53(9), 1017–31. Many other studies are cross-sectional and can only claim that these variables are correlated, but cannot identify what is causing what; e.g., do people become lonely because they spend so much time online? Or, alternatively, do they spend so much time online because they are lonely? This effect was documented in 2015 in a study of 414 university students in China found that the lonelier a person is, the more time they spend on their phone. Bian, M., and Leung, L. (2015). Linking Loneliness, Shyness, Smartphone Addiction Symptoms, and Patterns of Smartphone Use to Social Capital. *Social Science Computer Review*, 33(1), 61–79.

9 | twice as likely as obesity to precipitate our death: Sample, Ian (2014). Loneliness twice as unhealthy as obesity for older people, study finds. *The Guardian*. Feb. 16, 2014.

9 | read the typed page in addition to the writer: Mattox, Henry E. (1997). "Typewriter: Technology and Foreign Affairs: The Case of the Typewriter." *American Diplomacy*, October 1997. http://www.unc.edu/depts/diplomat/AD_Issues/amdipl_5/mattox_type.html

9 | the State Department called it a "necessary evil": Ibid.

10 | "must be continually on the jump": Schumpeter (2011). "Too Much Information: How to Cope with Data Overload." *The Economist*, June 30, 2011.

10 | "send messages through the air": WGBH, "Marconi Receives Radio Signal Over the Atlantic," in *A Science Odyssey: People and Discoveries*, Public Broadcasting Service. http://www.pbs.org/wgbh/aso/databank/entries/dt01ma.html

10 | "The only difference is that there is no cat": Albert Einstein, Quotation #26870 from Michael Moncur's (Cynical) Quotations, Quotations page. http://www.quotationspage.com/quote/26870.html

10 | "feel together, think together, live together": Fischer, C. S. (1992). *America Calling: A Social History of the Telephone to 1940.* Berkeley: University of California Press.

10 | will be around for a long time: Fischer, C. S. (2010). *Made in America: A Social History of American Culture and Character.* Chicago: University of Chicago Press.

11 | the receiver was replaced on the hook: McKenna, K., and Bargh, J. (2000). Plan 9 from cyberspace: The implications of the Internet for personality and social psychology. *Personality and Social Psychology*, 4(1), 57–75.

11 | "errand boys, and things of that kind": Vanderbilt, Tom (2012). "The Call of the Future," *The Wilson Quarterly*, Spring 2012: https://www.wilsonquarterly.com/quarterly/spring-2012-the-age-of-connection/the-call-of-the-future/

11 | "far-flung operations and far-flung relationships": Ibid.

11 | threatened neighborhood solidarity: Fischer, *America Calling*.

11 | the historical era that underwrote and enveloped this siesta": Vanderbilt, "The Call of the Future."

12 | 15 million cars worldwide: Frontenac Motor Company, "The Model T Ford." http://www.modelt.ca/background.html

12 | the "automotive paradox": Melosi, Martin V. "The Automobile and the Environment in American History," *Automobile in American Life and Society* blog: http://www.autolife.umd.umich.edu/Environment/E_Overview/E_Overview2.htm

12 | "isolated lives in the country and congested lives in the city": Fischer, *America Calling.*

12 | "bargains, library, and soda water": Fischer, *Made in America,* 171.

12 | destroying their bucolic tranquility: Fischer, *America Calling.*

13 | revived only long enough to give his notice of departure: "Early Adventures with the Automobile." http://www.eyewitnesstohistory.com/auto.htm

13 | consequent dilapidation of, central cities: Melosi, "The Automobile and the Environment in American History."

13 | the equivalent of $10,970 in 2018 dollars: American TV Prices, *Television History: The First 75 Years.* https://www.saving.org/inflation/inflation. php?amount=445

13 | "War would be a thing of the past": Schwartz, Evan (2002). *The Last Lone Inventor: A Tale of Genius, Deceit, and the Birth of Television.* New York: Harper Perennial.

14 | "the average American family hasn't time for it": Vanderbilt, "The Call of the Future."

14 | with only the television a close second: In terms of reaching 40 percent penetration of the US market; yet the TV grew from 40 to 75 percent of the US market faster than the Internet, as did the radio. DeGusta, Michael (2012). "Are Smart Phones Spreading Faster than Any Technology in Human History?" *MIT Technology Review.* May 9, 2012. https://www.technologyreview.com/s/427787/ are-smart-phones-spreading-faster-than-any-technology-in-human-history/

15 | a "national loneliness epidemic": Cigna (2018). New Cigna study reveals loneliness at epidemic levels in America. https://www.cigna.com/newsroom/ news-releases/2018/new-cigna-study-reveals-loneliness-at-epidemic-levels-in-america

15 | over three in five Americans are now lonely: Cigna (2020). Loneliness and the workplace. https://doi.org/10.2486/indhealth.2018-0055

15 | the Royal College of General Practitioners: National campaign needed to tackle loneliness "epidemic," says RCGP. http://www.rcgp.org.uk/about-us/ news/2018/may/national campaign-needed-to-tackle-loneliness-epidemic-says-rcgp.aspx

15 | 9 million British citizens are often or always lonely: Yeginsu, Ceylan (2018). "UK appoints a Minister for Loneliness." *The New York Times,* January 17, 2018. https://www.nytimes.com/2018/01/17/world/europe/uk-britain-loneliness.html

15 | less time outside than prison inmates: U.K. kids spend less time outside than prison inmates, study says. *Time,* March 25. http://time.com/4272459/u-k-kids-spend-less-time-outside-than-prison-inmates-study-says/

16 | the primary driver of untenable levels of loneliness: Hyland, P., Shevlin, M., Cloitre, M., Karatzias, T., Vallières, F., McGinty, G., Fox, R., and Power, J. M. H. (2018). Quality not quantity: Loneliness subtypes, psychological trauma, and mental health in the US adult population. *Social Psychiatry and Psychiatric Epidemiology* 54(9), 1089–99.

16 | attribute to the rise of social media: Konrath, O'Brien, and Hsing, Changes in dispositional empathy in American college students over time.

16 | suicide rates are rising to unprecedented levels: Twenge, *IGen*.

16 | not even one person to talk with about important issues: McPherson, M., Smith-Lovin, L., and Brashears, M. E. (2006). Social isolation in America: Changes in core discussion networks over two decades. *American Sociological Review*, 71(3), 353–375.

17 | "there aren't many good solutions at the moment": Weisberg, Jacob, "We Are Hopelessly Hooked." *The New York Review of Books*. February 25, 2016. https://www.nybooks.com/articles/2016/02/25/we-are-hopelessly-hooked/

20 | on average, over twenty-five hundred times per day: "Internet Users Reach to Phones ~150x a Day … Could Be Hands-Free with Wearables," Internet Trends, May 29, 2013. https://www.slideshare.net/kleinerperkins/kpcb-inter-net-trends-2013/52-Mobile_Users_Reach_to_Phone

Chapter 2: The Bait-and-Switch of the Internet

21 | "People feel not just addicted, but trapped": Huffington, Arianna (2013). "Our Unplugging Challenge: Seven Days without Our Devices," *Huffington Post*, December 17, 2013. https://www.huffpost.com/entry/unplugging-chal-lenge_n_4455733

21 | "Today, Apple is reinventing the phone!": Wright, Mic (2015). "The original iPhone announcement annotated: Steve Jobs' genius meets Genius." Sept. 9, 2015: https://thenextweb.com/apple/2015/09/09/genius-annotat-ed-with-genius/

22 | would have otherwise and saved 14 million lives: Copeland, Jack, University of Canterbury, Christchurch, New Zealand (2012). "Alan Turing: The codebreaker who saved 'millions of lives.'" BBC News. June 19, 2012: http://www.bbc.com/news/technology-18419691

22 | a posthumous pardon four years later: "Royal Pardon for Codebreaker Alan Turing." BBC News. Dec. 24, 2013. http://www.bbc.com/news/technology-25495315

23 | even an "extended self": Clayton, R. B., Leshner, G., and Almond, A. (2015). The extended iSelf: The impact of iPhone separation on cognition, emotion, and physiology. *Journal of Computer-Mediated Communication*, 20(2), 119–35.

23 | "highly addicted" to their electronic gadgets: Schumpeter (2012). "Slaves to the Smartphone." *The Economist.* March 30, 2012, 80.

23 | without access to their online social networks: Siew, Walden (2010). "Study: College students are Internet-addicted," Reuters, April 23, 2010.

23 | "landing like Wild West gunslingers": Wayne, Teddy (2014). "The 7-Day Digital Diet," *The New York Times.* Feb. 7, 2014.

23 | said they couldn't live without their smartphone: Sullivan, Andrew (2016). "I Used to Be a Human Being," *New York Magazine,* Sep. 18, 2016. http://nymag.com/intelligencer/2016/09/andrew-sullivan-my-distraction-sickness-and-yours.html

23 | "That made me so angry," she said: "Japanese Woman Arrested for Virtual-World 'Murder.'" Associated Press/Fox News, October 24, 2008. http://www.foxnews.com/story/2008/10/24/japanese-woman-arrested-for-virtual-world-murder/

23 | "I have suffered a real loss": *The Week,* Dec. 24, 2010–Jan. 7, 2011, 26.

24 | were upset she had been born prematurely: Tran, Mark (2010). "Girl Starved to Death While Parents Raised Virtual Child in Online Game." *The Guardian,* March 5, 2010. http://www.theguardian.com/world/2010/mar/05/korean-girl-starved-online-game

24 | "communicating with family and friends": *The Week,* September 3–10, 2010, 8.

24 | "longer than originally intended?": Young, K. (1996). Internet addiction: The emergence of a new clinical disorder. *CyberPsychology and Behavior,* 3, 237–244.

24 | "experienced as irresistible": Shapira, N., et al. (2003). Problematic Internet use: Proposed classification and diagnostic criteria. *Depression and Anxiety,* 17, 207–16.

25 | regulate through their own volition: Everitt, B. J., and Robbins, T. W. (2016). Drug addiction: Updating actions to habits to compulsions ten years on. *Annual Review of Psychology,* 67(1), 23–50.

25 | consequences of those behaviors, they are addicted: Malenka, R. C., Nestler, E. J., and Hyman, S. E., "Chapter 15: Reinforcement and Addictive Disorders," in A. Sydor and R. Y. Brown, *Molecular Neuropharmacology: A Foundation for Clinical Neuroscience,* 2nd ed. New York: McGraw-Hill Medical, 2009. 364–75.

25 | than seeking what we do: Baumeister, R. F. (2001). Bad is stronger than good. *Review of General Psychology,* 5(4), 323–70.

25 | "you can't make good things happen in your life": Alter, Adam. *Irresistible: The Rise of Addictive Technology and the Business of Keeping Us Hooked.* New York: Penguin, 2017.

25 | as an emotion without an object: May, R. (1980). Value conflicts and anxiety. In Kutash, I. L., and Schlesinger, L. B., eds., *Handbook on Stress and Anxiety*. San Francisco: Jossey-Bass, 241–48.

26 | "addictions are very, very similar": Alter, *Irresistible*.

26 | when we feel bored, distressed, or irritable: Barker, Eric. This Is How to Stop Checking Your Phone: 5 Secrets from Research. https://www.bakadesuyo.com/2017/03/how-to-stop-checking-your-phone/

26 | interacting with our phones about 150 times per day: "Internet Users Reach to Phones ~150x a Day."

27 | what many scholarly and popular writers claim: e.g., Young, K. (1998). *Caught in the Net: How to Recognize the Signs of Internet Addiction and a Winning Strategy for Recovery*. New York: Wiley.

29 | 61 percent of Americans are now lonely: Cigna (2020).

30 | "immersed in an ocean of romantic possibilities": Ansari, Aziz, and Klinenberg, Eric (2015), *Modern Romance*. New York: Penguin.

31 | someone who might share the pain: Sullivan, "I Used to Be a Human Being."

32 | "feeling helplessly and dangerously alone": Cacioppo, J. T., and Patrick, W. (2008). *Loneliness: Human Nature and the Need for Social Connection*. New York: W. W. Norton, 50–51.

32 | "less aware of the addictive qualities": Sinek, S. (2014). *Leaders Eat Last: Why Some Teams Pull Together and Others Don't*. New York: Penguin, 53.

34 | "having a problem with one specific area of content": Interview with David Greenfield, June 11, 2019.

34 | "the things they deliver can be addictive": McCarthy, Ellen (2018). "Breaking Up with Your Smartphone Is Really, Really Hard. Just Ask These People." *Washington Post*. February 8, 2018. https://www.washingtonpost.com/lifestyle/style/breaking-up-with-your-smartphone-is-really-really-hard-just-ask-these-people/2018/02/07/941f23bc-0906-11e8-8777-2a059f168dd2_story.html?noredirect=on&utm_term=.8af1ee805ed5

35 | even if it is a video game: Research from Philip Zimbardo, the social psychologist behind the famous Stanford Prison Experiment, has uncovered that this is a primary motive for young men who become hardcore gamers, in part because they do not feel comfortable in social situations or that they are able to make a name for themselves in real life. Zimbardo, P., and Coulombe, N. (2016). *Man Interrupted: Why Young Men Are Struggling and What We Can Do About It*. Newburyport, MA: Conari Press.

37 | *A Long Way Home* and the movie *Lion*: Brierly, Saroo (2015). *A Long Way Home: A Memoir*. New York: Berkley. *Lion* (2016), Fielder, Angie and Canning, Iain, producers.

37 | see his mother, brother, and sister: *The Week*. March 30, 2012, 6.

38 | "you are still good-looking": Nudd, Tim. "Perfect Match: Brazilian Kids Learn English by Video Chatting with Lonely Elderly Americans FCB's Touching Work for a Language School," *AdWeek*, May 14, 2014. http://www.adweek.com/adfreak/perfect-match-brazilian-kids-learn-english-video-chatting-lonely-elderly-americans-157523

39 | over half showed up: Cialdini, R. B. (1993). *Influence: The Psychology of Persuasion*. New York: HarperCollins.

Chapter 3: Social Information Versus Social Connection

40 | called this phenomenon the "Internet paradox": Kraut et al., Internet paradox.

40 | face-to-face cancer support groups: Klemm, P., and Hardie, T. (2002). Depression in internet and face-to-face cancer support groups. *Oncology Nursing Forum*, 29, 4.

40 | Stanford social scientist Norman Nie: Nie and Erbring, *Internet and Society*; Pinker, S. (2015). *The Village Effect: How Face-to-Face Contact Can Make Us Healthier and Happier*. Toronto: Vintage Canada.

41 | less enjoyment of their face-to-face interactions: Dwyer, R., Kushlev, K., and Dunn, E. (2017). Smartphone use undermines enjoyment of face-to-face social interactions. *Journal of Experimental Social Psychology* (March), 1–7.

42 | "lead to more boring interactions": Interview with Ryan Dwyer, June 7, 2019.

42 | when each partner is using their phone: Roberts, J. A., and David, M. E. (2016). My life has become a major distraction from my cell phone: Partner phubbing and relationship satisfaction among romantic partners. *Computers in Human Behavior*, 54, 134–41.

42 | "tend not to develop addiction": Alter, *Irresistible*.

44 | first identified by the social psychologist Leon Festinger: Festinger, L. (1954). A theory of social comparison processes. *Human Relations*, 7(2), 117–40.

44 | academic self-concept tends to decrease: Marsh, H., Kong, C., and Hau, K. (2000). Longitudinal multi-level models of the big-fish-little-pond effect on academic self-concept: Counterbalancing contrast and reflected glory effects in Hong Kong schools. *Journal of Personality and Social Psychology*, 78, 337–49.

44 | the last thing you'd want to gamble: In her Heart of Darkness Challenge Journal in Appendix A, Krystle shares how work pressures and feelings of self-doubt can combine to produce tremendous anxiety, which impelled her to check social media to alleviate this anxiety. Seeing the exaggerated successes of others, however, only made it worse.

45 | "they will remember how you made them feel": https://www.goodreads.com/quotes/663523-at-the-end-of-the-day-people-won-t-remember-what

46 | listening to and supporting others emotionally: Konrath, O'Brien, and Hsing, Changes in dispositional empathy in American college students over time.

47 | one of the most important ingredients of happiness: Pinker, *The Village Effect.*

47 | quitting Facebook causes an increase in well-being: Tromholt, The Facebook experiment.

47 | "the human desire to connect": Silverman, J. (September 8, 2008), quoted by Zaharov-Reutt, A., "Skype: The 'wow' started 5 years ago." www.itwire.com, 248.

47 | "why Facebook is here on this planet": https://www.azquotes.com/quote/1292381

48 | "We can't leave the casino—because it's in our pockets": McCarthy, "Breaking up with your smartphone is really, really hard."

48 | ride a metro or bus or taxi and just … think: Some of us chose instead to read a book, magazine, or newspaper while being transported; nonetheless, we could usually only peruse one book or magazine, as it was inconvenient to carry more, and our thoughts often focused on a few ideas emanating from these media. During an entire commute, we may have read just one or a few articles (rather than sifting through the first few sentences of countless articles on social media, any of which are hard to focus on as we are also replying to text messages from friends), making the distractibility factor much lower than when using our smartphones.

50 | hands-free cell phone calls increase the risk of driving accidents: Parker-Pope, Tara. "A Problem of the Brain, Not the Hands: Group Urges Phone Ban for Drivers." *New York Times.* January 13, 2009.

50 | report that they text behind the wheel: National Highway Traffic Safety Administration, "Distracted Driving." https://www.nhtsa.gov/risky-driving/distracted-driving

50 | legal maximum blood alcohol level: Parker-Pope, "A Problem of the Brain, Not the Hands."

50 | risk of collision compared to when they are not texting: Richtel, Matt. "In Study, Texting Lifts Crash Risk by Large Margin." *New York Times.* July 28, 2009. https://www.nytimes.com/2009/07/28/technology/28texting.html

50 | ability to effectively engage in other tasks: Willingham, Daniel (2010). "Have Technology and Multitasking Rewired How Students Learn?" *American Educator,* 34(2) (Summer 2010), 23–28.

50 | a four-hundred-pound black bear while texting: "Texting Man Runs into Bear," *Huffington Post,* April 11, 2012. http://www.huffingtonpost.com/mobileweb/2012/04/11/texting-man-runs-into-bear_n_1418128.html

53 | heart disease, and other life-threatening maladies: Cacioppo and Patrick, *Loneliness.*

Chapter 4: The Brogrammer Brigade

54 | all eight were men: Forbes Technology Council, "Eight Influential Tech Leaders Making a Difference," *Forbes,* July 10, 2018. https://www.forbes.com/sites/forbestechcouncil/2018/07/10/eight-influential-tech-leaders-making-a-difference/#1fdf872d476a

54 | Ninety-three percent were men: Maney, Kevin (2009). "25 Innovators in Technology," *Entrepreneur.* March 9, 2009. https://www.entrepreneur.com/article/200524

54 | 93 percent were Y-chromosome holders: Bastone, Nick (2018) "35 U.S. Tech Startups That Reached Unicorn Status in 2018," *Business Insider,* November 12, 2018. https://www.inc.com/business-insider/35-us-tech-startups-that-reached-unicorn-status-in-2018.html

54 | "engineering and computer science background": Miller, Claire (2012). "In Google's Inner Circle, a Falling Number of Women," *New York Times,* Aug. 24, 2012.

55 | "disdainful of anyone far from the machine": Madrigal, Alexis C. (2019). "The People Who Hated the Web Even Before Facebook," *The Atlantic,* March 15, 2019. https://www.theatlantic.com/technology/archive/2019/03/people-who-hated-web-even-before-facebook/584932/

55 | workforce at Google were women: Donnelly, Grace (2017). "Google's 2017 Diversity Report Shows Progress Hiring Women, Little Change for Minority Workers," *Fortune,* June 29, 2017. http://fortune.com/2017/06/29/google-2017-diversity-report/

55 | similarly occupied by women: Molla, Rani (2017). "It's not just Google— many major tech companies are struggling with diversity," Vox Recode, August 7, 2017. https://www.recode.net/2017/8/7/16108122/major-tech-companies-silicon-valley-diversity-women-tech-engineer

55 | taps their phone 2,617 times per day: Winnick, Michael (2016). "Putting a Finger on Our Phone Obsession: Mobile Touches—a Study on Humans and Their Tech," *dscout,* June 16, 2016. https://blog.dscout.com/mobile-touches

55 | every waking hour of life: "Internet Users Reach to Phones ~150x a Day."

55 | eighteen minutes per day on their phones: Barker, "This Is How to Stop Checking Your Phone."

56 | they similarly followed suit: Kramer, A. D. I., Guillory, J. E., and Hancock, J. T. (2014). Experimental evidence of massive-scale emotional contagion through social networks. *Proceedings of the National Academy of Sciences,* 111(29), 8788–90.

56 | based on the posts and photos they upload: Levin, Sam (2017). "Facebook Told Advertisers It Can Identify Teens Feeling 'Insecure' and 'Worthless,'" *The Guardian*, May 1, 2017. https://www.theguardian.com/technology/2017/may/01/facebook-advertising-data-insecure-teens

56 | "buttons you can push in a particular person": Lewis, P. (2017). "Our minds can be hijacked": the tech insiders who fear a smartphone dystopia. *The Guardian*, October 6, 2017. https://www.theguardian.com/technology/2017/oct/05/smartphone-addiction-silicon-valley-dystopia

56 | "just as their designers intended": Ibid.

56 | a red flag for the rest of us: Weller, Chris (2017). "Bill Gates and Steve Jobs Raised Their Kids Tech-free—and It Should've Been a Red Flag," *Business Insider*, January 10, 2018. https://www.businessinsider.com/screen-time-limits-bill-gates-steve-jobs-red-flag-2017-10

57 | "just how powerful it will be": Reingold, Jennifer, and Tkaczyk, Christopher (2008). "10 New Gurus You Should Know," *Fortune*, November 13, 2008. http://archive.fortune.com/galleries/2008/fortune/0811/gallery.10_new_gurus.fortune/

57 | "increased attitude and behavior change": Fogg, B., Cuellar, G., and Danielson, D. (2009). Motivating, influencing, and persuading users: An introduction to captology. In Sears, A., and Jacko, J., eds., *Human-Computer Interaction Fundamentals* (CRC Press, 2017), 109–22.

57 | "just not an accurate narrative": Interview with B. J. Fogg, June 10, 2019.

57 | "technologies are here and more are coming": "Protecting Consumers in the Next Tech-Ade," Federal Trade Commission Proceedings, Washington, DC, November 7, 2006. https://www.ftc.gov/sites/default/files/documents/public_events/protecting-consumers-next-tech-ade/transcript_061107.pdf

58 | "experiencing certain internal triggers": Weisberg, "We Are Hopelessly Hooked."

58 | addictive substances ranging from sugar to heroin: Anderson, Jenny (2018). "'It's Not a Drug, But It May As Well Be': Expert Opinions on Whether Kids Are Addicted to Tech," *Quartz*, February 9, 2018. https://qz.com/1202888/are-kids-actually-addicted-to-technology/

59 | "text that whizzes by our screens": Christakis, Erika (2018). "The Dangers of Distracted Parenting," *The Atlantic*. July/August 2018. https://www.theatlantic.com/magazine/archive/2018/07/the-dangers-of-distracted-parenting/561752/

59 | relate what they experience to their real lives: Pinker, *The Village Effect*.

60 | talking with them or giving them a hug: Anderson, "'It's Not a Drug, But It May As Well Be.'"

60 | fits of uninhibited anger and rage: Silard, A., and Watson-Manheim, M. B. (2015). The bait-and-switch of the Internet: The influence of connectivity on contactedness and connectedness. In Conference Proceedings of the Academy of Management. Vancouver, BC: Academy of Management. Walther, J. (1996). Computer-mediated communication: Impersonal, interpersonal, and hyperpersonal interaction. *Communication Research*, 23(1), 3–43.

60 | (textual messaging) of electronic communication: Spears, R., and Lea, M. (1992). Social influence and the influence of the "social" in computer-mediated communication. In Lea, ed., *Contexts of Computer-Mediated Communication*. New York: Harvester-Wheatsheaf, 30–65.

60 | strip our communication with others of context: Faraj, S., Jarvenpaa, S. L., and Majchrzak, A. (2011). Knowledge collaboration in online communities. *Organization Science*, 22(5), 1224–39.

60 | its originator, Stanford professor Albert Mehrabian: Koneya, M., and Barbour, A. (1976). *Louder Than Words: Nonverbal Communication.* Interpersonal Communication series. Columbus, OH: Merrill. Mehrabian, Albert. (1971). *Silent Messages: Implicit Communication of Emotions and Attitudes.* Belmont, CA: Wadsworth Publishing Co. Also see, for example, "The Mehrabian Myth: Article Questions Body Language Assumptions," Present with Ease. http://www.presentwithease.com/the-mehrabian-myth.html

61 | without overdoing their intensity: Silard and Watson-Manheim, The bait-and-switch of the Internet.

61 | "A small leak will sink a great ship": https://www.brainyquote.com/quotes/benjamin_franklin_135836

61 | delegate this responsibility to screens: Pinker, *The Village Effect.*

61 | problems when they are five and a half: Mistry, K. B., Minkovitz, C. S., Strobino, D. M., and Borzekowski, D. L. G. (2007). Children's Television Exposure and Behavioral and Social Outcomes at 5.5 Years: Does Timing of Exposure Matter? *Pediatrics*, 120(4), 762–69.

61 | from four years in 1970 to just four months at present: Christakis, "The Dangers of Distracted Parenting."

62 | "right from the beginning of people's lives": Rueb, Emily S. (2019). "W.H.O. Says Limited or No Screen Time for Children under 5," *New York Times*, April 24, 2019, https://www.nytimes.com/2019/04/24/health/screen-time-kids.html

62 | attentional problems at age seven: Christakis, D. A., Zimmerman, F. J., DiGiuseppe, D. L., and McCarty, C. A. (2004). Early television exposure and subsequent attentional problems in children. *Pediatrics*, 113(4), 708–13.

63 | "levels of stimulation that reality can't provide": Interview with Dimitri Christakis, June 5, 2019.

63 | "likely to develop more behavioral problems": Interview with Jenny Radesky, June 10, 2019.

63 | happier and more competent: Schonert-Reichl, K. A., Buote, D., Jaramillo, A., Foulkes, K., Rowcliffe, P., Calbick, J., and Cleathero, J. (2007). *Middle Childhood Inside and Out: The Psychological and Social World of Children 9–12.* Burnaby, BC: University of British Columbia/United Way.

64 | "mammalian reward and motivation": Aron, A., Li, H., Mashek, D. J., Strong, G., Fisher, H., and Brown, L. L. (2005). Reward, Motivation, and Emotion Systems Associated With Early-Stage Intense Romantic Love. *Journal of Neurophysiology,* 94(1), 327–37.

64 | continue seeking out the addictive habit or substance: Anderson, "It's Not a Drug, But It May As Well Be."

65 | than during actual copulation: Aron et al., Reward, Motivation, and Emotion Systems (2005).

65 | mundane and boring in comparison: Zimbardo and Coulombe, *Man Interrupted.*

66 | "comfort, heat, sex," admonishes Marcellino: Lewis, "Our minds can be hijacked."

66 | "behaviors that we know can produce that hit": Sinek, *Leaders Eat Last,* 53.

67 | Norman Nie and Canadian psychologist Susan Pinker have noted: Nie and Erbring, *Internet and Society.* Pinker, *The Village Effect.*

67 | a common symptom of schizophrenia: "Schizophrenia," Mayo Clinic. https://www.mayoclinic.org/diseases-conditions/schizophrenia/symptoms-causes/syc-20354443

67 | contain excessive dopamine receptors: Seeman, P., Guan, H., and Van Tol, H. (2007). Dopamine D4 receptors elevated in schizophrenia. *Nature,* 365, 441–45.

67 | reduce the symptoms of schizophrenia: Swerdlow, N., and Koob, G. (1987). Dopamine, schizophrenia, mania, and depression: Toward a unified hypothesis of cortico-stiato-pallido-thalamic function. *Behavioral and Brain Sciences,* 10, 197–46.

68 | tend to earn a lower GPA: Jacobsen, W. C., and Forste, R. (2010). The wired generation: Academic and social outcomes of electronic media use among university students. *Cyberpsychology, Behavior, and Social Networking,* 14(5), 275–80.

69 | "get pleasure and they can't even feel it": Interview with Rob Lustig, June 10, 2019.

70 | "I feel fine being sucked into the vortex after that": Wayne, "The 7-Day Digital Diet."

70 | reinforcement and approval only come in the long term, if at all: There is a similar dynamic with bonuses and incentives: they only tend to work when people feel they'll receive them soon (see Heath, C. (1999). On the Social Psychology of

Agency Relationships: Lay Theories of Motivation Overemphasize Extrinsic Incentives. *Organizational Behavior and Human Decision Processes*, 78(1), 25–62. Email frequently offers this short-term reward with its associated release of dopamine. Whereas, if you are writing a book or a proposal or working on a long-term project, the cost—cognitive attention—is higher, and the reward or benefit is lower because you don't receive as much of the short-term dopamine reward.

Chapter 5: You Are the Crash Test Dummy

71 | on a regular basis until the early to mid-90s: I remember returning from two years in Kenya as a Peace Corps volunteer in 1992 and buying my first desktop computer—a Compaq—just before starting my first master's degree a year later. Before I finished my two years at Harvard, I would also have a dial-up modem and an AOL account for sending and receiving emails. Still an enjoyable experience as at this time, this communication medium was primarily used for infrequent personal messaging with a few family members and friends.

74 | "We are sitting ourselves to death": The Active Times, "Sitting Is the New Smoking: Ways a Sedentary Lifestyle Is Killing You," *Huffington Post*, September 29, 2014. https://www.huffpost.com/entry/sitting-is-the-new-smokin_b_5890006

74 | "replaced with low-intensity activities" engaged in while standing: Reynolds, Gretchen (2014). "Sit Less, Live Longer?" *New York Times*, Sept. 17, 2014. https://well.blogs.nytimes.com/2014/09/17/sit-less-live-longer/?_r=0

75 | office worker sits for about ten hours per day: Schulte, Brigid (2015). "Health Experts Have Figured Out How Much Time You Should Sit Each Day," *Washington Post*, June 2, 2015. https://www.washingtonpost.com/news/wonk/wp/2015/06/02/medical-researchers-have-figured-out-how-much-time-is-okay-to-spend-sitting-each-day/?utm_term=.fb00f913cf4b

75 | playing *StarCraft* in an Internet café for fifty hours: Tran, "Girl Starved to Death While Parents Raised Virtual Child in Online Game."

76 | producing severe joint and muscle problems: Schulte, "Health Experts Have Figured Out How Much Time You Should Sit Each Day."

76 | "as you can when you're not exercising": Biswas, A., Oh, P. I., Faulkner, G. E., Bajaj, R. R., Silver, M. A., Mitchell, M. S., and Alter, D. A. (2015). Sedentary time and its association with risk for disease incidence, mortality, and hospitalization in adults a systematic review and meta-analysis. *Annals of Internal Medicine*, 162(2), 123–32.

77 | link between prolonged sitting and mortality: Ekelund, U., et al. (2016). Does physical activity attenuate, or even eliminate, the detrimental association of sitting time with mortality? A harmonised meta-analysis of data from more than 1 million men and women. *The Lancet*, 388, 1302–10.

80 | "the point is to just get off your rear end": Schulte, "Health Experts Have

Figured Out How Much Time You Should Sit Each Day."

81 | are "about making the shift from sedentary time to playtime": Rueb, "W.H.O. Says Limited or No Screen Time for Children under 5."

82 | "I think it's going to take time": Dretzin, Rachel, director, *Digital Nation: Life on the Virtual Frontier*. PBS Frontline Films, February 2, 2010. https://www. pbs.org/wgbh/frontline/film/digitalnation/

85 | "they're just so glued to their screen": Interview with B. J. Fogg.

85 | Turkle labeled this phenomenon "alone together": Turkle, S. (2012). *Alone Together: Why We Expect More from Technology and Less from Each Other*. New York: Basic Books.

86 | "'solitude' to express the glory of being alone": https://www.brainyquote. com/quotes/paul_tillich_107897

86 | over three of every five Americans are lonely: Cigna (2020).

Chapter 6: Your Digital Identity

88 | 6 percent of Silents had done the same: Choney, Suzanne (2010). "Just as You Thought: More Teens Are Texting," MSNBC, April 20, 2010.

88 | seniors over sixty-five have purchased a high-speed connection: O'Brien, Sara (2017). "One-third of U.S. Seniors Don't Use the Internet," CNN, May 17, 2017. http://money.cnn.com/2017/05/17/technology/pew-study-seniors-in-ternet/index.html

88 | writer and educator Marc Prensky: Prensky, M. (2001). "Digital Natives, Digital Immigrants," *On the Horizon: The Strategic Planning Resource for Education Professionals*, Vol. 9, No. 5, 2001.

90 | "I have no idea what the Internet is," she told reporters: *The Week*, April 22, 2011, 6.

91 | the fleeting joy we actually experience: Wilson, T. D., and Gilbert, D. T. (2005). Affective forecasting: Knowing what to want. *Current Directions in Psychological Science*, 14(3), 131–34.

91 | new affluence than they thought they would be: Brickman, P., Coates, D., and Janoff-Bulman, R. (1978). Lottery winners and accident victims: Is happiness relative? *Journal of Personality and Social Psychology*, 36(8), 917.

92 | eventually having to call us anyway: "Social Whirl," *The Economist*, June 23, 2012, 65.

92 | Zuckerberg replied "Senator, we run ads": Gutman, Rachel (2018). "The 13 Strangest Moments from the Zuckerberg Hearing," *The Atlantic*, April 10, 2018. https://www.theatlantic.com/technology/archive/2018/04/the-strang-est-moments-from-the-zuckerberg-testimony/557672/

93 | **"in a digital world, speaking social":** "Social Whirl."

94 | **"no rules or regulations in between them":** Interview with Rob Lustig.

95 | **still continued up to the highest voltage:** Milgram, S. (1965). Some conditions of obedience and disobedience to authority. *Human Relations*, 18, 57–76; Milgram, S. (1974). *Obedience to Authority*. New York: Harper and Row; Myers, D. (2010). *Social Psychology*, 10th ed. New York: McGraw-Hill.

95 | **kill orders with aircraft or more distant weapons:** Myers, *Social Psychology*.

95 | **relationship with the other person:** Caspi, A., Roberts, B. W., and Shiner, R. L. (2005). Personality Development: Stability and Change. *Annual Review of Psychology*, 56(1), 453–84.

95 | **Guy Davenport remarked, "Distance negates responsibility":** Myers, *Social Psychology*.

96 | **suffering would not be seen or heard by their killers:** Russell, N., and Gregory, R. (2005). Making the undoable doable: Milgram, the Holocaust, and modern government. *American Review of Public Administration*, 35, 327–49.

96 | **to join the jihadist cause:** "United Kingdom: Should ISIS brides be allowed home?" *The Week*, March 1, 2019. https://www.pressreader.com/usa/the-wee k-us/20190301/281930249258767

97 | **"I just wanted to grow up like a normal kid":** "Holocaust Survivor, Man Who Helped Free Him Reunite at College of the Ozarks," KSPR News, April 20, 2010.

99 | **better coping in adolescence:** Mischel, W., et al. (2011). "Willpower" over the life span: Decomposing self-regulation. *Social Cognitive and Affective Neuroscience*, 6(2), 252–56.

100 | **strengthen over a person's life span:** Baumeister, R. F., and Heatherton, T. (1996). Self-regulation failure: An overview. *Psychological Inquiry*, 7(1), 1–15; Diamond, L. M., and Aspinwall, L. G. (2003). Emotion regulation across the life span : An integrative perspective emphasizing self-regulation, positive affect, and dyadic processes. *Motivation and Emotion*, 27(2), 125–57; Mischel et al.,"Willpower" over the life span.

100 | **referred to as the "maturity principle":** Caspi, A., Roberts, B. W., and Shiner, R. L. (2005). Personality development: stability and change. *Annual Review of Psychology*, 56(1), 453–84. McAdams, D., and Olson, B. (2010). Personality development: Continuity and change over the life course. *Annual Review of Psychology*, 61, 517–42. While individuals generally become more conscientious and stable over time, openness to experience conversely tends to decrease in old age (Caspi, Roberts, and Shiner, 2005).

101 | **"dangerous health effects on teenagers":** Frank, Scott (2010). Hyper-texting and Hyper-Networking Pose New Health Risks for Teens: Case Western Reserve School of Medicine researcher presents study findings from the

American Public Health Association's 138th Annual Meeting & Exposition. Case Western Reserve School of Medicine website, November 9, 2010. https://casemed.case.edu/cwrumed360/news-releases/release.cfm?news_id=135&news_category=8

101 | lower GPAs supports these results: Jacobsen and Forste, The wired generation.

101 | times more texts than teenagers who pay per message: Lenhart, A., Ling, R., Campbell, S., and Purcell, K. (2010). "Teens and Mobile Phones," Pew Research Center, April 20, 2010. www.pewinternet.org/2010/04/20/teens-and-mobile-phones

103 | spend the most time on their phones: Gökçearslan, Ş., Mumcu, F. K., Haşlaman, T., and Çevik, Y. D. (2016). Modelling smartphone addiction: The role of smartphone usage, self-regulation, general self-efficacy and cyberloafing in university students. *Computers in Human Behavior*, 63, 639–49.

105 | often met with harsh responses: Radesky, J. S., et al. (2014). Patterns of mobile device use by caregivers and children during meals in fast food restaurants. *Pediatrics*, 133(4), e843–49.

106 | "how to soothe their emotions internally," Radesky explained: Interview with Jenny Radesky, June 10, 2019.

106 | frequent, continual, digitally unmediated presence: Carol shares how she became a less distracted parent during the Heart of Darkness Challenge in Appendix A.

108 | "It's the learning that they're doing by watching": Interview with Jenny Radesky, June 10, 2019.

108 | become more emotionally stable over time: Mischel et al., "Willpower" over the life span.

Chapter 7: The Kids Are Not Alright

110 | the only generation that can boast this claim: Mobile Fact Sheet, Pew Research Center, January 12, 2017. https://www.pewresearch.org/internet/fact-sheet/mobile/

110 | one in four before even getting out of bed: Marche, Stephen (2012). "Is Facebook Making Us Lonely?" *The Atlantic*, May 2012.

110 | depression since the release of the first iPhone in 2007: Eighth and tenth graders have been surveyed since 1991. Also see Twenge, *IGen*.

110 | their psychological well-being increased: Twenge, J. M., Martin, G. N., and Campbell, W. K. (2018). Decreases in psychological well-being among American adolescents. *Emotion*, 18(6), 765–80.

111 | all of which are in turn linked to depression: Kelly, Y., Zilanawala, A.,

Booker, C., and Sacker, A. (2018). Social media use and adolescent mental health: Findings from the UK Millennium Cohort Study. *EClinicalMedicine*, 6, 59–68.

111 | "in-person interaction plummeted": Twenge, *IGen*, 104.

111 | using social media more than boys: Kelly et al., Social media use and adolescent mental health; Twenge, *IGen*. In the UK survey, two-fifths of the fourteen-year-old girls surveyed reported spending at least three hours per day on social media compared with only one-fifth of the boys.

111 | depression as compared to 35 percent for boys: For those who spent 3 to 5 hours per day on social media, the increase in depressive symptoms was 26 and 21 percent, respectively. Recall that the more the fourteen-year-olds in this study used social media, the worse were their sleep, body image, and self-esteem, each of which produced higher depressive symptoms (Kelly, Zilanawala, Booker, and Sacker, 2018).

111 | more than double—over 50 percent—for girls: Twenge, *IGen*.

112 | "that manner in which we find mastery": Interview with David Greenfield.

112 | irrational, risky behaviors: Twenge, J. M., Baumeister, R. F., Tice, D. M., and Stucke, T. S. (2001). If you can't join them, beat them: Effects of social exclusion on aggressive behavior. *Journal of Personality and Social Psychology*, 81(6), 1058–69; Twenge, Catanese, and Baumeister, Social exclusion causes self-defeating behavior.

113 | "one has failed to satisfy that need": Interview with Roy Baumeister, December 8, 2018.

113 | highly sensitized to detect social exclusion: Pinker, *The Village Effect*.

113 | half of Baby Boomers (50 percent): Cigna (2020).

113 | a sense of meaningfulness in life: Stillman, T., Baumeister, R., Lambert, N., Crescioni, C., DeWall, N., and Fincham, F. (2009). Alone and without purpose: Life loses meaning following social exclusion. *Journal of Experimental Social Psychology*, 45(4), 211–17.

113 | ostracized by the KKK—can be hurtful: Gonsalkorale, K., and Williams, K. D. (2007). The KKK won't let me play: Ostracism even by a despised outgroup hurts. *European Journal of Social Psychology*, 37(6), 1176–86.

114 | 73 percent of teens had access to a smartphone: Twenge, J. M., Joiner, T. E., Rogers, M. L., and Martin, G. N. (2018). Increases in depressive symptoms, suicide-related outcomes, and suicide rates among U.S. adolescents after 2010 and links to increased new media screen time. *Clinical Psychological Science*, 6(1), 3–17.

114 | the largest gap since these statistics were recorded: Twenge, *IGen*.

114 | Director of the Human Nature Lab at Yale University: Nicholas is the brother of Dimitri, the pediatrician mentioned in a previous chapter who led the study on early television exposure and subsequent attentional problems in children.

115 | mental health, and life satisfaction in a future year: Shakya, H. B., and Christakis, N. A. (2017). "A New, More Rigorous Study Confirms: The More You Use Facebook, the Worse You Feel," *Harvard Business Review*, April 10, 2017. https://hbr.org/2017/04/a-new-more-rigorous-study-confirms-the-more-you-use-facebook-the-worse-you-feel

115 | "the real world interaction we need for a healthy life": Ibid.

115 | psychological distress, anxiety, and depressive symptoms: Kawachi, I., and Berkman, L. F. (2001). Social ties and mental health. *Journal of Urban Health: Bulletin of the New York Academy of Medicine*, 78(3), 458–467.

115 | 2015 and found no correlation: Twenge, Joiner, Rogers, and Martin, Increases in depressive symptoms, suicide-related outcomes, and suicide rates among U.S. adolescents.

116 | currently feeling to seek relief from it: Van der Kolk, B. (2015). *The Body Keeps the Score: Brain, Mind, and Body in the Healing of Trauma*. New York: Penguin.

117 | a primary risk factor for and can often lead to suicide: Mercado, M., et al. (2017). "Trends in Emergency Department Visits for Nonfatal Self-inflicted Injuries Among Youth Aged 10 to 24 Years in the United States, 2001–2015." *Journal of the American Medical Association*, November 21, 2017. https://jamanetwork.com/journals/jama/article-abstract/2664031

117 | "cheap prostitute that stands on the corner": Twenge, *IGen*, 86.

117 | "I could feel his pain": Ibid.

118 | more clinically depressed than those of in-person bullying: Wang, J., Nansel, T., and Iannotti, R. (2011). Cyber bullying and traditional bullying: Differential association with depression. *Journal of Adolescent Health*, 48(4), 415–17.

120 | overuse their smartphones than those lower in self-esteem: Mazmanian, M., Orlikowski, W. J., and Yates, J. (2013). The autonomy paradox: The implications of mobile email devices for knowledge professionals. *Organization Science*, 24(5), 1337–57.

120 | their emails and social media messages: Ibid.

121| in an attempt to feel worthy: Festinger, A theory of social comparison processes.

121 | speed comparable to the smartphone: the television: Sebastian, A. (2012). "Smartphones Set to Become the Fastest Spreading Technology in Human History," ExtremeTech, May 9, 2012. https://www.extremetech.com/computing/129058-smartphones-set-to-become-the-fastest-spreading-technology-in-human-history

121 | others they observed on the silver screen: Hennigan, K., et al. (1982). Impact of the introduction of television on crime in the United States: Empirical findings and theoretical implications. *Journal of Personality and Social*

Psychology, 42(3), 461–477.

122 | post selfies doctored with shrinking software: Turkle, *Alone Together*.

124 | "I started to embrace the uniqueness of my own": Bergmann, E. (2018). "Advice from a Formerly Lonely College Student," *New York Times*, October 9, 2018. https://www.nytimes.com/2018/10/09/well/family/advice-from-a-formerly-lonely-college-student.html

125 | rather than as a medium for active socializing: Krasnova, H., Wenninger, H., Widjaja, T., and Buxmann, P. (2013). Envy on Facebook: A hidden threat to users' life satisfaction? In 11th International Conference on Wirtschaftsinformatik, 27 February–1 March 2013, Leipzig, Germany.

125 | more motivated by envy than admiration: Van de Ven, N., Zeelenberg, M., and Pieters, R. (2011). Why envy outperforms admiration. *Personality and Social Psychology Bulletin*, 37(6), 784–95.

125 | low self-esteem, and emotional instability: Nadkarni, A., and Hofmann, S. (2012). Why do people use Facebook? *Personality and Individual Differences*, 52(3), 243–49.

Chapter 8: Digital Drift

128 | until three in the morning: This incident occurred before I had children, who are now my daily alarm clock at around six or seven each morning. Now that I know I can't sleep in, it's much easier to resist these digital temptations. This has been one of the benefits of having children; they have helped me to avert the late-night Digital Drift sessions and go to bed early so I experience much more of the next day.

129 | no real purpose other than to pass the time: Mark Rendeiro, "Using the Internet for Nothing in Particular," *Badoo News*, December 14, 2011.

129 | more information to suppress it: Evgeny Morozov, "Only Disconnect," *The New Yorker*, October 28, 2013. https://www.newyorker.com/magazine/2013/10/28/only-disconnect-2

129 | "every picture taken of your friends since they were 12": *Mad* #509, June 2011.

132 | "supposed to be doing the opposite of this?": Lewis, "Our minds can be hijacked."

133 | to get to the building: Darley, J., and Batson, D. (1973). "From Jerusalem to Jericho": A study of situational and dispositional variables in helping behavior. *Journal of Personality and Social Psychology*, 27(1), 100–108.

134 | "attitude-behavior consistency": Ajzen, I. (1985). From intentions to actions: A theory of planned behavior. In Kuhl, J. and Beckmann, J., eds., *Action-Control: From Cognition to Behavior, Springer*, 11–39; Ajzen, I. (1991). The theory of planned behavior. *Organizational Behavior and Human Decision*

Processes, 50, 179–211. It has also been called "value-behavior correspondence." Magee, J. C., and Smith, P. K. (2013). The social distance theory of power. *Personality and Social Psychology Review*, 17(2), 158–86.

134 | even if it is turned off: Ward, A. F., Duke, K., Gneezy, A., and Bos, M. W. (2017). Brain drain: The mere presence of one's own smartphone reduces available cognitive capacity. *Journal of the Association for Consumer Research*, 2(2), 140–54.

134 | goals afforded by the current situation: Cantor, N. (1994). Life task problem solving: Situational affordances and personal needs. *Personality and Social Psychology Bulletin*, 20(3), 235–43.

137 | are Hispanics and African Americans: Cigna (2020).

137 | receive the lowest grades in school: Rideout, V. J., Foehr, U. G., and Roberts, D. F. (2010). *Generation M 2: Media in the lives of 8- to 18-year-olds.* Menlo Park, CA: Henry J. Kaiser Family Foundation; Pinker, *The Village Effect.*

137 | "a lot of dysfunction in society": Thornhill, John, "Boldness in Business Person of the Year: Sir Tim Berners-Lee," *Financial Times*, March 14, 2019. https://www.ft.com/content/9d3205a8-15af-11e9-a168-d45595ad076d

137 | four times more likely to smoke tobacco: QEV Analytics, Ltd. Knowledge Networks, "The Importance of Family Dinners VII," The National Center on Addiction and Substance Abuse at Columbia University, September 2011. https://www.centeronaddiction.org/download/file/fid/374

138 | "It's why I'm so tired on Monday": Richtel, Matt, "Wasting Time Is New Divide in Digital Era," *New York Times*, May 29, 2012.

139 | do something even remotely educational: Twenge, *IGen.*

139 | watching TV has been found to be a myth: "The U.S. Digital Consumer Report," Nielsen, February 10, 2014. https://www.nielsen.com/us/en/insights/reports/2014/the-us-digital-consumer-report.html

139 | average adult spends at a full-time job: Rideout et al., *Generation M 2.*

Chapter 9: The Meta-Democratization

142 | the forefront of a movement of painters: Boorstin, D. J. (2012). *The Creators: A History of Heroes of the Imagination.* New York: Vintage.

142 | "air and light, which constantly change": Ibid., 523.

143 | "a world perceived momentarily by the senses": Ibid., 515.

143 | an original and "positive" for its copy: Ibid.

143 | "could be diffused to the millions": Ibid., 527.

146 | supplant human-driven cars within our generation: It's already beginning: at the time of publication, the latest Tesla drives, brakes, and switches lanes automatically.

146 | "Internet connection at his workplace is writing good fiction": Wayne, Teddy, "The 7-Day Digital Diet."

147 | "data to the users who generate it": Thornhill, "Boldness in Business Person of the Year."

147 | "the opposite of what it was intended to be": "WWW: This Is Not the Internet We Imagined," *The Week*, March 29, 2019.

148 | are satisfied with the experience: Pinker, *The Village Effect*.

Chapter 10: The Brand Is You

151 | Coca-Cola plants in Morocco and Algeria: Allen, Frederick, *Secret Formula: How Brilliant Marketing and Relentless Salesmanship Made Coca-Cola the Best-Known Product in the World*. New York: Harper Business, 1995.

152 | participants preferred in over 190,000 taste tests: Ibid.

153 | "Page-Ranking for people": Quote by Peter Gloor. "What Makes Heroic Strife," *The Economist*, April 21, 2012, 94.

154 | when their confidence is shaken: Mazmanian, M. (2013). Avoiding the trap of constant connectivity. When congruent frames allow for heterogeneous practices. *Academy of Management Journal*, 56(5), 1225–50.

156 | "touchscreen devices don't transfer to the real world": Interview with Dimitri Christakis, June 5, 2019.

157 | poorly tended, unhygienic public swimming pool: I must note that, while I am aware that such pools exist, I have never experienced such a pool. All of the public pools I've swum in have been very clean.

158 | Pamela Qualter calls the "reaffiliation motive": Qualter, P., et al. (2015). Loneliness across the life span. *Perspectives on Psychological Science*, 10(2), 250–64.

158 | Twitter, Facebook, which end up increasing it: Eco, U. (2013). Internet ha multiplicado la soledad. *Cuba Debate*, May 24.

159 | paradoxical effect of the Internet: Kraut et al., Internet paradox.

159 | truly been there for you in your life: Dwyer, Kushlev, and Dunn, Smartphone use undermines enjoyment of face-to-face social interactions.

Chapter 11: Convenience over Enjoyment

162 | renders life stunningly convenient: My wife, despite living in the United States for over twelve years now, only recently stopped having trouble pumping gas. In the town in Mexico where she grew up, this skill is generally unnecessary. Due to lower labor costs, gas station attendants are always at the ready and there is no self-service option as is the custom here in the US.

165 | as productive as face-to-face communication: Ferrazi, Keith, "How Virtual Teams Can Create Human Connections Despite Distance," *Harvard Business Review Blog Network*, January 31, 2014.

166 | with some mutual creativity, it will: A good friend and his wife adamantly deny meeting on the web; they claim they had friends in common and found each other through a mutual friend's social network, a predecessor of Facebook. Neither is meeting face-to-face always glorious: The comedian Chris Rock comically shares on his comedy album *Never Scared* how meeting in a club can also create problems for the how-we-met story.

167 | meeting people for the first time: Kraut et al., Internet paradox.

Chapter 12: Your Netflix Time

172 | referring to Netflix as a "very small niche business": Chong, Celena, "Blockbuster's CEO Once Passed Up a Chance to Buy Netflix for Only $50 million," *Business Insider*, July 17, 2015. https://www.businessinsider.com/block-buster-ceo-passed-up-chance-to-buy-netflix-for-50-million-2015-7

172 | Netflix was worth $148 billion: "Netflix Net Worth 2006-2019," Macro-tends. https://www.macrotrends.net/stocks/charts/NFLX/netflix/net-worth

175 | They were precious things: Richards, Keith, *Life*. London: Phoenix Books, 2011, 89–91.

175 | face-to-face much less often today: Twenge, *IGen*.

175 | "Social media has killed the music group": *Ebony*, June 2016, 125.

176 | "And then you die": Brooks, David, "Intimacy for the Avoidant," *New York Times*. October 7, 2016.

177 | That's what we lived for, basically: Richards, *Life*, 89–91.

Chapter 13: So Much Information, So Little Wisdom

181 | a task my mind is set on no matter what: Another professor who has never owned a cell phone (she became disenchanted with them when one started ringing during her wedding vows) shared with me a few days after the San Bernardino fire that many students trying to leave the university were in height-ened danger because they only knew one or two ways to exit the campus due to their dependence on Google Maps. She, on the other hand, looked at real (i.e., paper) maps and sometimes printed directions from Google Maps (as she owned no smartphone) and had discovered numerous paths to and from the university. Clearly, I was no better off than these smartphone-reliant students.

181 | its map of the border was erroneous: *The Week*, November 19, 2010, 8.

183 | Harvard Business School professor Leslie Perlow: Schumpeter, "Too Much Information."

183 | **"during that contraction—things are looking up!":** *The Week*, December 24, 2010–January 7, 2011, 8.

183 | **"on the level on which it was created":** https://www.brainyquote.com/quotes/albert_einstein_143191

185 | **"whatever responsibility I can maintain":** *The Week*, December 22–29, 2017, 49.

185 | **hunters and gatherers in the electronic data forest:** *The Week*, June 11, 2010, 14. Quoted from *Wired*.

186 | **external to us yet accessible:** Sparrow, Betsy, Liu, Jenny, and Wegner, Daniel, "Google Effects on Memory: Cognitive Consequences of Having Information at Our Fingertips," *Science*, Vol. 333, issue 6043 (August 5, 2011), 776–78.

187 | **"destroying how society works":** Manjoo, Farhad, "From Our NYT Files: Even the Tech Elite Are Worrying About Tech Addiction," *New York Times*, February 15, 2018. https://www.nytimes.com/interactive/2018/02/09/technology/the-addiction-wrought-by-techies.html

188 | **induce the coveted right swipe:** At a recent conference, the woman sitting next to me started telling me, "I love to travel. I have some special places in my country I love to go, quiet places where I am surrounded by nature." I immediately recognized the common verbiage of dating websites and started talking about my wife. I now always try to remember to wear my wedding ring to conferences.

189 | **"in the satisfaction of our needs":** Madrigal, "The People Who Hated the Web Even Before Facebook."

189 | **"fantasies onto the images before us":** Sullivan, "I Used to Be a Human Being."

189 | **album *Purple Rain*, titled "Electric Intercourse":** "Everybody Want What They Don't Got," *Uptown* #44, September 8, 2000.

189 | **if they view them at all:** I am painfully aware that over the past five years I have spent untold hours taking pictures of our children on my smartphone, and less than an hour during the same period looking at these photos.

192 | **"That's the model":** Interview with David Greenfield.

193 | **one of every four adults:** McPherson, Smith-Lovin, and Brashears, *Social isolation in America.*

194 | **marginal or inadequate counseling support:** Fischer, C. S. (1982). *To Dwell Among Friends: Personal Networks in Town and City.* University of Chicago Press.

194 | **grown to almost half of the population:** McPherson, Smith-Lovin, and Brashears, *Social isolation in America.*

Chapter 14: Direct Your Use of Technology, Not the Other Way Around

196 | **"not as free as we think they are":** Lewis, "Our minds can be hijacked."

196 | **respond to any given stimulus:** Covey, S. (2013). *The Seven Habits of Highly Effective People.* New York: Simon and Schuster.

198 | **"Circumstances don't make the man, they only reveal him":** https://www.goodreads.com/quotes/22144-circumstances-don-t-make-the-man-they-only-reveal-him-to

199 | **"instead of it being his master?":** Fischer, *America Calling.*

200 | **connecting his house to the Internet:** "Mapping the Tubes," *The Economist,* June 23, 2012, 86.

201 | **"that alarming fact may slip from your grasp":** Tolkien, J. R. R., *On Fairy Stories,* California Lutheran University (n.d.). https://www.yumpu.com/en/document/read/11579323/jrr-tolkien-on-fairy-stories-california-lutheran-university

202 | **"of course everyone used it":** Lewis, "Our minds can be hijacked."

202 | **decision to buy a car:** Power, Rhett, "Research Shows Color Is Critical in Consumer Purchasing Decisions," *Inc.,* April 17, 2017. https://www.inc.com/rhett-power/research-shows-color-is-critical-in-consumer-purchasing-decisions.html

202 | **exciting, daring, and modern:** Ibid.

202 | **invited to a pricier outing:** Elliot, A. J., and Niesta, D. (2008). Romantic red: Red enhances men's attraction to women. *Journal of Personality and Social Psychology,* 95(5), 1150–64.

202 | **per day for the average user:** "Internet Users Reach to Phones ~150x a Day."

203 | **"That's why it's used as an alarm signal":** Lewis, "Our minds can be hijacked."

203 | **excitement, enthusiasm, and vitality:** Spreitzer, G. M., Lam, C. F., and Quinn, R. W. (2012). Human energy in organizations: Implications for POS from six interdisciplinary streams. In Cameron, K., and Spreitzer, G., ed., *The Oxford Handbook of Positive Organizational Scholarship.* New York: Oxford University Press, 155–67.

203 | **perpetually preparing for action:** Thayer, R. E. (1989). *The Biopsychology of Mood and Arousal.* New York: Oxford University Press.

203 | **"escaping from a predator":** Huffington, "Our Unplugging Challenge."

204 | **fight, flight, or freeze behaviors:** Quinn, R. W., Spreitzer, G. M., and Lam, C. F. (2012). Building a sustainable model of human energy in organizations: Exploring the critical role of resources. *The Academy of Management Annals,* 6(November), 337–96; Staw, B. M., Sandelands, L. E., and Dutton, J. E. (1981). Threat rigidity effects in organizational behavior: A multilevel analysis. *Administrative Science Quarterly,* 26(4), 501–24.

204 | **"diffuse contentment":** Silard, A., and Lee, Y. (2016). The differential temporal effects of leader emotion display on follower engagement. In Conference Proceedings of the Academy of Management. Anaheim, CA: Academy of Management.

205 | now-ubiquitous design feature: Lewis, "Our minds can be hijacked."

205 | "horrific unintended consequences": Ibid.

205 | increases rather than decreases boredom: Dwyer et al., Smartphone use undermines enjoyment of face-to-face social interactions.

206| discern between viewing and seeing: Interestingly, my kids no longer try to grab my phone since I stripped it of its tense-arousal-inducing colorful allure; it's not very interesting to them anymore either. Their mother's multicolored display, on the other hand, has risen in comparative value.

206 | "Android (or iPhone) display to grayscale": While Googling how to set your specific phone to grayscale is probably the best option given the rapid rate of technological change, here are some general instructions that were working at the time this book went to press. For Android: Go to the Settings app on your phone. Inside the app, scroll down, and choose the General setting. Among the numerous options available under the General option, find the Accessibility option. Finally, turn on the grayscale option, which can be found under the Vision section. For iPhone: General—Display Accommodations—Color filters—Turn on (grayscale should automatically turn on; if not, there should be a box you can check to turn it on).

207 | choice, or "controlled attention": Bowles, Nellie, "Is the Answer to Phone Addiction a Worse Phone?" *New York Times*, January 12, 2018. https://www.nytimes.com/2018/01/12/technology/grayscale-phone.html

207 | "not as delightful a distraction as it once was": Ibid.

208 | "because it won't look very good": Interview with David Greenfield.

209 | "some type of reward there, waiting for us": Doucleff, Michaeleen, Aubrey, Allison, and Johnson, Ryan, "Smartphone Detox: How to Power Down in a Wired World," *Morning Edition*, NPR, February 12, 2018. https://www.npr.org/sections/health-shots/2018/02/12/584389201/smartphone-detox-how-to-power-down-in-a-wired-world

209 | it induces stress and anxiety: Gazzaley, A., and Rosen, L. (2016). *The Distracted Mind: Ancient Brains in a High-Tech World.* Cambridge, MA: MIT Press.

Chapter 15: Downgrade Social Media, Upgrade Your Relationships

213 | Lonely people do not sleep as well: Cacioppo, J., and Hawkley, L. (2002). Loneliness and health: Potential mechanisms. *Psychosomatic Medicine*, 64, 407–17. http://www.psychosomaticmedicine.org/content/64/3/407.short

213 | are more depressed: Leary, M. R. (1990). Responses to social exclusion: Social anxiety, jealousy, depression, and low self-esteem. *Journal of*

Social and Clinical Psychology, 9(2), 221–29.

213 | **and anxious:** Baumeister, R. F., and Tice, D. M. (1990). Point-counterpoints: Anxiety and social exclusion. *Journal of Social and Clinical Psychology*, 9(2), 165–95.

213 | **and possess less self-control:** Williams, K., Cheung, C., and Choi, W. (2000). Cyberostracism: Effects of being ignored over the Internet. *Journal of Personality and Social Psychology*, 79(5), 748–62.

213 | **and lower self-esteem:** Leary, M., Tambor, E., Terdal, S., and Downs, D. (1995). Self-esteem as an interpersonal monitor: The sociometer hypothesis. *Journal of Personality and Social Psychology*, 68(3), 518–30.

213 | **reduced blood pressure regulation:** Uchino, B., Cacioppo, J., and Kiecolt-Glaser, J. (1996). The relationship between social support and physiological processes: a review with emphasis on underlying mechanisms and implications for health. *Psychological Bulletin*, 119(3), 488–531.

213 | **(tension of heart contractions):** Cacioppo and Hawkley, Loneliness and health.

213 | **increased risk for heart attacks:** Case, R. B. (1992). Living alone after myocardial infarction. *Journal of the American Medical Association*, 267, 515–19.

213 | **sooner than their non-lonely counterparts:** House, J., Landis, K., and Umberson, D. (1988). Social relationships and health. *Science*, 241(4865), 540–45.

213 | **than the wounds of those who are not lonely:** Cacioppo, J., and Hawkley, L. (2003). Social isolation and health, with an emphasis on underlying mechanisms. *Perspectives in Biology and Medicine*, 46(3), S39–S52.

213 | **over 60 percent of Americans are lonely:** Cigna (2020).

213 | **more time on Facebook than non-lonely people:** Song, H., Zmyslinski-Seelig, A., Kim, J., Drent, A., Victor, A., Omori, K., and Allen, M. (2014). Does Facebook make you lonely?: A meta analysis. *Computers in Human Behavior*, 36, 446–52.

213 | **"infinite streams of information and entertainment":** Morozov, "Only Disconnect."

214 | **the lonelier they became:** Fogel, J., Albert, S. M., Schnabel, F., Ditkoff, B. A., and Neugut, A. I. (2002). Internet use and social support in women with breast cancer. *Health Psychology*, 21(4), 398.

214 | **everyday activities as stress provoking:** Cacioppo and Hawkley, Social isolation and health.

214 | **more stress and burnout:** Cubitt, S., and Burt, C. (2002). Leadership style, loneliness and occupational stress in New Zealand primary school principals. *New Zealand Journal of Educational Studies*, 37(2), 159–69.

214 | **do not perform as well:** Ozcelik, H., and Barsade, S. (2018). No employee

an island: Workplace loneliness and job performance. *Academy of Management Journal*, 61(6).

215 | most effective form of emotion regulation: Gross, J. (1998). The emerging field of emotion regulation: An integrative review. *Review of General Psychology*, 2(3), 271–99; Gross, J. J. (2015). Emotion regulation: Current status and future prospects. *Psychological Inquiry*, 26(1), 1–26.

215 | meaningful as you would like them to be: Holt-Lunstad, J., Smith, T. B., Baker, M., Harris, T., and Stephenson, D. (2015). Loneliness and social isolation as risk factors for mortality: A meta-analytic review. *Perspectives on Psychological Science*, 10(2), 227–37; Qualter, P., et al. Loneliness across the life span. While many confuse the two, loneliness and depression are actually distinct emotions. Whereas loneliness is an emotion associated with the cognitive belief that your *social relationships* are not what you would like them to be, depression is an emotion associated with the cognitive belief that your *life* is not what you would like it to be. See Cacioppo and Patrick, *Loneliness*.

215 | this emotion—loneliness—very quickly: Gardner, W. L., Pickett, C. L., and Brewer, M. B. (2008). Social exclusion and selective memory: How the need to belong influences memory for social events. *Personality and Social Psychology Bulletin*, 26(4), 486–96; Stenseng, F., Belsky, J., Skalicka, V., and Wichstrom, L. (2014). Preschool social exclusion, aggression, and cooperation: A longitudinal evaluation of the need-to-belong and the social-reconnection hypotheses. Personality and Social Psychology Bulletin, 40(12), 1637–47.

216 | fear before giving a speech in public: This study is still in process and not yet published. We will be replicating it in another country.

216 | more effective strategy than suppression: Gross, J. J. (2015). Emotion regulation: Current status and future prospects. *Psychological Inquiry*, 26(1), 1–26; Gross, J., and John, O. (2003). Individual differences in two emotion regulation processes: implications for affect, relationships, and well-being. *Journal of Personality and Social Psychology*, 85(2), 348–62. I recently put cognitive reappraisal into practice during a vasectomy. I shifted my thoughts from how uncomfortable I felt that the friendly doctor had my *vas deferens* outside of my scrotum and in her hands and that my testicles felt like they were in a clamp, to the contribution I was making to my family. When that stopped working, I imagined myself outside of my body looking down at myself on the operating table. I observed myself going through a rite of passage, an important stage of my life. These thoughts helped me reduce the angst and anxiety I associated with what was happening and feel more positive emotions such as calmness and peace.

216 | was much less effective: Mischel, et al., "Willpower" over the life span.

217 | who will actually answer the phone: McPherson, Smith-Lovin, and Brashears, Social isolation in America.

218 | almost impossible-to-find, coveted commodity: Barney, J. B. (1991). Firm resources and sustained competitive advantage. *Journal of Management*, 17(1), 99–120.

218 | the root of ethnic conflict: Myers, *Social Psychology*.

218 | "only a limited amount of global harmony is possible": Wilson, E. O. (1978). *On Human Nature*. Cambridge, MA: Harvard University Press.

219 | victims of successful abductions in the US per year: Paula Fass, "Child Kidnapping in America," *Origins: Current Events in Historical Perspective*, Ohio State University and Miami University History Departments, Vol. 3, Issue 4, January 2010.

220 | media-poor reply (e.g., a text or email): I turn the other cheek when most people respond to one of my social overtures with a Communication Reciprocation Downgrade, primarily because I don't want them to feel uncomfortable. Yet sometimes, refusing to accommodate their downgrade, I don't reply to their electronic message and just call again a few weeks later.

221 | access a new career opportunity: Granovetter, M. S. (1973). The strength of weak ties. *American Journal of Sociology*, 1360–80; Granovetter, M. S. (1983). The strength of weak ties: a network theory revisited. *Sociological Theory* 1, 201–33.

222 | "unexpected emotional needs": Sullivan, "I Used to Be a Human Being."

223 | dancing, sports, ferret racing: Ferret racing is quite amusing and can be observed in Wales.

224| those using social media the least: "An epidemic of loneliness," *The Week*, January 11, 2019.

Chapter 16: Digital Limiting Strategies

226 | little knowing the outcome, I bought for her: I have wrestled with the existential question Should I have bought my mother her iPad? for years. In the end, I do not regret my decision. It's her use of the iPad, not the iPad itself, that has been so challenging. I can say the same about my decision to purchase a smartphone for myself about ten years ago. When we point our finger at someone, after all, three fingers are pointed back at ourselves.

228 | but not with my own mother: It turns out I'm not alone. As I mentioned in Chapter 15, parents have been the unexpected beneficiaries of the digital age, at least in that (on average, but of course not for any specific offspring) their children call them more than ever before.

229 | a specific app, on a particular day: At the time of publication, for iPhones there is Screen Time, and a similar such app for Android phones is ActionDash.

229 | "noise, overload, and distraction": Morozov, "Only Disconnect."

230 | emails are opened within six seconds: Alter, *Irresistible*.

230 | impede healthy organizational functioning: Blodget, H. (2011). BOMBSHELL: Huge Company Bans Internal Email, Switches Totally To

Facebook-Type-Stuff And Instant Messaging. *Business Insider*. http://www.
businessinsider.com/company-bans-email-2011-12#ixzz3H35JR8sw; BBC News.
(March 8, 2012). Volkswagen turns off Blackberry email after work hours. http://
www.bbc.com/news/technology-16314901

230 | "pass on family plans": Shellenbarger, Sue, "A Day Without Email Is Like ...",
Wall Street Journal, October 11, 2007.

232 | and they want one of their own: Interview with Dimitri Christakis, June
5, 2019.

233 | after the lights are turned off at night: American Academy of Pediat-
rics, "Children, Adolescents, and the Media," *Pediatrics*, 132(5), November
2013. https://pediatrics.aappublications.org/content/132/5/958; Zimbardo and
Coulombe, *Man Interrupted*.

233 | more trustworthy, honest, and kinder than the average person: Jarrett,
Christian, "What Are We Like? 10 Psychology Findings That Reveal the Worst
of Human Nature," *The British Psychological Society Research Digest*, October 12,
2018. https://digest.bps.org.uk/2018/10/12/what-are-we-like-10-psychology-
findings-that-reveal-the-worst-of-human-nature/

234 | "It has solved the problem," the priest shared: *The Week*, December 26,
2014.

234 | "screen-free Sundays" in his home: McCarthy, "Breaking Up with Your
Smartphone Is Really, Really Hard."

234 | "a river that had been polluted for decades": Kutnowski, Martin,
"Fighting the Internet Invasion of Childhood," *Wall Street Journal*, September 9,
2014. https://www.wsj.com/articles/martin-kutnowski-fighting-the-internet-in-
vasion-of-childhood-1410304231

238 | automatically and unintentionally: Duhigg, C. (2012). *The Power of
Habit: Why We Do What We Do in Life and Business*. New York: Random House;
Ebenbach, D. H., and Keltner, D. (1998). Power, emotion, and judgmental
accuracy in social conflict: Motivating the cognitive miser. *Basic and Applied
Social Psychology*, 20(1), 7–21.

238 | central findings of social psychology: Myers, *Social Psychology*.

238 | has won a presidential debate: Sears, D. O., and Kinder, D. (1985). Public
opinion and political action. In G. Lindsey and E. Aronson, eds., *The Handbook
of Social Psychology*, 3rd ed. New York: Random House.

239 | "logistical stuff like navigating": McCarthy, "Breaking Up with Your
Smartphone Is Really, Really Hard."

240 | "we can use them in pathological ways": Doucleff, Aubrey, and Johnson,
"Smartphone Detox."

242 | each moment occurs on average every six minutes: "Internet Users Reach
to Phones ~150x a Day."

Chapter 17: The Heart of Darkness

245 | 7 percent of the full experience of communication: Koneya and Barbour, *Louder Than Words.*

246 | in a small town in Mexico, I realized why: There's an important lesson in how I discovered the Heart of Darkness and Side Door models: we go through much of our busy lives on automatic pilot. Taking time on a vacation or stay-cation and observing and reflecting on how we use our phones and digital devices, and in which contexts they're helping or hindering us from realizing our goals and values, as I did on my end-of-year vacation, can be an extremely powerful and life-transforming endeavor. I invite you to devote some time on your next vacation—or even this weekend—to reflect on your digital etiquette. Consider how you can bring the use of your phone, tablet, and laptop into alignment with your vision of how you would like to live your life.

246 | feelings of anxiety to increase: Clayton et al., *The extended iSelf*; Gazzaley and Rosen, *The Distracted Mind.*

247 | no longer be controlled by social media companies: Our puppeteers are few these days: Facebook owns WhatsApp, just as Match, Tinder, and OKCupid are all owned by the same company.

248 | 70 percent of office emails are read within six seconds: Alter, *Irresistible.*

248 | email, the more stressed you become: Barley, S. R., Meyerson, D. E., and Grodal, S. (2011). E-mail as a source and symbol of stress. *Organization Science*, 22(4), 887–906; Kushlev, K., and Dunn, E. (2015). Checking e-mail less frequently reduces stress. *Computers in Human Behavior*, 43, 1458–66.

248 | and the less you check the less stress you experience: Clive Thompson, "Are You Checking Work Email in Bed? At the Dinner Table? On Vacation?" *Mother Jones*, May/June 2014. https://www.motherjones.com/politics/2014/04/smartphone-addiction-research-work-email/

249 | why did all of my previous experimenting not work?: I subscribe to the view on innovation of Thomas Edison, who once said about his efforts to invent the light bulb: "I have not failed. I've just found 10,000 ways that won't work." https://www.brainyquote.com/quotes/thomas_a_edison_132683

251 | the final screen on my phone—the Heart of Darkness: I also say to myself, "Okay, so when I check my text messages, that's also the time that I will make any (free international) WhatsApp calls" because I know if I go there and see the WhatsApp messages, I'll want to check them.

253 | "thought that generates from your own brain": Doucleff, Aubrey, and Johnson, "Smartphone Detox."

253 | social media sites such as Facebook: McPherson, Smith-Lovin, and Brashears, Social isolation in America.

253 | tremendous impact on one's life: In her journal in Appendix A, Nancy shares how the Heart of Darkness Challenge can reinvigorate relationships and transform your life through more face-to-face and phone time.

254 | "more of a guideline than a rule": Joseph Gelmis, "*Ghostbusters:* Newsday's 1984 review of original film," *Newsday,* June 8, 2016. https://www.newsday.com/entertainment/movies/ghostbusters-newsday-s-1984-review-of-original-film-1.11891998

256 | produce too much anxiety: Clayton et al., The extended iSelf; Gazzaley and Rosen, *The Distracted Mind.*

257 | Samantha, a bank manager from the Philippines, told me: In Appendix A, Carol shares how the Side Door model helped her to keep tabs on her sick daughter.

Chapter 18: Contain Your Phone, Expand Your Life

259 | "as well as when you do them one at a time": Willingham, "Have Technology and Multitasking Rewired How Students Learn?"

259 | which causes more stress: Ebenbach and Keltner, Power, emotion, and judgmental accuracy in social conflict.

259 | produces more mistakes: Kleiman, Jessica, "How Multitasking Hurts Your Brain (and Your Effectiveness at Work)," *Forbes,* January 15, 2013. https://www.forbes.com/sites/work-in-progress/2013/01/15/how-multitasking-hurts-your-brain-and-your-effectiveness-at-work/

259 | do not remember facts or solve problems very well: Ophir, E., Nass, C., and Wagner, A. (2009). Cognitive control in media multitaskers. *Proceedings of the National Academy of Sciences,* 106(37), 15583–87.

259 | "a test of task-switching ability": Ibid., 15583.

260 | ways you'll later regret (i.e., engaging in an addiction): Ajzen, From intentions to actions; Ajzen, I., and Fishbein, M. (2005). The influence of attitudes on behavior. In Albarracin, D., Johnson, B. T., and Zanna, M. P., eds., *The Handbook of Attitudes,* New York: Psychology Press, 173–222; Darley and Batson, "From Jerusalem to Jericho."

260 | neurons that fire together wire together: Supercamp by Quantum Learning, April 28, 2014. https://www.supercamp.com/what-does-neurons-that-fire-together-wire-together-mean/

261 | communicate with one or two: Dunbar, R. I. M., Arnaboldi, V., Conti, M., and Passarella, A. (2015). The structure of online social networks mirrors those in the offline world. *Social Networks,* 43, 39–47.

262 | "please just call me": The advantage of saying you only check once per day is that it removes any expectation of a response that day, as you may have already checked before they send their message.

270 | twice per week for the next seven weeks: Why seven weeks? Daphne, a former client who undertook the Heart of Darkness Challenge, shared "There is a mantra that goes 'It takes 21 days to create a habit and 90 days to create a lifestyle.'" Seven weeks is long enough to create an entrenched habit that, if you experience enough benefits in association with it—developing new neuronic associations in relation to your phone as per the saying "neurons that fire together wire together"—can lead to continuing the habit and creating a new lifestyle. At the same time, seven weeks is short enough not to feel overwhelming so you can give it a try.

Commencement

271 | to be insufficient: Ajzen, From intentions to actions; Ajzen and Fishbein, The influence of attitudes on behavior; Darley and Batson, "From Jerusalem to Jericho."

272 | from 25 percent in 1981 to 41 percent in 2007: Myers, *Social Psychology*; Pryor, J., Hurtado, S., Sharkness, J., and Korn, W. (2007). *The American freshman: National norms for fall 2007*. Los Angeles: Higher Education Research Institute, UCLA.

272 | *If not you, who? If not now, when?*: https://www.goodreads.com/quotes/527445-if-not-now-when-if-not-you-who